T0306089

Theory of Macroeconomic Hysteresis

Theory of Macroeconomic Hysteresis

Isaak D Mayergoyz
University of Maryland, USA

Can E Korman
George Washington University, USA

NEW JERSEY · LONDON · SINGAPORE · BEIJING · SHANGHAI · HONG KONG · TAIPEI · CHENNAI · TOKYO

Published by

World Scientific Publishing Co. Pte. Ltd.

5 Toh Tuck Link, Singapore 596224

USA office: 27 Warren Street, Suite 401-402, Hackensack, NJ 07601

UK office: 57 Shelton Street, Covent Garden, London WC2H 9HE

Library of Congress Control Number: 2024008417

British Library Cataloguing-in-Publication Data
A catalogue record for this book is available from the British Library.

THEORY OF MACROECONOMIC HYSTERESIS

Copyright © 2024 by World Scientific Publishing Co. Pte. Ltd.

All rights reserved. This book, or parts thereof, may not be reproduced in any form or by any means, electronic or mechanical, including photocopying, recording or any information storage and retrieval system now known or to be invented, without written permission from the publisher.

For photocopying of material in this volume, please pay a copying fee through the Copyright Clearance Center, Inc., 222 Rosewood Drive, Danvers, MA 01923, USA. In this case permission to photocopy is not required from the publisher.

ISBN 9789811290466 (hardcover)
ISBN 9789811290473 (ebook for institutions)
ISBN 9789811290480 (ebook for individuals)

For any available supplementary material, please visit
https://www.worldscientific.com/worldscibooks/10.1142/13766#t=suppl

Desk Editors: Nandha Kumar/Yulin Jiang

Typeset by Stallion Press
Email: enquiries@stallionpress.com

Printed in Singapore

To Charlotte, Izzy, Ali, Liva,
Alya and Nurhan

Preface

Macroeconomics can be viewed as a system with a discrete memory of past shocks. These shocks result in macroeconomic hysteresis which affects future economic evolution.

This book deals with the mathematical theory of macroeconomic hysteresis. This is the theory of aggregation of microeconomic hysteresis. This aggregation results in the emergence of new economic phenomena. Indeed, microeconomic sunk cost hysteresis is usually represented by relatively simple hysteresis loops. This type of hysteresis has a local (i.e., Markovian) memory, and in the economic literature it is often referred to as weak hysteresis. It turns out that macroeconomic aggregation results in the formation of discrete memory of past economic shocks. As a consequence, this aggregation elevates microeconomic hysteresis to the level of non-Markovian history-dependent multibranch hysteresis. In the economic literature, this history-dependent multi-branch hysteresis is referred to as strong hysteresis.

In the book, the basic properties of macroeconomic hysteresis are mathematically studied. It is demonstrated that certain important properties of macroeconomic hysteresis (such as history-dependent branching, erasure of effects of some past economic shocks, geometric features of macroeconomic hysteresis loops, etc.) are insensitive to specific structures of microeconomic hysteresis subject to aggregation. This suggests that the above properties may be viewed as universal. Furthermore, it is pointed out that these aggregation models have the prediction power of future macroeconomic branching, which may be employed for the prediction of future economic evolution.

The presentation in the book is largely based on the past publications of the authors in the field of mathematical modeling of hysteresis phenomena. In writing this book, special efforts have been made to make it accessible to a large audience of readers. To achieve this goal, a strong emphasis has been placed on the clarity of exposition of various mathematical concepts related to hysteresis. It is for the readers to judge to what extent these efforts have been successful.

Our thanks to Yulin Jiang and Nandha Kumar from World Scientic Publishing for their valuable assistance and patience. Finally, the first author of the book gratefully acknowledges the financial support derived from the Alford L. Ward professorship that made this project possible.

Isaak D. Mayergoyz and Can E. Korman

Contents

Chapter 1

Introduction

It is known that economic activities (such as employment, trade or, in general, investment) exhibit hysteresis. The notion of economic hysteresis has a long and instructive history whose origin can be traced back to the classical book of Alfred Marshall *Principles of Economics* [69]. In a nutshell, the essence of economic hysteresis is the history dependence of economic activities.

There are two distinct forms of economic hysteresis: microeconomic and macroeconomic hysteresis. Microeconomic hysteresis occurs on the level of individual firms and companies. Whereas, macroeconomic hysteresis is the result of the aggregation of large number of heterogenous (but qualitatively similar) cases of microeconomic hysteresis. Macroeconomic hysteresis is observed on the level of industry branches or an entire country's economy.

This book deals with the mathematical theory of macroeconomic hysteresis. Basically, this is the theory of hysteresis aggregation which results in the emergence of new economic phenomena. Indeed, microeconomic hysteresis is usually represented by relatively simple hysteresis loops. This type of hysteresis has local (i.e., Markovian) memory, and in the economic literature it is often referred to as **weak** hysteresis [7]. The situation is quite different in the case of macroeconomic hysteresis. Here, as a result of aggregation of weak microeconomic hysteresis, a new type of hysteresis emerges which has nonlocal (i.e., non-Markovian) memory. This memory has a discrete structure and its elements can be associated with past economic shocks. The main manifestation of this discrete memory is **history-dependent branching**. In the economic literature, this history-dependent branching is referred to as **strong** hysteresis [4]. Remarkably, it turns out that the main properties of macroeconomic hysteresis are by and large insensitive to (or, practically independent of) the underlying structures of microeconomic hysteresis subject to aggregation. In this sense, these aggregation properties may be viewed as universal.

In this book, mathematical models of macroeconomic hysteresis are discussed. These models are endowed with discrete memories corresponding to memories of actual macroeconomic hysteresis caused by past shocks. Furthermore, the highly desirable feature of any theory is its predictive power. It turns out that the discussed models, due to their mathematical structure, have the ability to predict future macroeconomic hysteresis branches. Needless to say, that the prediction of future economic evolution, i.e., branching, can be of significant value.

This book consists of five chapters. This first chapter is introductory in nature. It summarizes the main content of the book without invoking any mathematical formulas. This chapter can be read in parallel with other chapters of the book.

The second chapter starts with the definition of hysteresis. This definition is given by using the input-output approach which has been the foundation of systems theory. The input-output method has long been used in the economics literature as well. Here, it was introduced by Wassily Leontief who won the Nobel Memorial Prize in Economic Sciences in 1973 for the development of the input-output method and its applications. The input-output definition of hysteresis is quite general in nature because the actual economic meaning of input and output are left unspecified. This makes the above definition applicable to various forms of economic hysteresis.

In Chapter 2, hysteresis is first defined for periodic variations of input. For such variations, input-output relations are represented by hysteresis loops. In the simplest case, these are rectangular hysteresis loops (see Fig. 2.4) which are extensively used in the book for mathematical representation of complex economic hysteresis. In the case of nonperiodic piece-wise monotonic input variations, hysteresis manifests itself as history-dependent branching (see Fig. 2.5). Here, each new branch is formed after each new input extrema. This branching is controlled by past input extrema, which form discrete memories of multi-branch hysteresis.

The second chapter also contains a brief discussion of microeconomic hysteresis. The origin of this hysteresis is due to the fact that firms operate by employing binary actions such as hiring-firing, buying-selling or, in general, investing-disinvesting. These binary actions are of opposite nature. However, they are not reversible versions of one another. In other words, these binary actions are asymmetric, and this asymmetry occurs due to the **market entry sunk costs**. This sunk cost can be viewed as market entry investment which may have many different components, such as the development of a new product, acquisition of new special equipment for new product fabrication, marketing, creation of sales and distribution networks, hiring of workers and their training, etc. Such investments are firm specific and, by and large, nonrecoverable. Usually, firms make sunk cost investments and enter the market at the time when they can generate sufficiently large revenue to gradually recover the market entry investments and make some profit. Firms may also continue to operate when they are unprofitable. This is usually done with some foresight of a certain likelihood that profitable times may return and current losses will be recovered by future profits. At the time, when unprofitability becomes intolerable and the return of profitability is assessed to be quite remote, firms may exit the market.

It is apparent from the above discussion that microeconomic hysteresis is **sunk cost hysteresis**. In simple situations, it can be characterized by two triggers α and β corresponding to the values of the forcing input at which market entry and exit may occur, respectively. This corresponds to the case when microeconomic hysteresis can be represented by rectangular hysteresis loops. More complex loops which can be used for modelling of microeconomic hysteresis are briefly discussed in the chapter as well, and it is pointed out that these loops **can be mathematically represented in terms of rectangular loops.**

It turns out that microeconomic hysteresis may be strongly affected by the uncertainty of the economic environment. This uncertainty is reflected in the fact that the forcing inputs (such as exchange rate, interest rate, etc.) may not be deterministic but rather stochastic in nature. This stochasticity affects the choice of α and β triggers [10], [41], [83] and it leads to the **broadening** of the width $\alpha - \beta$ of the hysteresis loops describing **microeconomic hysteresis**. In economic literature, this width is often called the "band of inaction". The stochastic nature of forcing input results in random dynamics of the investment process. In the second chapter, the modeling of random dynamics of investment under (input) uncertainty is discussed by using independent identically distributed (i.i.d.) processes for random forcing inputs. First, the case of a rectangular hysteresis loop driven by i.i.d. processes is discussed and simple analytical expressions are derived for the expected value of the output and its variance. The described analysis is then extended to more complex microeconomic hysteresis loops by using their representation in terms of rectangular loops.

The second chapter is concluded with a very brief discussion of macroeconomic hysteresis and its modeling. It is stressed that macroeconomic hysteresis emerges as a result of aggregation of very large cases of heterogeneous microeconomic hysteresis. Consequently, it can be stated that the **microeconomic sunk cost and aggregation** are the main causes of macroeconomic hysteresis. Due to the very large number of heterogeneous firms involved in the aggregation, this aggregation process can be mathematically represented as the integration of microeconomic hysteresis models with respect to their trigger values α and β corresponding to different firms. This leads to the mathematical models of macroeconomic hysteresis. The comprehensive analysis of such models of macroeconomic hysteresis is carried out in the subsequent chapters of the book.

The third chapter of the book deals with the Preisach aggregation model of macroeconomic hysteresis. In this model, microeconomic hysteresis of individual firms is represented by rectangular loops with different trigger values α and β, and different vertical (output) heights which are functions of α and β. Historically, the Preisach model was first introduced in 1935 for the description of magnetic hysteresis (see [85] and [86]), and it was regarded for many years as a physical model. In the late 1970s and the beginning of 1980s, it was realized (see [62], [70] and [71]) that the Preisach model contains a new mathematical idea and can be defined without referring to any physical phenomena by using the input-output approach. As a result, this model was separated from its physical connotations and represented in purely mathematical terms. In this way, a new mathematical tool has evolved that can be used for the mathematical description of hysteresis of various nature. For instance, this model has been used for the description and analysis of hysteresis in superconductors, optics, nonlinear elasticity, biology and neural science.

In economics, the Preisach model is constructed by the integration of outputs of rectangular hysteresis loops which represent microeconomic hysteresis of individual firms. It turns out that as a result of the aforementioned integration, the Preisach model has unique properties of detecting input extrema, storing them in its structure and choosing the appropriate future branches of macroeconomic hysteresis according to the accumulated history of past input extrema. In other words, the Preisach model reveals that macroeconomic aggregation elevates weak microeconomic hysteresis to the level of non-Markovian history-dependent multibranch hysteresis with discrete memory of past economic shocks. To demonstrate how the above properties emerge, a special **diagram technique** has been developed. This diagram technique constitutes the mathematical foundation of the analysis of macroeconomic aggregation of microeconomic hysteresis, and it is extensively used throughout the book.

The above diagram technique is based on the simple fact that there is a one-to-one correspondence between rectangular loops and points (α, β) of the half-plane $\alpha \geq \beta$. In other words, each point on the above half-plane can be identified with only one rectangular loop whose trigger values α and β coincide respectively with the α and β coordinates of the point. At any instant of time, all points (α, β) on the half-plane are subdivided into two sets: the set of points for which the corresponding rectangular loops are in the upward position (this is the so-called "upward" set) and the set of points for which the corresponding rectangular loops are in the downward position (this is the so-called "downward" set). It is demonstrated in the book that these two sets are separated by a staircase line whose vertices have α and β coordinates coinciding respectively with local maxima and minima of input at past instants of time. This separating (i.e., interface) line consists of horizontal and vertical links. The final link is attached to the line $\alpha = \beta$, and it moves when the input is changed (see Figs. 3.12 and 3.13). This final link is a horizontal one and it moves upwards as the input is monotonically increased. On the other hand, the final link is a vertical one and it moves leftward as the input is monotonically decreased. Since the "downward" output values of rectangular loops are equal to zero, the output value of the Preisach model is equal to the integral over the "upward" set. The boundary of this set is the aforementioned staircase line whose α and β vertex coordinates coincide with the past input maxima and minima, respectively. Consequently, the output values of the Preisach macroeconomic model are controlled by the values of past input extrema as well as by instantaneous values of input. This implies that the Preisach model is endowed with a discrete memory structure consisting of past input extrema.

The above discussion clearly reveals the mechanism of the above memory formation. Namely, this memory formation occurs as a result of two different ways of modification of the staircase interface between "upward" and "downward" sets. Indeed, for a monotonically increasing input, a horizontal final link is formed which moves upwards, while for a monotonically decreasing input a vertical link is formed which moves leftwards. These two different ways of modification of the separating line results in the formation of a staircase interface line, whose vertices have α and β coordinates equal to past input extrema. Furthermore, the above mechanism of memory formation is also responsible for sequential branching, which is a clear manifestation of hysteresis.

By using the above diagram technique, the basic properties of the Preisach macroeconomic model are discussed in the book. The first important property of the aggregation described by the Preisach model is the **Erasure Property**. According to this property, not all past input extrema may be stored by the Preisach model at any instant of time. This means that some of the input extrema may be erased, i.e., eliminated, by new input extrema that occur as a result of subsequent time variations of input. It turns out that, at any instant of time, the stored input extrema form the **alternating sequence of dominant input maxima and minima**, while all intermediate input extrema are erased. The term "dominant maximum" implies that all past erased maxima are below a dominant maximum. Similarly, the term "dominant minimum" implies that all past erased minima are above a dominant minimum. The term "alternating sequence" implies that there is a single dominant minimum between any two consecutive in time dominant maxima, and the other way around (see Fig. 3.18).

It is clear from the previous discussion that past input extrema affect future values of the output of the Preisach aggregation model. This suggests that these extrema may have lasting economic consequences. The past input extrema are also exogenous in nature. Consequently, the past input extrema can be viewed as manifestations of **shocks**. As a result, the **Erasure Property** of macroeconomic aggregation of microeconomic hysteresis implies that **not all** shocks affect the future branching of macroeconomic hysteresis. In other words, the persistence and protracted effects of some past shocks can be eliminated by strong, i.e., dominant, future shocks. This is quite natural from the economic point of view. This is because the dominant shocks may usually result in appreciable and irreversible structural changes in industry, technology or society. This may render the structural changes caused by erased intermediate shocks to be irrelevant as far as the future development of the economy is concerned.

Next, the **Property of Congruency** of macroeconomic hysteresis loops is discussed. These loops are formed as a result of periodic in time variations of input between two consecutive extrema. It turns out that all macroeconomic hysteresis loops will be congruent for periodic variations of input between the **same** two consecutive extremum values (see Fig. 3.21). This congruency is not affected by the past input variations occurring before the onset of the above periodic variations of input. These past input variations affect the positions of macroeconomic hysteresis loops on the input-output plane. However, due to their congruency, the coincidence of these loops can be achieved by translating them on the above plane along the output-axis. This implies that congruent macroeconomic loops have the same geometric shapes. The independence of their shapes from past input extrema preceding such periodic input variations suggests that their shapes are completely determined by the last two input extrema. This means that the **last two shocks** completely control the shapes of macroeconomic hysteresis loops. The previous past dominant shocks may affect their positions on the input-output plane but not their geometric shapes.

The congruency of macroeconomic hysteresis loops implies the validity of the **Property of Equal Vertical Chords**. This property may have important economic implications, especially in the case of cyclic unemployment. In this case, the length of vertical chords of macroeconomic hysteresis loops can be viewed as a measure of economic recovery. This is because the length of vertical chords can be used as a measure of persisting cyclic unemployment. Since geometric shapes of macroeconomic hysteresis loops are controlled by the last two shocks, this means that the degree of gradual recovery is dependent on these shocks, while all other past shocks have no protracted effects on recovery.

Finally, the **Property of Zero Initial Slopes** is discussed. This property means that newly formed branches of multi-branch macroeconomic hysteresis have zero initial slopes **immediately** following new branch formations (see Fig. 3.31). The smallness of the slopes of newly formed branches may persist. It is shown that this is the case because the initial slopes' gradual increase are controlled by the number of firms whose microeconomic hysteresis is described by narrow hysteresis loops. These numbers tend to be relatively small because of the broadening of the band of inaction $\alpha - \beta$ may be beneficial for efficient firm operations under uncertain economic environments. In the case of branches corresponding to economic recovery, these almost flat and protracted initial parts of hysteresis branches may lead to lingering high unemployment rates. This may mask the onset of recovery. Similarly, the persisting flatness of the initial parts of recession branches of hysteresis loops may also mask the onset of a recession.

In the third chapter, the multi-branch property of macroeconomic hysteresis, the erasure property and the property of equal vertical chords are established by using the Preisach aggregation model. In this model, microeconomic hysteresis is represented by simple rectangular loops. This may lead to the point of view that the above properties are the consequences of the rectangular loop representation of microeconomic hysteresis.

However, in the next chapter, the multi-branch property of macroeconomic hysteresis, the erasure property and the property of equal vertical chords are established for generalized aggregation models. In these models, microeconomic hysteresis is represented by more realistic and more complex hysteresis loops. This suggests that the above properties may be **insensitive** to the structure of the underlying microeconomic hysteresis subject to aggregation. This means that their origin may be due to the hysteresis aggregation itself. In this sense, the above properties may be viewed as **universal**.

The last section of the third chapter deals with alternative forms of the Preisach aggregation model of macroeconomic hysteresis. First, the special alternative form is discussed which reveals that the Preisach macroeconomic model has a **reversible component**. This fact may be surprising because this model is constructed as the aggregation of heterogeneous rectangular loops. These loops do not contain locally reversible non-constant components. Indeed, these hysteresis loops describe locally irreversible jumps between two constant values. For this reason, the emergence of locally reversible non-constant components in macroeconomic hysteresis can be viewed as the effect of aggregation. To explicitly reveal and separate the reversible and irreversible (i.e., hysteretic) components, the region of integration in the Preisach model is subdivided into three specific subregions. Then, it is mathematically demonstrated that the part of the Preisach model corresponding to the integration over one of these three subregions describes the irreversible component of hysteresis, while the two other parts represent the reversible component of that hysteresis. If only the irreversible component of macroeconomic hysteresis is of interest, then the above reversible part can be ignored.

Finally, two other alternative forms of the Preisach aggregation model are discussed. These forms are **algebraic** in nature. This means that the output of the Preisach model can be explicitly expressed by using some algebraic formulas instead of integration. These algebraic formulas are represented in terms of specially defined functions, and these formulas are derived by using the diagram technique. The above formulas have finite number of terms. These terms depend on the values of past dominant input extrema, and only the last term depends on the current value if input. This last term describes the time output evolution for the last (i.e., the newly formed) hysteresis branch. These formulas can be useful for numerical implementation of the Preisach model. More importantly, the above formulas may provide some **prediction power** of history-dependent branching of macroeconomic hysteresis. The latter is only possible if sufficient information about the underlying microeconomic hysteresis is available. The accuracy of branching prediction may be affected by the somewhat simplistic rectangular loop representation of microeconomic hysteresis. Furthermore, the Preisach model does not account for continuous structural evolutions of the economy and its effects on macroeconomic hysteresis. It turns out that the last two limitations of the Preisach model can be relaxed by using generalized macroeconomic hysteresis models.

These models are discussed in the fourth chapter. In the case of the Preisach aggregation model, macroeconomic hysteresis is constructed as the aggregation of heterogenous rectangular loops describing microeconomic hysteresis. As mentioned above, such loops represent an idealization of actual microeconomic hysteresis, because they describe this hysteresis in terms of only two possible outcomes corresponding to "downward" and "upward" values of output. In the case of the generalized aggregation model, these rectangular loops are replaced by general hysteresis loops whose ascending and descending branches are monotonic functions of input (see Figs. 4.1 and 4.3). Such hysteresis loops may provide the opportunity to account for gradual binary actions. In such hysteresis loops, the transitions between ascending and descending branches occur at triggers α and β, respectively. As mentioned before, in the case of rectangular hysteresis loops the range of input values between β and α is called the band of inaction. This terminology is misleading in the case of generalized hysteresis loops. For such hysteresis loops, it is better to call the above range as the **irreversibility range**. Indeed, for the above range the output values along the two loop branches are different for the same values of input, which is the manifestation of irreversibility.

It is remarkable that general hysteresis loops discussed above can be represented mathematically in terms of rectangular loops with trigger values α and β. This representation has two distinct terms, corresponding to irreversible and reversible components of microeconomic hysteresis, respectively. The irreversible part is given in terms of rectangular loops with triggers α and β. The height of these loops are equal to the differences between the output values along two branches. For this reason, these heights not only depend on α and β but on input values as well. It is apparent that the above irreversible component is equal to zero outside the irreversibility range.

The generalized macroeconomic model is constructed by aggregating heterogenous hysteresis loops discussed above. As in the case of the Preisach model, this aggregation is mathematically accomplished through integration with respect to α and β. This aggregation model has two terms corresponding to the irreversible and reversible components, respectively. In this sense, the mathematical structure of this model is similar to the structure of the alternative form of the Preisach model when its irreversible and reversible components are separated. The main difference is that in the case of the generalized model, the irreversible component has rectangular loops with input dependent heights. Such loops can be represented as products of rectangular loops (with unit heights) and some functions depending on α, β and instantaneous values of input as well. It is shown in the book that this representation leads to another interpretation of the generalized Preisach model. In this interpretation, the above input dependence can be attributed to the fact that switching triggers α and β of microeconomic hysteresis loops may not remain constant as a result of changing economic conditions. In other words, these triggers may be shifted and become input dependent as the economy evolves. It is demonstrated in the book that these shifts can be accounted for in the framework of the generalized aggregation model.

The fact that general hysteresis loops can be represented in terms of rectangular loops makes the diagram technique discussed in the third chapter very instrumental for the analysis of the generalized aggregation model of macroeconomic hysteresis as well. By using this technique, it is demonstrated that the generalized aggregation model has the same three properties as in the case of the Preisach aggregation model. These are the multi-branch property of macroeconomic hysteresis, the erasure property and the property of equal vertical chords for macroeconomic hysteresis loops formed for periodic input variations between the same two consecutive input extrema. This implies that the above properties may be insensitive to the structure of the underlying microeconomic hysteresis subject to aggregation. However, the generalized aggregation model also has two distinct features as well. First, it is demonstrated that macroeconomic loops formed for the same two last extremum values of input have the same vertical chords regardless of the past input histories, however, **they are not congruent**. In other words, in contrast with the Preisach aggregation model, they have different geometrical shapes. Their geometrical shapes are controlled by past dominant input extrema, i.e., by past dominant shocks. Nevertheless, according to Cavalieri's principle, these incongruent macroeconomic loops will have the same area, which is controlled by the last two input extrema.

This implies that the economic hysteresis losses caused by sunk adjustment costs [1], [56] will be the same. The values of these economic losses are controlled by the last two shocks.

Another distinct feature of the generalized aggregation model is that it is endowed with a much more general mechanism of branching than the Preisach aggregation model. Indeed, in the case of the Preisach model, there exists only **one** last branch of macroeconomic hysteresis regardless of the past input history. The geometric shape of this branch is determined only by the last input extrema, i.e., the last shock, and it does not depend on past alternating dominant input extrema, i.e., past dominant shocks. In contrast, in the case of the generalized model, infinite number of last branches of macroeconomic hysteresis is possible (see Figs. 4.23 and 4.24). Geometric shapes of these branches depend on particular past histories of past alternating dominant input extrema, i.e., past dominant shocks. This fact is established by using the algebraic form of the generalized model. This form is the sum of finite number of terms, and **each term** depends on particular past dominant extrema as well as **an instantaneous value of input**.

The next section of the fourth chapter deals with the discussion of macroeconomic hysteresis models based on the aggregation of heterogeneous microeconomic "**play**" hysteresis models. Play hysteresis models may properly and accurately describe the patterns of gradual investments by individual firms. In these models, there are ascending and descending branches which form a major hysteresis loop, and there is also a continuous set of parallel flat inner lines inside this loop which connect the above branches (see Fig. 4.25). Only one of these lines passes through each point inside the major loop. These inner parallel lines are fully reversible and they can be traced in opposite directions for monotonically increasing and decreasing inputs, respectively. Within the framework of play hysteresis, patterns of investment can be briefly described as follows. An investment starts for a monotonically increasing input and the ascending branch of play hysteresis is gradually traced. The input may reach some maximum value and start to decrease before the planned total investment is completed. Under these conditions, the process of investment is stopped and one of the parallel flat inner lines is traced leftward from the ascending branch toward the descending one. If the input achieves some minimum value before the descending branch is reached and then starts to monotonically increase again, then the same inner line is traced in the opposite direction until the ascending branch is reached. After that moment in time, the further monotonic increase in the input results in the renewal of the investment process. This is represented by further upward tracing of the ascending branch until the investment is completed. On the other hand, if the above monotonic decrease in the input is not interrupted, then the inner line is completely traced until the descending branch is reached. The further monotonic decrease in input results in gradual disinvestment. The latter may proceed by tracing the descending branch until the disinvestment process is completed. The described transitions from investment to disinvestment and the other way around may occur as many times as there are input extrema. It is apparent that the described play microeconomic hysteresis accounts for gradual and prudent investment actions. These actions are more realistic and sophisticated than the investment actions represented by rectangular loops or general hysteresis loops without fully reversible inner lines. It is clear that during tracing of parallel inner lines no investment (or disinvestment) actions occur. For this reason, these inner lines can be viewed as **numerous inner bands of inaction** of the same width w.

Despite its complexity, play hysteresis is Markovian (i.e., weak) hysteresis. In other words, this is hysteresis with local memory. This is because the value of output at any instant of time and the value of input at all subsequent instants of time uniquely define the value of output at these subsequent instants of time. This means that for any point on the input-output plane there is only one curve that represents the future time evolution of output for a specific input.

It is remarkable, that despite its complexity, the play hysteresis can be represented in terms of rectangular loops with triggers α and $\alpha - w$. This representation consists of the integration of outputs of the above loops with respect to α. The validity of this representation is mathematically established by using the diagram technique. On the basis of this representation, the macroeconomic hysteresis model as the aggregation of heterogeneous microeconomic play hysteresis models is constructed. This is done through the integration of the above rectangular loop representation of play hysteresis with respect to width w of inner bands of inaction. As a result of this integration, a macroeconomic hysteresis model emerges which is mathematically identical to the Preisach aggregation model. This implies that the Preisach model and the macroeconomic model based on the aggregation of play hysteresis have identical properties, such as the multi-branch property, the erasure property and the equal vertical chords property. This in turn suggests once again that the above properties are insensitive to the specific nature of the underlying microeconomic hysteresis subject to aggregation and their emergence is by and large the aggregation effect.

It is interesting to point out that play hysteresis and its aggregation are extensively used in the study of mechanical hysteresis. In the corresponding literature, this approach is referred to as the Prandtl-Ishlinskii model. It is clear from the above discussion, that the Prandtl-Ishlinskii model can be viewed as a particular case of the Preisach model. This implies that all properties established for the Preisach model are also valid for the Prandtl-Ishlinskii model.

The last section of the fourth chapter deals with the feedback and multi-input macroeconomic hysteresis models. Baldwin and Krugman had pointed out on the existence of a feedback between the output and input in the case of macroeconomic hysteresis. In foreign trade hysteresis, this is the feedback between the trade volume and the exchange rate. In cyclic unemployment, this is the feedback between the unemployment rate and the interest rate. In the Preisach hysteresis model of macroeconomic hysteresis, this feedback is neglected. Mathematically, the above feedback can be accounted for by using a modified input to the Preisach model. This input is equal to the difference between the actual input and the output multiplied by some feedback constant. The comprehensive analysis of this type of feedback model is mathematically quite complicated. It is demonstrated in the book that this analysis is still doable in the case when the feedback constant is relatively small. In the latter case, the feedback model can be mathematically construed as a perturbation of the Preisach aggregation model. In the book, this perturbation analysis of the feedback model is performed. This analysis is based on the algebraic form of the Preisach model introduced in the third chapter. By using this algebraic form, linear equations for the perturbed output values of the feedback model are derived, and it is explained how they can be used in computations. It is also remarked that by using analog circuit modeling of the Preisach model, the analysis of the feedback model can be performed for any values of the feedback constant.

The fourth chapter is concluded with the discussion of multi-input hysteresis models. In our previous analysis of economic hysteresis, it was assumed that a firm's market entry and exit depend on a single input. This may be possible for firms with only one business segment. However, many firms may have several distinct business segments, For example, Apple Inc. has several business segments which include personal computers, smart phones, tablets, wearables and services. For distinct business segments, the structures of entry sunk cost (i.e., market entry investments) may be quite different. This may result in different microeconomic hysteresis structures for distinct business segments. Furthermore, the market entries and exits for distinct business segments may depend on different exogenous inputs. This implies the existence of macroeconomic hysteresis with many inputs. For the sake of presentation simplicity, economic hysteresis with two distinct inputs $u(t)$ and $v(t)$ is first discussed and its generalization to the multi-input case is outlined at the end of the section. On the microeconomic level, hysteresis of two segments is modelled by two rectangular loops with triggers (α, β) and (α', β'), respectively. The heights of these loops may depend on other segment inputs. This dependence reflects the possible coupling between two business segment investments. One example of such a coupling may be the transfer of workers and/or capital from one business segment to another within the same firm caused by exogenous input variations.

The aggregation of two input microeconomic hysteresis can be mathematically modelled through integration with respect to triggers (α, β) and (α', β'). As a result, the two input macroeconomic model is constructed which has two integral terms. These terms are very similar to the integral form of the Preisach aggregation model. This suggests that the diagram technique can be used for the analysis of the two input aggregation model. By using this analysis, the following properties can be established: history dependent multi-branch hysteresis property, the erasure property and the property of equal vertical chords for macroeconomic hysteresis loops. These properties are analogous (but not fully identical) to similar properties of the Preisach aggregation model with a single input. It turns out that the two input model of macroeconomic hysteresis also has the distinct **path independence property**. According to this property, output increments of the two input macroeconomic model corresponding to monotonic variations of two inputs between two points (u_1, v_1) and (u_2, v_2) on the (u, v)-input plane do not depend on a path between the above points on the above plane (see Fig. 4.41). The path independence property suggests that, in the analysis of two input hysteresis, it is always possible to chose the path consisting of horizontal and vertical lines on which one of the two inputs is constant. Such a choice simplifies appreciably the analysis of the two input model. The section is concluded with the remark that it would be very interesting to investigate the use of multi-input hysteresis models for the generalization of the Leontief multi-sector input-output model of economy.

In the third and fourth chapters of the book, macroeconomic hysteresis is mathematically studied under the assumption of deterministic forcing inputs. The purpose of the fifth chapter is to remove this limitation and to consider the macroeconomic aggregation under stochastic conditions. This requires the analysis of hysteresis driven by random processes.

The fifth chapter is the most sophisticated and advanced chapter in the book from the mathematical point of view. To make it accessible to a large audience of readers, the very basic facts of the theory of random processes are summarized in the first section of the chapter. This summary is presented without going into subtle mathematical discussions and proofs. The section starts with the definition of stochastic processes, which is done on two levels: on the level of **random realizations (i.e., samples)** and on the level of **joint** and **transition probability densities**. The discussion is concerned with stochastic processes with continuous samples. The simplest and most studied example of such processes is the Wiener process. This is the process with independent increments which are Gaussian random variables. It turns out that by using the Wiener process, the broad class of Markov stochastic processes can be generated and studied by introducing stochastic differential (Itô or Stratonovich) equations. This is the class of Markov processes with continuous samples which are called diffusion processes. Diffusion processes can also be studied by using the transition probability density function. This function has "forward" and "backward" coordinates. With respect to the forward coordinates, it satisfies the forward Kolmogorov equation, while with respect to the backward coordinates, it satisfies the backward Kolmogorov equation. These are **linear deterministic partial differential equations**, while the Itô or Stratonovich equations are **nonlinear stochastic ordinary differential** equations. The latter equations are used in Monte Carlo simulations. The discussion of hysteresis driven by stochastic diffusion processes presented in the book is by and large based on the Kolmogorov backward and forward equations.

The general discussion of stochastic diffusion processes is illustrated by the example of the Ornstein-Uhlenbeck process. This process is quite unique because it is the **stationary Gaussian Markov** process. This process has been used in economics to model the stochasticity of interest rates, currency exchange rates and commodity prices. The Ornstein-Uhlenbeck process captures mean reversion of interest rate fluctuations (for instance). There are two terms (diffusion and drift) in the stochastic differential equation for the Ornstein-Uhlenbeck process. The diffusion term is proportional to the time derivative of the Wiener process and it is the source of random fluctuations. The drift term is proportional to the difference between the mean and the random current value of the interest rate. If the interest rate drops below its mean value, then the drift term is positive resulting in the tendency for the interest rate to move upwards towards its mean value. On the other hand, if the interest rate rises above its mean value, then the drift term is negative resulting in the tendency for the interest rate to move down towards its mean value. This is the mechanism of mean reversion.

The section is concluded with the discussion of how the theory of stochastic processes can be used in the analysis of the Preisach aggregation model driven by a stochastic input. It is pointed out that the main step in this analysis is the study of random outputs of rectangular hysteresis loops driven by a diffusion process. Then, the expected value of the Preisach model output can be found as the aggregation (i.e., integration) of expected output values of individual rectangular loops. It is pointed out that two techniques can be used for the analysis of random outputs of randomly driven rectangular loops. The first technique treats random triggering (i.e., random switching of rectangular loops) as the **exit problem** for diffusion processes. The second and entirely different approach is based on the **theory of stochastic processes on graphs**. This theory was originally developed to study random perturbations of Hamiltonian dynamic systems. It turns out that the mathematical machinery of this theory is naturally suitable for the analysis of the outputs of randomly driven rectangular hysteresis loops.

In the second section of the chapter, the analysis of random outputs of rectangular hysteresis loops driven by a stationary stochastic diffusion process is discussed by using the theory of exit problems. First, it is pointed out that the above random outputs are binary processes represented by sequences (i.e., trains) of rectangular pulses of constant height. The widths of these rectangular pulses and their separations are random. Thus, if the above randomness is completely characterized, then the stochastic binary output process will be properly defined as well. This characterization of the random width and random separation of rectangular output pulses can be accomplished by using the theory of exit problem for stationary diffusion processes. Indeed, it is clear that the random width of rectangular pulses is equal to the random time during which a rectangular hysteresis loops is in the upward state. On the other hand, the above random time is equal to the random exit time of the diffusion process from the semi-infinite interval whose lower boundary is defined by the downward trigger β. Similarly, it is apparent that the random separation between rectangular pulses is equal to the random time the rectangular hysteresis loop is in the downward (i.e., zero) state. The above random time is equal to the random exit time of the diffusion process from the semi-infinite interval whose upper boundary is defined by the upward trigger α (see Figs. 5.4 and 5.5).

The described two exit problems corresponding to these random downward and upward switchings of rectangular loops, respectively, may be useful for microeconomic hysteresis analysis under uncertainty. Indeed, in microeconomics, firms' market entry and market exit are often characterized by two triggers α and β, which can be identified with switching thresholds of rectangular loops. On the basis of microeconomic analysis, the market entry may be chosen to occur when the random input reaches some specific value α. This implies that a firm which is ready for investment at some instant of time, when the input value is quite different and below α, has to wait until the input α-value is reached. This waiting time is equal to the random exit time resulting in the upward switching of the rectangular hysteresis loop. If the solution of the corresponding exit problem suggests a very long (on average) waiting time for market entry, this may lead to the adjustment of the microeconomic analysis resulting in the selection of the α-trigger. Similarly, the firm market exit time occurs when the random input reaches some value β. This implies that the time during which a firm remains in the market is equal to the random exit time resulting in downward rectangular loop switching. The statistics of this random exit time can be used to determine the average time that the firm remains in the market, which in turn may lead to the estimate of the expected value of a firm's revenue.

The discussed exit problems are among the most well-studied problems of stochastic diffusion process theory. These problems are reduced to the solution of specific initial-boundary value problems for the backward Kolmogorov equation. This initial-boundary value problem is presented in the book for a general stationary diffusion process as well as for the Ornstein-Uhlenbeck process. The latter is justified because in economics a random volatility of forcing input is often described by the Ornstein-Uhlenbeck process. The above initial-boundary value problem for the backward Kolmogorov equation can be solved numerically. In the case of the Ornstein-Uhlenbeck forcing input, the **analytical** solution can also be found by using the Laplace transform and parabolic cylinder functions.

In the third section of the fifth chapter, another approach is developed for the analysis of randomness in hysteretic systems. This approach is based on the theory of stochastic processes on graphs. The foundation of this approach is based on the following simple fact. The output of a randomly driven rectangular hysteresis loop is a random binary process, which is not Markovian. However, it is possible to construct the two-component process which is Markovian, and it contains the above random output as its first component. This two-component Markov process is defined on the graph representing a rectangular hysteresis loop (see Fig. 5.11). This graph has four edges and two vertices, with coordinates equal to trigger values α and β, respectively. Each of the two so-called inner graph edges are connected to the two vertices, and they form a loop. Two other so-called outside graph edges are infinitely long, and each of them is connected to a single (but different) vertex. For the outside edges, the second component of the above two-component process coincides with the input stochastic process. This process is split into the sum of two stochastic processes, which are the second components of the Markovian two-component process on the inner edges of the graph. It is demonstrated that the analysis of the above two-component process is reduced to the solution of an initial-boundary value problem for the forward Kolmogorov equation on the described graph. It turns out that simple analytical expressions can be obtained for the stationary solution of the two-component process in the case when the random input is the Ornstein-Uhlenbeck process. This leads to simple formulas for the expected value and the variance of the output of randomly driven rectangular hysteresis loops. Furthermore, the above formulas can be used for the calculation of the expected value of the random output of the Preisach aggregation model. The third section is concluded with the analysis of the second moment and variance of the output. This analysis is more involved, and it requires the introduction of a three component Markov process. This process is defined on more complex graphs than the graphs for rectangular hysteresis loops. Nevertheless, it is shown that analytical expressions can still be derived for the second moment and variance of the random output of the Preisach aggregation model.

The fourth section of the fifth chapter deals with the stochastic analysis of generalized models of macroeconomic hysteresis. As demonstrated in the fourth chapter, these models can also be represented in terms of rectangular hysteresis loops. For this reason, the results obtained in the second and third sections can be used in this analysis with some modifications accounting for the specifics of the generalized models. These modifications are discussed briefly in the fourth section.

In the book, rate-independent macroeconomic hysteresis models are discussed. The term "rate-independent" implies that in these models only past input extrema (i.e., past shocks) may leave their mark upon future evolution of macroeconomics, while the speed of input (or output) variations has no influence on future hysteresis branching. The last assumption can be relaxed and dynamic hysteresis models can be developed. Some of such dynamic models are discussed in the book [75]. The relevance of such dynamic models in economics may be still in question, because it undermines the main assumption of macroeconomics that due to its huge scale it is mostly driven by some past shocks.

Chapter 2

Economic Hysteresis

2.1 What is Economic Hysteresis?

The hysteresis phenomenon is ubiquitous. It is encountered in many different areas of science, engineering and social life. The most known example of this phenomenon is magnetic hysteresis which found applications in magnetic data storage devices, such as hard disk drives and magnetic tapes as well as in the design of permanent magnets. Other examples of hysteresis include mechanical hysteresis, superconducting hysteresis, optical hysteresis, electron-beam hysteresis, adsorption hysteresis, economic hysteresis, etc. The phenomenon of hysteresis is also encountered in biology and neuroscience (see [76]).

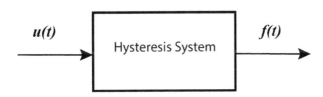

u(t)   Hysteresis System   *f(t)*

Fig. 2.1

To make our subsequent discussion very general and precise, it is desirable to give the mathematical definition of hysteresis based on its common features observed in its various manifestations. This can be done by adopting the language of systems theory. Namely, we consider a system that converts an input $u(t)$ into an output $f(t)$ (see Fig. 2.1). This system is called a hysteresis system (HS), if its input-output relationship exhibits hysteresis. The most known and simplest manifestation of hysteresis is a hysteresis loop (see Fig. 2.2). Such a loop is formed for periodic back and

forth variations of the input between two consecutive extremum values. For
symmetric loops, these extremum values are the minimum value $-u_m$ and
the maximum value u_m. A hysteresis loop has two branches: a lower (ascending) branch corresponding to monotonic increase of input from $-u_m$ to
u_m and an upper (descending) branch corresponding to monotonic decrease
of input from u_m to $-u_m$. In Fig. 2.2, the tracing of these branches are
marked by upward and downward arrows.

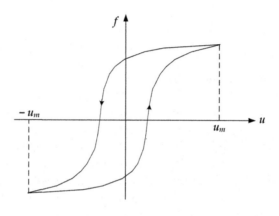

Fig. 2.2

The term "hysteresis" was introduced by the British physicist
J.A. Ewing. This word is of Greek origin with the meaning of "lagging
behind". Indeed, when a symmetric hysteresis loop is traced, variations of
output $f(t)$ lag behind variations of input $u(t)$. Namely, when the descending branch is traced, the input $u(t)$ reaches zero, while the output $f(t)$ is
still positive. Furthermore, output $f(t)$ reaches zero, when input $u(t)$ is
already negative. Similar lagging behind variations of the output $f(t)$ are
observed in Fig. 2.2 in tracing the ascending branch of a symmetrical hysteresis loop.

Symmetric hysteresis loops are formed when the input $u(t)$ varies
between two consecutive extremum values of the same magnitude. In general, hysteresis loops are formed for back and forth input variations between
any two consecutive extremum values u_1 and u_2 (see Fig. 2.3).

The simplest and most elementary hysteresis nonlinearities are rectangular loops (see Figs. 2.4a and 2.4b). These types of loops are used as the
main building blocks for sophisticated mathematical models of economic
hysteresis discussed in subsequent chapters.

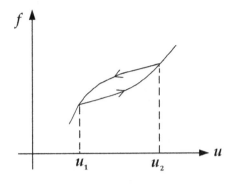

Fig. 2.3

It is easy to see that hysteresis nonlinearities represented by hysteresis loops have **local** memories. The latter means that the value of output $f(t_0)$ at any instant of time t_0 and the values of input $u(t)$ at all subsequent instants of time $t \geq t_0$ uniquely define the values of output $f(t)$ for all $t \geq t_0$. This is because the initial output value $f(t_0)$ specifies the (upper or lower) branch of the hysteresis loop along which the subsequent variations of output occur. This implies that in the case of hysteresis with local memory the past exerts its influence upon the future through the current values of output. By analogy with the theory of random processes, hysteresis with local memory can be called Markovian hysteresis. In the economic literature [7], the term **weak hysteresis** is used for Markovian hysteresis.

Although loops are the most known manifestation of hysteresis, they do no fully reflect the essence of hysteresis phenomenon. **The essence of this phenomenon is the history dependent branching.** In other words, hysteresis can be defined as a multibranch input-output relation for which transitions from one branch to another occur after each input extremum. Such a multi-branch nonlinearity is shown in Fig. 2.5. It is apparent that the formation of hysteresis loops is a particular case of history-dependent branching. This case is realized for periodic variations of inputs, while branching occurs for **arbitrary input variations**.

In summary, hysteresis can be viewed as an input-output nonlinearity with memory of past history which reveals itself through branching. This memory of past history has a relatively simple structure in the case of **rate-independent hysteresis**. The term "rate-independent" means that hysteresis branching is controlled only by the past extremum values of input, while the speed and particular manner of monotonic input variations

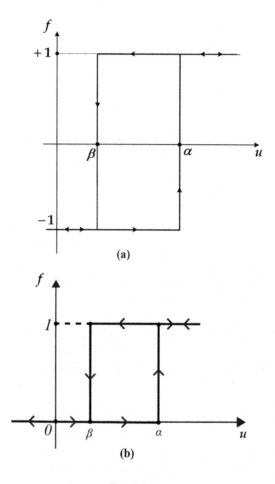

(a)

(b)

Fig. 2.4

between input extremum points has no influence on branching. The above statement is illustrated by Figs. 2.6a, 2.6b and 2.6c. Here, Figs. 2.6a and 2.6b represent two different inputs $u^{(1)}(t)$ and $u^{(2)}(t)$ which successively assume the same extremum values u_1, u_2, u_3 and u_4 but vary in time differently between these values. Then, in the case of rate-independent hysteresis these two inputs will result in the same branching as shown in Fig. 2.6c. This implies that rate-independent hysteresis is endowed with a discrete memory structure consisting of past-extremum values of input. The notion of rate-independent hysteresis is naturally applicable in economics. This is because of high economic inertia caused by the huge scale of the

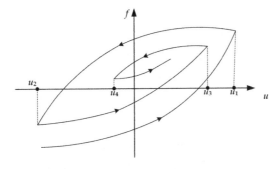

Fig. 2.5

economy as well as by the innate nature of any bureaucracy to maintain stability by resisting to fast changes (or any changes).

It is clear that multibranch hysteresis has **nonlocal** memory. For this reason, this is non-Markovian hysteresis. In the economic literature [4], the term **strong hysteresis** is used for non-Markovian hysteresis.

Up to this point, we have discussed counter clock-wise hysteresis where the tracing of hysteresis loops and consecutive hysteresis branches occurs in the counter clock-wise direction. It turns out that there exists clock-wise hysteresis phenomena, as well. Examples of clock-wise hysteresis are shown in Figs. 2.7a and 2.7b. The properties of this hysteresis are very similar to counter clock-wise hysteresis. For this reason, its analysis is omitted in the subsequent discussions.

Having defined the notion of hysteresis, we next proceed to the discussion of how this definition is relevant to economic hysteresis. However, some general remarks concerning economic hysteresis are first in order. Economic hysteresis has a long and interesting history. Over the years, many facts related to economic hysteresis were discussed in the literature (for instance, see [1], [2], [4]–[8], [9]–[13], [16]–[20], [23], [24], [28]–[33], [38]–[42], [48], [54]–[56], [65], [69], [77], [78], [83], and [89]). This list of references is not complete but rather suggestive. Nevertheless, as of today, a concept of economic hysteresis is still lacking an unambiguous and precise definition accepted by the majority of researchers in economics. As a result the term hysteresis means different things to different researchers. For instance, some researchers maintain that the main manifestation of hysteresis is **remanence**, while other researchers believe that the key feature of hysteresis is **strong persistence**. It turns out that these two features are simultaneously present in hysteresis phenomena. Indeed, the remanence can be

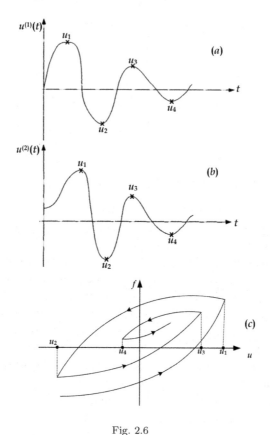

Fig. 2.6

defined as a difference of two output values at two consecutive branches for the same value of input. Consequently, the remanence is represented by vertical chords between two consecutive hysteresis branches. This is illustrated in Fig. 2.8. It is clear from this figure that this remanence persists until a new hysteresis loop is formed. Consequently, it can be concluded that the important manifestation of hysteresis is the **persisting remanence**. It is worthwhile to mention that remanence implies **irreversibility**. The latter term is also often used in the economic literature for the characterization of hysteresis [41].

The presented definition of hysteresis is quite general because the actual economic meanings of input $u(t)$ and output $f(t)$ are left unspecified. This makes the above definition applicable to various forms of economic hysteresis. Examples include trade hysteresis, unemployment hysteresis, investment hysteresis, etc. The input-output formalism has long been used

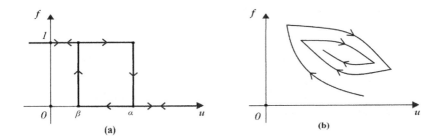

Fig. 2.7

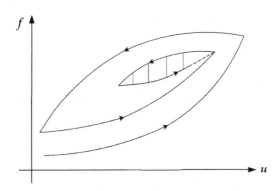

Fig. 2.8

in the economic literature. The origin of this formalism can be traced back
to the foundational work of Wassily Leontief who won the Nobel Memorial
Prize in Economic Sciences in 1973 "for the development of the input-
output method and for its application to important economic problems."
The essence of this method is to describe input-output interactions between
different sectors of the economy. In contrast with hysteresis, this is a linear
technique in which the input-output interactions are mathematically modeled by matrices. A nonlinear generalization of this technique is discussed
by Sandberg in [87].

As will be discussed later in the book, hysteresis loops (see Figs. 2.4b
and 2.7a) are typical for **microeconomic** hysteresis, while multi-branch
hysteresis (see Figs. 2.6c and 2.7b) describes **macroeconomic** hysteresis. This multibranch macroeconomic hysteresis occurs due to the aggregation of very large number of **heterogeneous** microeconomic hysteresis
loops. By using this aggregation, mathematical models of macroeconomic
hysteresis are constructed.

The given definition of macroeconomic hysteresis as history-dependent branching is consistent with observed economic activities which typically consist of numerous upward and downward output variations. These output variations are usually caused by upward and downward variations of input, which in the economic literature is often called as the "forcing variable". These output variations as function of the input can be viewed as hysteresis branches which sequentially follow one another in time. In the case of rate-independent hysteresis, this branching is controlled not only by the current input variations but by the past extremum values of the input as well.

In the economic literature on hysteresis, the term of **"economic shock"** is frequently used. There is no consensus among scholars concerning the precise definition of an economic shock. It is usually and tacitly assumed that shocks are short-term exogenous events that have long-term consequences for the economy in general and economic hysteresis in particular. It is apparent from the given definition of rate-independent multi-branch hysteresis that past input extrema can be viewed as mathematical manifestations of shocks. Indeed, these past input extrema are usually exogenous in nature and they control future hysteresis branching. The latter implies that they have long-term economic consequences. It is discussed later in the book, that in the case of macroeconomic hysteresis models constructed as aggregations of a large number of heterogeneous microeconomic hysteresis models, not all past extrema can be viewed as shocks at a given instant of time t. This is due to the **erasure property** of aggregation of microeconomic hysteresis, which will be discussed later in the book.

The notion of hysteresis as a history dependent multibranch nonlinearity was introduced in [70], [71] and [73]. This notion has been gradually accepted and used in the economic literature. For instance, it is stated in the paper of B. Amable, J. Henry, F. Lordon and R. Topol [5] that:

" ... *following Mayergoyz, we may say that a system is hysteretic if 'the input-output relationship is non-linear multibranch, the transitions from branch to branch occurring each time the input reaches an extremum'*"

Similarly, it is stated in the conclusion of the paper of M. Göcke [54] that:

"... *all types of 'genuine' hysteresis show the common feature of multibranch non-linearity.*"

Next, we proceed to the brief review of existing approaches to economic hysteresis modeling. It turns out that two approaches to the modeling and analysis of macroeconomic hysteresis are most dominant in the existing economic literature. The first approach is due to the pioneering work of R. Baldwin, P. Krugman, B. Amable, J. Henry, F. Lordon, R. Topol, R. Cross,[1] M. Göcke and A. Belke. The central idea of this approach is to investigate first the nature of microeconomic hysteresis and then proceed to the analysis of the corresponding macroeconomic hysteresis obtained through the aggregation procedure. In this book, this approach is adopted for the study of macroeconomic hysteresis with the main emphasis on the theoretical analysis of new phenomena emerging as a result of aggregation.

The important feature of the above approach is that it clearly reveals the **origin** of economic hysteresis. On the microeconomic level, this origin is due to **binary actions** such as buying-selling in the case of trade hysteresis, hiring-firing in the case of unemployment hysteresis or, in general, investment-disinvestment. These binary actions are of opposite nature. However, they are not reversible versions of one another. They occur in a different manner due to **entry sunk costs**. This leads to the origin of microeconomic hysteresis described by hysteresis loops. The macroeconomic aggregation of the above microeconomic hysteresis leads to the formation of history dependent multibranch hysteresis.

The highly desirable feature of any theory is its **predictive power**. It turns out that macroeconomic aggregation models of hysteresis represent unique mathematical tools endowed with the **predictive power of future macroeconomic hysteresis branching**. Namely, it is shown in this book that, due to their structure, these mathematical tools detect input extrema, store them and choose the future hysteresis branches in accordance with the accumulated history of past input extrema. Needless to say that the prediction of future economic evolution, i.e., branching, can be of significant economic value.

The second and entirely different approach to the macroeconomic unemployment hysteresis was introduced by O. Blanchard and L. Summers [23]. During the 1980s, it was perceived that the unemployment natural rate hypothesis was inconsistent with observed long-lasting unemployment rates in Europe. As a way out of this predicament, Blanchard and Summers suggested that unemployment rates are history-dependent and exhibit hysteresis. This was stated in their paper in the following manner:

"The sustained upturn in European unemployment challenges the premise of most macroeconomic theories that there exists some 'natural' or 'nonaccelerating inflation' rate of unemployment toward which the economy

---

[1]The authors acknowledge that they were encouraged by the late R. Cross to work on the mathematical models of macroeconomic hysteresis.

tends to gravitate and at which the level of inflation remains constant. The European experience compels consideration of alternative theories of 'hysteresis' which contemplate the possibility that increases in unemployment have a direct impact on the 'natural' rate of unemployment.

This article explores theoretically and empirically the idea of macroeconomic hysteresis—the substantial persistence of unemployment and the protracted effects of shocks on unemployment."

The mathematical concept of hysteresis used in the paper of Blanchard and Summers is spelled out in the first footnote of the paper as follows:

"Formally, a dynamic system is said to exhibit hysteresis if it has at least one eigenvalue equal to zero (unity, if specified in discrete time). In such a case, the steady state of the system will depend on the history of the shocks affecting the system. Thus, we should say that unemployment exhibits hysteresis when current unemployment depends on past values with coefficients summing to 1. We shall instead use 'hysteresis' more loosely to refer to the case where the degree of dependence on the past is very high, where the sum of coefficients is close but not necessarily equal to 1."

The paper of Blanchard and Summers resulted in two benchmarking shifts in economic discussions. First, this paper has led to the growing discontent with the concept of natural rate of unemployment. Second, the paper was very influential in bringing the notion of hysteresis to the center of economic research.

The concept of natural rate of unemployment was introduced in 1967 and 1968 independently by E. Phelps [81] and [82] and M. Friedman [51]. It was suggested that this rate corresponds to some economic equilibrium, and an actual unemployment rate gradually tends to the natural rate under constant inflation. The actual unemployment mostly consists of three distinct components: cyclical, structural and frictional. The cyclical unemployment is temporary, and it can be controlled by the appropriate monetary policy through interest rates, for instance. Frictional unemployment is due to the workers who are between jobs. Structural unemployment is due to shifts in demands for different types of labor. This unemployment reflects the mismatch between the labor structure of the existing work force and the labor demand of existing and newly developed technologies. The natural rate of unemployment is the sum of frictional and structural unemployment. In other words, the natural rate of unemployment is the rate that would occur in the absence of cyclical unemployment fluctuations. However the structural unemployment changes with time as well, and this makes the determination of the natural rate imprecise and elusive. This and other factors resulted in the criticism of the concept of the natural rate hypothesis and the development of new ideas. For instance, Blanchard and Summers suggested the idea of "fragile equilibria" to account for the strong unemployment dependence on its past history. The criticism of the natural rate hypothesis and its relation to hysteresis is discussed in the book "The Natural Rate of Unemployment: Reflections on 25 Years of the Hypothesis" edited by Rod Cross [30]. Here, it is also worthwhile to mention the paper of Blanchard "Should We Reject the Natural Rate Hypothesis?" [24].

As far as unemployment hysteresis analysis is concerned, it is clear from the cited above footnote in the paper of Blanchard and Summers, that this analysis is performed at the **macroeconomic level** by using unemployment time series and the **concept of the unit root** for such series. According to this concept, it is assumed that actual unemployment time series can be viewed as solutions of randomly perturbed **linear** discrete time equations. Such equations define discrete time stochastic processes. For the deterministic parts of such equations, algebraic characteristic equations can be introduced. If 1 is a root of these algebraic equations, then it is said that the corresponding stochastic processes have a unit root. For a unit root stochastic process, any nonzero value of the noise term will **permanently affect** the values of the stochastic process at subsequent instants of time. In economics, this mathematical fact is interpreted as **persistent** dependence of economic time series on past shocks which reveals the existence of hysteresis.

The above concept of economic hysteresis is fundamentally different from the notion of macroeconomic hysteresis previously discussed in this section. The very detailed analysis of the unit root hysteresis and its comparison with multibranch hysteresis is performed in the papers of Amable, Henry, Lordon and Topol (see [6], [7] and [8]). The main points of this analysis can be summarized as follows. First, the unit root type hysteresis is defined above for **linear** systems while it is well-known that hysteresis is an intrinsically **nonlinear** phenomenon. Second, the unit root type of unemployment hysteresis is introduced by using only unemployment time series without any reference to "forcing" variables responsible for the existence of hysteresis. Finally, the unit root unemployment hysteresis is introduced on the macroeconomic level without any discussion of the origin of such hysteresis as a result of aggregation of microeconomic unemployment hysteresis. On the microeconomic level, the origin of unemployment hysteresis is due to the binary actions of hiring and firing by numerous businesses. These actions are of opposite nature, but they occur in a different manner because (at least) there are always barriers to firing workers once they are hired. These barriers can be interpreted as a part of the employment sunk costs. This leads to microeconomic hysteresis described by hysteresis loops. The macroeconomic aggregation elevates this hysteresis to the level of multibranch history-dependent hysteresis. As was already mentioned, this approach will be pursued in this book.

2.2   Microeconomic Hysteresis

We shall now discuss microeconomic hysteresis, which reveals the **origin** of economic hysteresis. As has already been mentioned, this origin is due to the fact that firms operate using binary actions such as buying-selling, hiring-firing or, in general, investing-disinvesting. These binary actions are of opposite nature. However, they are not reversible versions of one another. In other words, these binary actions are asymmetric due to the **market entry sunk costs**. This leads to microeconomic hysteresis which is usually described by relatively simple hysteresis loops. The theory of microeconomic hysteresis has been extensively developed due to the work of Baldwin ([9], [10]), Baldwin and Krugman [11], Dixit ([38]–[40], [42]), Dixit and Pindyck [41] and Pindyck [83].

It turns out that microeconomic hysteresis may be strongly affected by the uncertainty of the economic environment. This uncertainty is reflected in the fact that the "forcing" input (such as exchange rate, interest rate, etc.) is not deterministic but rather stochastic in nature. First, we shall ignore this stochasticity and consider the case when a firm may perfectly anticipate variations of forcing input. This is done to demonstrate that the origin of microeconomic hysteresis has nothing to do with stochasticity of input, but it is rather due to market entry sunk costs. For this reason, microeconomic hysteresis can be viewed as the **sunk cost hysteresis**. Of course, this deterministic approach is an idealization, and the uncertainty of input may affect the microeconomic hysteresis. This issue will be discussed later in the subsequent section.

To discuss sunk cost hysteresis in some generality, we consider two binary actions: investment and disinvestment. To enter the market, a firm must make some investment. In general, this investment is irreversible in nature because it is firm specific. This means that it is not recoverable. This market entry investment may have many different components such as acquisition of special equipment for new product fabrication and manufacturing, research and development of a new product, marketing, creation

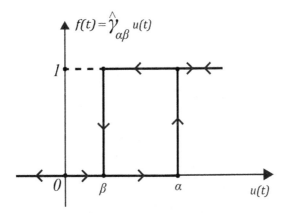

Fig. 2.9

of sales and distribution networks, hiring of workers and their training, etc. This irreversible investment is the market entry sunk cost. Usually, a firm makes this sunk cost investment and enters the market at the time when it expects to generate sufficiently large revenue to gradually recoup the market entry sunk cost and make some profit. In the case of sunk cost hysteresis, firms may also continue to operate when they are unprofitable and they are losing money. This is usually done with some foresight of a certain likelihood that profitable times may return and current losses will be recovered through future profits. This staying in the market may also avoid market exit losses related to the value of market entry sunk cost investment. At the time, when unprofitability becomes intolerable and the return of profitability is assessed to be quite remote, the firm may exit the market.

It is clear from the above discussion that there are two triggers α and β corresponding to the values of forcing input at which market entry and market exit may occur. In the simplest case this leads to the hysteresis loop shown in Fig. 2.9. According to this figure, if the firm originally is not in the market, it will remain this way until the forcing input reaches the entry trigger value α. At this time, the firm enters the market and it remains in the market until the forcing input reaches the exit trigger value β. It is apparent from the above figure that when the input varies between β and α, the firm can be out of the market if the input $u(t)$ entered the interval

$$\beta < u(t) < \alpha \qquad (2.1)$$

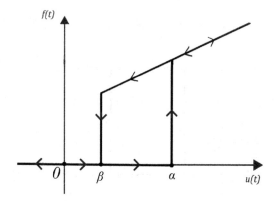

Fig. 2.10

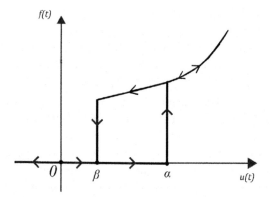

Fig. 2.11

trom the β-side. On the other hand, if the input $u(t)$ varies in this interval and entered it from the α-side, then the firm will remain in the market. Thus, it is clear that when the input $u(t)$ varies between trigger values β and α, the state of the firm depends on the past history. Namely, this state depends on the past states of the firm before the input enters the interval (2.1). This means that when input $u(t)$ varies within this interval, then there are two persistent remanent states of the firm which are determined by its past states immediately before the input entrance to this interval. This phenomenon is the clear manifestation of hysteresis.

The hysteresis loop shown in Fig. 2.9 is a rectangular hysteresis loop. This is the simplest and most elementary hysteresis loop. In the case when the output $f(t)$ represents a firm's investment, this loop represents the idealized case when this investment remains constant for the very wide range of input variations. More realistic loops for the sunk cost hysteresis are shown in Figs. 2.10 and 2.11. Similar loops can be found, respectively, in the papers of Baldwin and Krugman [11] and Amable, Henry, Lordon and Topol [4], [8]. These figures reflect the fact that the firm's investment may monotonically decrease with decreasing input, which eventually results in the firm's exit from the market.

It is remarkable that hysteresis loops shown in Figs. 2.10 and 2.11 can be mathematically represented in terms of the rectangular hysteresis loop $\hat{\gamma}_{\alpha\beta}u$ shown in Fig. 2.9. We shall demonstrate this for the case of the loop shown in Fig. 2.11. First, we introduce ascending $f^+_{\alpha\beta}(u)$ and descending $f^-_{\alpha\beta}(u)$ branches for the above loop as shown in Figs. 2.12a and 2.12b, respectively. Here, we note that the ascending and descending branches are fully reversible within the intervals $-\infty < u < \alpha$ and $\beta < u < \infty$, respectively. Now, it is easy to verify that the hysteresis loop shown in Fig. 2.11 can be mathematically represented by the formula:

$$\hat{\Gamma}_{\alpha\beta}(u) = \left(f^-_{\alpha\beta}(u) - f^+_{\alpha\beta}(u)\right)\hat{\gamma}_{\alpha\beta}u + f^+_{\alpha\beta}(u), \qquad (2.2)$$

where $\hat{\Gamma}_{\alpha\beta}(u)$ is the mathematical notation for the hysteresis loop shown in Fig. 2.11.

Indeed, when the input $u(t)$ is monotonically increasing from $-\infty$ to α then $\hat{\gamma}_{\alpha\beta}u(t) = 0$. Consequently, according to formula (2.2), we find that $f = \hat{\Gamma}_{\alpha\beta}(u) = f^+_{\alpha\beta}(u)$ which is zero according to Fig. 2.12(a). When $u(t)$ exceeds α and continues to increase then $\hat{\gamma}_{\alpha\beta}u(t) = 1$. Consequently, according to formula (2.2), we find that $f = \hat{\Gamma}_{\alpha\beta}(u) = f^-_{\alpha\beta}(u)$, which is the same as $f^+_{\alpha\beta}(u)$ when $u > \alpha$. On the other hand, if upon exceeding α input $u(t)$ is monotonically decreasing but does not reach β, then still $\hat{\gamma}_{\alpha\beta}u(t) = 1$. According to formula (2.2) this implies that $f(t) = \hat{\Gamma}_{\alpha\beta}\big(u(t)\big) = f^-_{\alpha\beta}(u)$. Finally, when input $u(t)$ decreases below β, then $\hat{\gamma}_{\alpha\beta}u(t) = 0$ and $f(t) = f^+_{\alpha\beta}(u)$, which for $u(t) < \beta$ coincides with $f^-_{\alpha\beta}(u)$.

It is worthwhile to mention that formula (2.2) is quite general and can be used for the representation of various hysteresis loops. For instance, it is easy to show by using literally the same line of reasoning as before that this formula can be used for the representation of the loop shown in Fig. 2.13. Such a hysteresis loop may describe not an abrupt but rather an incremental investment occurring gradually.

The importance of formula (2.2) is due to the representation of complex hysteresis loops by the simpler rectangular loops which are fully

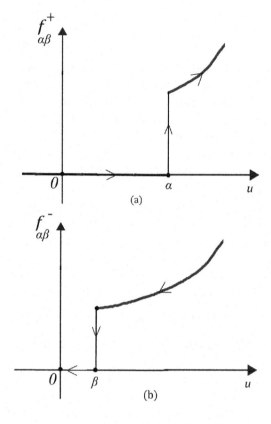

(a)

(b)

Fig. 2.12

characterized by only two numbers: α and β. This fact will be extensively used in the next two chapters to study macroeconomic hysteresis models and their properties.

Rectangular loops $\hat{\gamma}_{\alpha\beta}u$ can also be used for the representation of weak (i.e., Markovian) hysteresis nonlinearities which are more complex than simple hysteresis loops. One of such examples is the Prandtl-Ishlinskii play hysteresis, which was historically used for the description of mechanical hysteresis. The use of such hysteresis for the analysis of economic hysteresis was proposed by Göcke [55] and more recently by Mota [77], [78]. It is shown in Sec. 4.3 that the play hysteresis may properly describe the patterns of gradual investments by individual firms. The play hysteresis can be geometrically represented by Fig. 2.14. Here, there is a set of inner straight lines within the major loop which is outlined by bold lines. Only one line

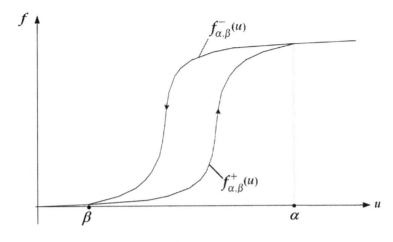

Fig. 2.13

passes through each point inside of the major loop. These lines are fully reversible and can be traversed in opposite directions, for monotonically increasing and decreasing input $u(t)$. It turns out that this hysteresis can be also represented in terms of rectangular loops $\hat{\gamma}_{\alpha\beta}u$ by the following formula:

$$f(t) = \frac{m_s}{\alpha_2 - \alpha_1} \int_{\alpha_1}^{\alpha_2} \hat{\gamma}_{\alpha,\alpha-w} u(t) d\alpha. \tag{2.3}$$

The derivation of the above formula will be discussed in Sec. 4.3.

In our preceding discussion, it has been tacitly assumed that the market entries and exits are controlled by a single forcing input (e.g. exchange rate or interest rate for trade or unemployment hysteresis, respectively). In reality, several exogenous variables may jointly control each firm decision to enter or exit the market. These variables may be accounted for by introducing one synthetic (i.e. composite) controlling input. It belongs to the area of microeconomics to properly ascertain the structure of such synthetic forcing inputs. The main advantage of such synthetic inputs is that market entries and exits may still be characterized by only two trigger values α and β, respectively.

Up to this point, we have not discussed the delicate and critical issue of choosing the trigger values α and β. The first discussion of this issue can be traced back to the classical work of Alfred Marshall [69]. According to his approach, firms invest when expected returns exceed long-run average expenditures and exit the market otherwise. Much later, the modern

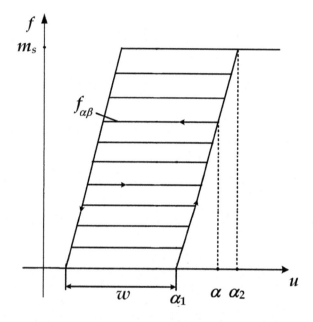

Fig. 2.14

orthodox approach to investment has emerged and it is based on the net present value (NPV) rule. In simplistic terms, the NPV is the difference between the present value of cash inflow and the present value of cash outflow over some period of time. The NPV rule favors the investment when the net present value is positive and suggests to avoid investment otherwise. It is clear that this rule can be used to determine the market entry threshold α. However, the NPV rule does not account for investment irreversibility. For this reason, this rule can not be used for the determination of market exit threshold β. Furthermore, the NPV rule does not account for market uncertainties caused by stochastic variations of forcing inputs such as exchange rates, interest rates, etc. This implies that the NPV rule is not applicable to irreversible (hysteretic) investments under uncertainty. Under this uncertainty, waiting to invest may have positive value. This is because the passage of time may bring more information concerning possible future profits and may make a later decision to be a better one. At the same time, there may be a risk to delay investment decisions due to the possibility of market entry by other competing firms. It is apparent that this risk must be weighted against the benefit of waiting for new information.

2.3 Investment Under Uncertainity

The mathematical analysis of investment under uncertainty was studied in detail in the ground breaking works of Baldwin [10], Dixit and Pindyck [41] and Pindyck [83]. The theory of stochastic processes in combination with the mathematical machinery of dynamic programming were used in their analysis. Stochastic processes, such as i.i.d. (independent identically distributed), geometric Brownian motion and Ornstein-Uhlenbeck type processes were employed for the description of the randomness. It was demonstrated in the above research that the investment under uncertainty benefits from the broadening of the width, $\alpha - \beta$, of the hysteresis loop. In the economic literature, this width is often called as the "**band of inaction**". In the mentioned works of Baldwin, Dixit and Pindyck the shape of the microeconomic hysteresis loop is not specified. However, the very fact that these authors characterize microeconomic hysteresis by only two numbers (i.e. triggers α and β), suggests that they deal with rectangular hysteresis loops. Indeed, only a rectangular hysteresis loop can be fully characterized (up to its vertical scale) by **only two** numbers α and β.

In this section, we shall discuss a different issue appearing in the modeling of investment under uncertainty. This issue is related to the fact that the **stochastic nature of the forcing input results in random dynamics of investment**. This implies that the investment is a stochastic process as well. The analysis of this random investment process is performed below by assuming that random forcing input can be modelled as an i.i.d. process. First, the case of the rectangular hysteresis loop driven by an i.i.d. process is discussed and simple analytical expressions for the expected value of the random output and its variance are derived. This analysis is then extended to more complex microeconomic hysteresis loops by using their representation in terms of rectangular hysteresis loops discussed in the previous section. The use of the i.i.d. process may seem to be somewhat unrealistic in some economic applications. Nevertheless, it is interesting to point out that Baldwin (see [10]) uses the dynamic programming technique and comes to the conclusion that the use of this technique *"reduces the problem with a general forcing variable process to be formally equivalent to the iid case."* Furthermore, in the fifth chapter, the random output dynamics is analysed when the stochastic random input is modelled by time continuous diffusion processes, and the exit problem technique as well as the stochastic processes on graphs technique are developed.

To start the discussion, we consider the output process f_n defined by the formula

$$f_n = \hat{\gamma}_{\alpha\beta} x_n, \qquad (2.4)$$

where

$$x_n = u + X_n. \qquad (2.5)$$

Here, X_n is the discrete time i.i.d. process with the property that for different time indices n the random variables are independent and identically distributed. The latter means that they have the same probability density function. It will be assumed that

$$\bar{X}_n = 0, \qquad (2.6)$$

where $\bar{X}_n$ stands for the expected value of X_n.

According to (2.5) and (2.6), this means that

$$\bar{x}_n = u, \qquad (2.7)$$

where u is the constant in time deterministic value of the input. If $\bar{X}_n \neq 0$, then the value $\bar{X}_n$ can be accounted for in the value of u. It is clear that x_n is also an iid process.

The purpose of the subsequent derivation is to find expressions for the mean of the output $\bar{f}_n$ and its variance $\sigma_{f_n}^2$ in terms of α and β. It is clear that f_n can be considered as the expected value of random investment of a firm at future instants of time corresponding to different values of n. Consequently, the above mentioned expression can be useful for choosing the trigger values α and β to achieve the desired expected values of investment at different times n. It is apparent that the above expression can also be used for other economic modeling purposes as well.

To start the derivation, we shall first introduce the notation:

$$q_{\alpha\beta}(n) = P(\hat{\gamma}_{\alpha\beta} x_n = 1), \qquad (2.8)$$

where the symbol P stands for probability. It is clear that

$$P(\hat{\gamma}_{\alpha\beta} x_n = 1) + P(\hat{\gamma}_{\alpha\beta} x_n = 0) = 1. \qquad (2.9)$$

Consequently,

$$P(\hat{\gamma}_{\alpha\beta} x_n = 0) = 1 - q_{\alpha\beta}(n). \qquad (2.10)$$

It is also clear that

$$\bar{f}_n = E(\hat{\gamma}_{\alpha\beta} x_n) = P(\hat{\gamma}_{\alpha\beta} x_n = 1) = q_{\alpha\beta}(n), \qquad (2.11)$$

where E stands for the expected value.

To find the analytical expression for $\bar{f}_n = q_{\alpha\beta}(n)$, we shall first derive the finite difference equation for $\bar{f}_n$. This derivation is based on the following total probability relation:

$$P\big(\hat{\gamma}_{\alpha\beta}x_{n+1} = 1\big) = P\big(\hat{\gamma}_{\alpha\beta}x_{n+1} = 1\big|\hat{\gamma}_{\alpha\beta}x_n = 1\big)P\big(\hat{\gamma}_{\alpha\beta}x_n = 1\big)$$
$$+ P\big(\hat{\gamma}_{\alpha\beta}x_{n+1} = 1\big|\hat{\gamma}_{\alpha\beta}x_n = 0\big)P\big(\hat{\gamma}_{\alpha\beta}x_n = 0\big). \quad (2.12)$$

Next, we introduce the following switching probabilities

$$P_{\alpha\beta}^{++}(n) = P\big(\hat{\gamma}_{\alpha\beta}x_{n+1} = 1\big|\hat{\gamma}_{\alpha\beta}x_n = 1\big), \quad (2.13)$$

$$P_{\alpha\beta}^{+0}(n) = P\big(\hat{\gamma}_{\alpha\beta}x_{n+1} = 0\big|\hat{\gamma}_{\alpha\beta}x_n = 1\big). \quad (2.14)$$

It is apparent that

$$P_{\alpha\beta}^{++}(n) + P_{\alpha\beta}^{+0}(n) = 1. \quad (2.15)$$

Similarly,

$$P_{\alpha\beta}^{0+}(n) = P\big(\hat{\gamma}_{\alpha\beta}x_{n+1} = 1\big|\hat{\gamma}_{\alpha\beta}x_n = 0\big), \quad (2.16)$$

$$P_{\alpha\beta}^{00}(n) = P\big(\hat{\gamma}_{\alpha\beta}x_{n+1} = 0\big|\hat{\gamma}_{\alpha\beta}x_n = 0\big), \quad (2.17)$$

and

$$P_{\alpha\beta}^{0+}(n) + P_{\alpha\beta}^{00}(n) = 1. \quad (2.18)$$

By using formulas (2.8) and (2.10) as well as the above definitions of the switching probabilities, the formula (2.12) can be written in the form:

$$q_{\alpha\beta}\big(n+1\big) = P_{\alpha\beta}^{++}(n)q_{\alpha\beta}(n) + P_{\alpha\beta}^{0+}(n)\Big[1 - q_{\alpha\beta}(n)\Big], \quad (2.19)$$

which can be further transformed as follows:

$$q_{\alpha\beta}\big(n+1\big) = q_{\alpha\beta}(n)\Big[P_{\alpha\beta}^{++}(n) - P_{\alpha\beta}^{0+}(n)\Big] + P_{\alpha\beta}^{0+}(n). \quad (2.20)$$

Now, by using formula (2.15), the last equation can be written as:

$$q_{\alpha\beta}\big(n+1\big) = q_{\alpha\beta}(n)\Big[1 - \big(P_{\alpha\beta}^{+0}(n) + P_{\alpha\beta}^{0+}(n)\big)\Big] + P_{\alpha\beta}^{0+}(n). \quad (2.21)$$

Due to the dependence on n, the probabilities in the above equation are difficult to evaluate in general. However, the problem is significantly simplified when we deal with the i.i.d. process. In this case, the probabilities $P_{\alpha\beta}^{+0}(n)$ and $P_{\alpha\beta}^{0+}(n)$ do not depend on n. Indeed, due to the definition of these probabilities (see formulas (2.14) and (2.16), respectively) as well as due to the properties of independence and identical distribution of the iid process, we find

$$P_{\alpha\beta}^{0+}(n) = P\big(x_{n+1} > \alpha\big) = \int_\alpha^\infty \rho(x)dx, \quad (2.22)$$

$$P_{\alpha\beta}^{+0}(n) = P(x_{n+1} < \beta) = \int_{-\infty}^{\beta} \rho(x)dx, \qquad (2.23)$$

where $\rho(x)$ is the common probability density function for all x_n.

Now, we introduce the notation:

$$r_{\alpha\beta} = 1 - \left[P_{\alpha\beta}^{0+}(n) + P_{\alpha\beta}^{+0}(n) \right] \qquad (2.24)$$

and taking into account formula (2.11), we obtain

$$\bar{f}_{n+1} = r_{\alpha\beta}\bar{f}_n + P_{\alpha\beta}^{0+}. \qquad (2.25)$$

This is the linear first-order finite difference equation for $\bar{f}_n$ with constant coefficients. The general solution of this equation has the form:

$$\bar{f}_n = A_{\alpha\beta}r_{\alpha\beta}^n + B_{\alpha\beta}. \qquad (2.26)$$

By substituting the last formula into equation (2.25), we find:

$$A_{\alpha\beta}r_{\alpha\beta}^{n+1} + B_{\alpha\beta} = A_{\alpha\beta}r_{\alpha\beta}^{n+1} + B_{\alpha\beta}r_{\alpha\beta} + P_{\alpha\beta}^{0+}, \qquad (2.27)$$

which leads to

$$B_{\alpha\beta} = \frac{P_{\alpha\beta}^{0+}}{1 - r_{\alpha\beta}}. \qquad (2.28)$$

From formula (2.22), (2.23) and (2.24), it follows that

$$0 < r_{\alpha\beta} < 1. \qquad (2.29)$$

According to equation (2.26), this implies that with the increase of time, i.e., the increase of n, the expected value of investment $\bar{f}_n$ becomes almost constant and equal to $B_{\alpha\beta}$. Consequently, according to (2.28), we find that for sufficiently large n the following relation is valid:

$$\bar{f}_n \approx \frac{P_{\alpha\beta}^{0+}}{1 - r_{\alpha\beta}}. \qquad (2.30)$$

By using formulas (2.22)–(2.24), the last expression can be written as follows:

$$\bar{f}_n \approx \frac{\displaystyle\int_{\alpha}^{\infty} \rho(x)dx}{1 - \displaystyle\int_{\beta}^{\alpha} \rho(x)dx}. \qquad (2.31)$$

The last formula suggests that the broadening of the band of inaction $\alpha - \beta$, due to the decrease of β, leads to the decrease of the denominator in the last formula. This may lead to the

increase in the "steady-state" expected investment. It can also be shown that the broadening of the band of inaction due to the increase of α has the opposite effect. Next, we shall derive the formula for $\bar{f}_n$ which is valid for any n. To do this, we have to find the expression for $A_{\alpha\beta}$ in formula (2.26). This can be done by using the initial condition for $q_{\alpha\beta}(n)$. Indeed, from formulas (2.11) and (2.26) we conclude that

$$q_{\alpha\beta}(0) = A_{\alpha\beta} + B_{\alpha\beta}. \qquad (2.32)$$

On the other hand,

$$q_{\alpha\beta}(0) = 0. \qquad (2.33)$$

This is true because the firm is initially not in the market and, consequently, $\hat{\gamma}_{\alpha\beta}x_0 = 0$.

From formulas (2.32) and (2.33) it follows that

$$A_{\alpha\beta} = -B_{\alpha\beta}, \qquad (2.34)$$

and, according to expression (2.26) we have

$$\bar{f}_n = B_{\alpha\beta}(1 - r_{\alpha\beta}^n). \qquad (2.35)$$

From formulas (2.22), (2.23) and (2.24), it follows that

$$r_{\alpha\beta} = \int_\beta^\alpha \rho(x)dx. \qquad (2.36)$$

Finally, from equations (2.22), (2.28), (2.35) and (2.36), we find

$$\bar{f}_n = \frac{\displaystyle\int_\alpha^\infty \rho(x)dx}{1 - \displaystyle\int_\beta^\alpha \rho(x)dx}\left[1 - \left(\int_\beta^\alpha \rho(x)dx\right)^n\right]. \qquad (2.37)$$

The last formula is the explicit expression for the expected investment $\bar{f}_n$ at any "instant of time" n in terms of market trigger values α and β as well as of the probability density function $\rho(x)$ of the i.i.d. process. It is apparent from the above formula that broader the "band of inaction" $\alpha - \beta$, the larger $r_{\alpha\beta}$ and the smaller the initial expected investment. Furthermore, it takes a longer "time", i.e., larger n to reach the steady-state expected investment value.

By using the derived formulas, it is easy to find the expression for the variance of the output, $\sigma_{f_n}^2$, as well. Indeed, it is clear that

$$\sigma_{f_n}^2 = \overline{(f_n - \bar{f}_n)^2} = \overline{f_n^2} - (\bar{f}_n)^2. \qquad (2.38)$$

From Fig. 2.9, it can be seen that $f_n^2 = f_n$. Therefore,

$$\overline{f_n^2} = \overline{(\hat{\gamma}_{\alpha\beta}u_n)^2} = \overline{(\hat{\gamma}_{\alpha\beta}u_n)} = \bar{f}_n. \tag{2.39}$$

Therefore, we find that

$$\sigma_{f_n}^2 = \bar{f}_n - (\bar{f}_n)^2. \tag{2.40}$$

Since $0 \le \bar{f}_n \le 1$, it is apparent that $\sigma_{f_n}^2$ reaches its maximum value of $1/4$ when $\bar{f}_n = 1/2$. This is the case when the input i.i.d. process has a symmetric probability density function around a mean value in the middle of the rectangular hysteresis loop, i.e, when $u = (\alpha + \beta)/2$. The variance decreases to zero as the mean value of the input deviates from the middle of the rectangular hysteresis loop.

By using the formula (2.31) in equation (2.40), we arrive at the following expression for $\sigma_{f_n}^2$ for large n:

$$\sigma_{f_\infty}^2 \approx \left(\frac{\int_\alpha^\infty \rho(x)dx}{1 - \int_\beta^\alpha \rho(x)dx} \right) - \left(\frac{\int_\alpha^\infty \rho(x)dx}{1 - \int_\beta^\alpha \rho(x)dx} \right)^2. \tag{2.41}$$

On the other hand, by substituting formula (2.37) into (2.40) we can find the variance valid for any n:

$$\sigma_{f_n}^2 = \left[\frac{\int_\alpha^\infty \rho(x)dx}{1 - \int_\beta^\alpha \rho(x)dx} \left(1 - \left[\int_\beta^\alpha \rho(x)dx \right]^n \right) \right]$$
$$- \left[\frac{\int_\alpha^\infty \rho(x)dx}{1 - \int_\beta^\alpha \rho(x)dx} \left(1 - \left[\int_\beta^\alpha \rho(x)dx \right]^n \right) \right]^2. \tag{2.42}$$

The above analysis was performed for the rectangular microeconomic hysteresis model shown in Fig. 2.9. This analysis can be easily extended to the more general microeconomic hysteresis loops expressed by formula (2.2). Accordingly, we consider the output process f_n defined by the formula

$$f_n = \hat{\Gamma}_{\alpha\beta}(x_n) = \left(f_{\alpha\beta}^-(x_n) - f_{\alpha\beta}^+(x_n) \right) \hat{\gamma}_{\alpha\beta}x_n + f_{\alpha\beta}^+(x_n), \tag{2.43}$$

where x_n is the discrete time i.i.d. process defined in the previous analysis by expressions (2.5)–(2.7).

Next, we will proceed with the derivation of the mean $\bar{f}_n$ and the variance $\sigma^2_{f_n}$ of the random output process f_n in terms of trigger values α and β.

The mean of the output, $\bar{f}_n$, is given in terms of the following expected values:

$$\bar{f}_n = \mathbb{E}\left\{ \left(f_{\alpha\beta}^-(x_n) - f_{\alpha\beta}^+(x_n) \right) \hat{\gamma}_{\alpha\beta} x_n \right\} + \mathbb{E}\left\{ f_{\alpha\beta}^+(x_n) \right\}, \qquad (2.44)$$

where the first term is the expected value of the irreversible component of the output, while the second term represents the expected value of the reversible component. The expected value of the irreversible component can be evaluated by using the following expression:

$$\mathbb{E}\left\{ \left(f_{\alpha\beta}^-(x_n) - f_{\alpha\beta}^+(x_n) \right) \hat{\gamma}_{\alpha\beta} x_n \right\}$$
$$= \int_\beta^\alpha \left(f_{\alpha\beta}^-(x) - f_{\alpha\beta}^+(x) \right) P\left\{ x < x_n < x + dx, \hat{\gamma}_{\alpha\beta} x_n = 1 \right\} dx$$
$$+ \int_\alpha^\infty \left(f_{\alpha\beta}^-(x) - f_{\alpha\beta}^+(x) \right) \rho(x) dx, \qquad (2.45)$$

where $P\left\{ x < x_n < x + dx, \hat{\gamma}_{\alpha\beta} x_n = 1 \right\}$ is a joint probability. In order to evaluate this expression, the joint probability needs to be determined. This is the probability that the random variable x_n is between x and $x + dx$ within the interval (α, β) *and* that the rectangular hysteresis loop is in the upper state, i.e., $\hat{\gamma}_{\alpha\beta} x_n = 1$. It is clear that the only way for this to occur at time step n is for the rectangular loop to have been in the upper state at time step $n - 1$, i.e., $\hat{\gamma}_{\alpha\beta} x_{n-1} = 1$. Therefore, we have

$$P\left\{ x < x_n < x + dx, \hat{\gamma}_{\alpha\beta} x_n = 1 \right\}$$
$$= P\left\{ x < x_n < x + dx, \hat{\gamma}_{\alpha\beta} x_{n-1} = 1 \right\}. \qquad (2.46)$$

Since x_n is an i.i.d. process, it is clear that x_n and $\hat{\gamma}_{\alpha\beta} x_{n-1}$ are *independent*. Therefore, the above joint probability can be expressed as the following product:

$$P\left\{ x < x_n < x + dx, \hat{\gamma}_{\alpha\beta} x_{n-1} = 1 \right\}$$
$$= \underbrace{P\left\{ x < x_n < x + dx \right\}}_{\rho(x)} \underbrace{P\left\{ \hat{\gamma}_{\alpha\beta} x_{n-1} = 1 \right\}}_{q_{\alpha\beta}(n-1)}, \qquad (2.47)$$

where $\rho(x)$ is the probability density function of the i.i.d. process and $q_{\alpha\beta}$ is the probability as defined earlier in formula (2.8). Substituting this expression into (2.45) and noting that $f_{\alpha\beta}^- = f_{\alpha\beta}^+$ in the interval (α, ∞), the expected value of the irreversible component is determined to be

$$\mathbb{E}\left\{ \left(f_{\alpha\beta}^-(x_n) - f_{\alpha\beta}^+(x_n) \right) \hat{\gamma}_{\alpha\beta} x_n \right\}$$
$$= \int_{\beta}^{\alpha} \left(f_{\alpha\beta}^-(x) - f_{\alpha\beta}^+(x) \right) \rho(x) q_{\alpha\beta}(n-1) dx. \qquad (2.48)$$

On the other hand, it is clear that the expected value of the reversible component in expression (2.44) can be calculated as follows

$$\mathbb{E}\left\{ f_{\alpha\beta}^+(x_n) \right\} = \int_{\alpha}^{\infty} f_{\alpha\beta}^+(x)\rho(x)dx. \qquad (2.49)$$

Substituting expressions (2.48) and (2.49) into expression (2.44) and noting that $f_{\alpha\beta}^+ = 0$ in the interval (α, β) results in the following expression for the expected value of the output:

$$\bar{f}_n = q_{\alpha\beta}(n-1) \int_{\beta}^{\alpha} f_{\alpha\beta}^-(x)\rho(x)dx + \int_{\alpha}^{\infty} f_{\alpha\beta}^+(x)\rho(x)dx. \qquad (2.50)$$

From this expression and formula (2.8), it can be concluded that the expected value of the output for the more general microeconomic hysteresis model can be calculated from the expected value $q_{\alpha\beta}(n-1)$ previously found for the case of the simpler rectangular hysteresis loop model. Furthermore, it is straightforward to show that the above expected value expression (2.50) for the more general microeconomic hysteresis model is reduced to the expected value (2.25) for the simpler rectangular loops. Indeed, taking into account the definition of $q_{\alpha\beta}$ given in expression (2.8) and formulas (2.21)–(2.24), it is clear that expression (2.50) is reduced to (2.25).

Next, we will calculate the variance of the output process, $\sigma_{f_n}^2$. Similar to the earlier analysis, the variance of the output can be calculated starting from expression (2.38), as follows:

$$\sigma_{f_n}^2 = \overline{f_n^2} - (\bar{f}_n)^2. \qquad (2.51)$$

From expression (2.43) we first calculate f_n^2. Noting that $\left(\hat{\gamma}_{\alpha\beta} x_n \right)^2 = \hat{\gamma}_{\alpha\beta} x_n$, it can be shown that

$$f_n^2 = \left[f_{\alpha\beta}^{-2}(x_n) - f_{\alpha\beta}^{+2}(x_n) \right] \hat{\gamma}_{\alpha\beta} x_n + f_{\alpha\beta}^{+2}(x_n). \qquad (2.52)$$

Starting from this expression, the expected value of the square of the output, $\overline{f_n^2}$, is calculated employing the line of reasoning used for the calculation of $\bar{f}_n$ shown in expressions (2.44)–(2.50). Accordingly, it can be shown that

$$\overline{f_n^2} = q_{\alpha\beta}(n-1) \int_{\beta}^{\alpha} f_{\alpha\beta}^{-2}(x)\rho(x)dx + \int_{\alpha}^{\infty} f_{\alpha\beta}^{+2}(x)\rho(x)dx. \qquad (2.53)$$

Substituting expressions (2.50) and (2.53) into (2.51) results in the following expression for the variance:

$$\sigma_{f_n}^2 = q_{\alpha\beta}(n-1) \int_\beta^\alpha {f_{\alpha\beta}^-}^2(x)\rho(x)dx + \int_\alpha^\infty {f_{\alpha\beta}^+}^2(x)\rho(x)dx$$

$$- \left[q_{\alpha\beta}(n-1) \int_\beta^\alpha f_{\alpha\beta}^-(x)\rho(x)dx + \int_\alpha^\infty f_{\alpha\beta}^+(x)\rho(x)dx \right]^2 . \quad (2.54)$$

2.4 Macroeconomic Hysteresis

To conclude this chapter, we shall briefly discuss macroeconomic hysteresis. The detailed discussion of this hysteresis will be provided in the next two chapters.

Macroeconomic hysteresis describes hysteresis phenomena occurring on a very large scale. The typical and most studied examples of macroeconomic hysteresis are foreign trade and unemployment. In the case of foreign trade hysteresis, a very large number of firms are involved in the same part of the market selling the same product. In the case of unemployment hysteresis, huge number of firms contribute to unemployment.

The **origin** of macroeconomic hysteresis is due to the aggregation of microeconomic hysteresis of a very large number of heterogeneous firms involved in international trade or contributing to unemployment. Mathematically, this aggregation is equivalent to summation. This summation is performed over a huge number of **heterogeneous** firms whose microeconomic hysteresis is qualitatively similar but quantitatively different. Since the summation is performed over huge numbers of firms, contributions of individual firms to macroeconomic hysteresis are relatively small. This implies that the above summation can be replaced with high accuracy by integration. In this way, the mathematical models of macroeconomic hysteresis emerge.

To illustrate the above origin of mathematical models of macroeconomic hysteresis, let us consider a very large number of firms whose microeconomic hysteresis is described, for instance, by formula (2.2). Due to heterogeneity of firms, triggers α and β will be different for different firms. As a result, the aggregation process can be mathematically realized as the following integration with respect to these trigger values:

$$f(t) = \iint\limits_{\alpha \geq \beta} \hat{\Gamma}_{\alpha,\beta} u(t) d\alpha d\beta, \quad (2.55)$$

where $f(t)$ is a macroeconomic output, while all firms are subject to the same exogenous forcing input.

Formula (2.55) is actually a mathematical model of macroeconomic hystersis. Such models of complex hysteresis through the integration of heterogeneous elementary hysteresis were first constructed in magnetics and their origin can be traced back to the classical work of Preisach [85], [86]. In economics, this aggregation approach to macroeconomic hysteresis was proposed by Amable, Henry, Lordon and Topol, and by Cross.

It turns out that as a result of aggregation (2.55) of weak microeconomic hysteresis represented by relatively simple but heterogeneous hysteresis loops a new type of strong hysteresis emerges. This is a multibranch hysteresis with the property that its branching is controlled by some past input extremum values. The latter occurs because mathematical models of the type (2.55) are endowed with the unique mathematical property to detect extremum values of the input, to store them and to generate hysteresis branches controlled by the stored past input extrema. In this sense, the mathematical models of the type (2.55) have the **predictive power** of branching.

It was pointed out by Baldwin and Krugman [11] that there exists a feedback between the output and input in the case of macroeconomic hysteresis. In foreign trade hysteresis, this is the feedback between the trade volume and the exchange rate. In cyclic unemployment hysteresis, this is the feedback between the unemployment rate and the interest rate. Mathematically, this type of feedback can be accounted for by the following modification of the macroeconomic hysteresis model defined in (2.55):

$$f(t) = \iint\limits_{\alpha \geq \beta} \hat{\Gamma}_{\alpha,\beta}\Big[u(t) - Kf(t)\Big]\,d\alpha d\beta, \qquad (2.56)$$

where K can be interpreted as a feedback strength.

The outlined issues related to macroeconomic hysteresis are discussed in detail in the following two chapters.

Chapter 3

Preisach Aggregation Model of Macroeconomic Hysteresis

3.1 Preisach Model

It was mentioned in the previous chapter that the origin of macroeconomic hysteresis is due to the aggregation of very large number of cases of similar but heterogeneous microeconomic hysteresis entities. It turns out that as a result of this aggregation of **weak** microeconomic hysteresis, represented by relatively simple but heterogeneous hysteresis loops, a new type of **strong** hysteresis emerges. This is a **multibranch** hysteresis with the property that **its branching is controlled by some past input extremum values**. In other words, macroeconomic hysteresis manifests itself as **history dependent branching** (see Fig. 2.5).

In this chapter, as well as in the next chapter, we shall discuss the properties of macroeconomic hysteresis. It is remarkable that certain important economic properties of such hysteresis are **insensitive** to the specific nature of underlying microeconomic hysteresis subject to aggregation. This implies that these economic properties are due **to the aggregation process itself**.

The very efficient and simple mathematical approach to study the **aggregation properties** of macroeconomic hysteresis is by using the classical Preisach model. In this model, microeconomic hysteresis is represented by rectangular loops $\hat{\gamma}_{\alpha\beta}$ (see Fig. 2.4) with different trigger values α and β. This study is performed in this chapter. In the next chapter, the aggregation properties of macroeconomic hysteresis are studied by using the generalized models. In these models, microeconomic hysteresis is represented by more realistic and more complex hysteresis loops (see, for instance, Figs. 2.10, 2.11, 2.13 and 2.14. Nevertheless, it is demonstrated that certain important properties of macroeconomic hysteresis remain the same as in the case when aggregation is described by the classical Preisach model. The latter clearly reveals that the important properties of macroeconomic hysteresis are indeed insensitive to the underlying nature of microeconomic hysteresis. This means, as has already been mentioned above, that **the true origin of these properties is the aggregation itself**.

Next, we proceed to the discussion of the classical Preisach model of hysteresis. This model has a long and instructive history that can be best characterized by the following eloquent statement of J. Larmor in his preface to the book of H. Poincare [84]: " ... *scientific progress, considered historically, is not a strictly logical process, and does not proceed by syllogisms. New ideas emerge dimly into intuition, come into consciousness from nobody knows where, and become the material on which the mind operates, forging them gradually into consistent doctrine, which can be welded on to existing domains of knowledge.*"

This is exactly what has happened with the Preisach model of hysteresis. The origin of this model can be traced back to the paper of F. Preisach "On the Magnetic Aftereffect" [85] published in 1935, where the idea of the hysteresis model is briefly outlined. Its English translation has appeared in [86]. This paper dealt exclusively with magnetic hysteresis. For this reason, the Preisach model was first regarded as a physical model. It was primarily known in the area of magnetics, where it was the focus of considerable research for many years (see for instance: [14], [22], [26], [35], [36] and [79]).

Somewhat in parallel, the Preisach model was independently discovered and then extensively studied for adsorption hysteresis by D.H. Everett and his collaborators [44], [45], [46]. This clearly indicated the generality of the Preisach model, and that its applications were not limited to specific areas, such as magnetics and adsorption.

The next step in the development of the Preisach model was made in the late 1970s and the beginning of 1980s. At that time, it was realized in the work of M. Krasnoselskii, A. Pokrovskii and I. Mayergoyz, that the Preisach model contained a new mathematical idea and can be stated without referring to any physical phenomena. As a result, this model was separated from its physical connotations and represented in purely mathematical terms that are similar to the spectral decomposition of operators [52]. In this way, a new mathematical tool has evolved that can now be used for the mathematical description of hysteresis of various physical nature. For instance, this model is widely used in the description and analysis of hysteresis of naturally consolidated rocks, nonlinear elasticity and plasticity,

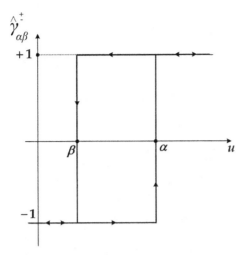

Fig. 3.1

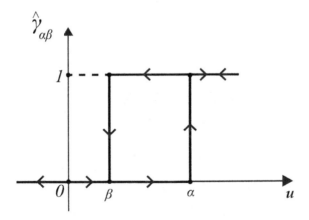

Fig. 3.2

shape memory alloys and piezoelectric materials. In those areas, this model is often referred to as "Preisach-Mayergoyz (PM) space".

We next proceed to the purely mathematical definition of the Preisach model. To do this, let us consider an infinite set of simplest hysteresis nonlinearities (i.e., operators) $\hat{\gamma}_{\alpha\beta}$. Each of these operators can be represented by a rectangular loop on the input-output diagram (see Fig. 2.4).

In physics and engineering, rectangular loops shown in Fig. 3.1 are used in the definition of the Preisach model. In economics, rectangular loops shown in Fig. 3.2 are more appropriate for the definition of the Preisach model. These rectangular loops will be used in our subsequent discussion. The two rectangular loops: $\hat{\gamma}^{\pm}_{\alpha\beta}$ shown in Fig. 3.1 and $\hat{\gamma}_{\alpha\beta}$ shown in Fig. 3.2 are mathematically equivalent. This equivalence is due to the following relation between these two rectangular loops:

$$\hat{\gamma}^{\pm}_{\alpha\beta}u(t) \;=\; 2\hat{\gamma}_{\alpha\beta}u(t) - 1. \tag{3.1}$$

The last formula is easily verifiable by using the previously mentioned Figs. 3.1 and 3.2.

Numbers (i.e., trigger values) α and β for the loops $\hat{\gamma}_{\alpha\beta}$ correspond to "up" and "down" switching values of input, respectively. It will be assumed as before that $\alpha \geq \beta$. Outputs of the above elementary hysteresis operators $\hat{\gamma}_{\alpha\beta}$ may assume only two values, $+1$ and 0. In other words, these operators can be interpreted as two-position elements with "up" and "down" positions, respectively,

$$\hat{\gamma}_{\alpha\beta}u(t) = +1, \tag{3.2}$$

and

$$\hat{\gamma}_{\alpha\beta}u(t) = 0. \tag{3.3}$$

As the input, $u(t)$, is monotonically increased, the ascending branch of a rectangular loop is followed. When the input is monotonically decreased, the descending branch is traced. It is clear that the operators $\hat{\gamma}_{\alpha\beta}$ represent hysteresis nonlinearities with local (weak) memories.

Along with the set of operators $\hat{\gamma}_{\alpha\beta}$, consider an arbitrary weight function $\mu(\alpha, \beta)$ that is often referred to as the Preisach function. Then, the Preisach model can be written as follows:

$$f(t) = \hat{\Gamma}u(t) = \iint\limits_{\alpha \geq \beta} \mu(\alpha, \beta)\hat{\gamma}_{\alpha\beta}u(t)d\alpha d\beta. \tag{3.4}$$

Here $\hat{\Gamma}$ is used for the concise notation of the Preisach hysteresis operator that is defined by the integral in (3.4).

It is apparent that the Preisach model (3.4) can be represented by the diagram shown in Fig. 3.3. According to this diagram, the same input $u(t)$ is applied to each of the rectangular loops $\hat{\gamma}_{\alpha\beta}$. Their individual outputs are multiplied by $\mu(\alpha, \beta)$ and then integrated over all appropriate values of α and β. As a result, the output, $f(t)$, is obtained.

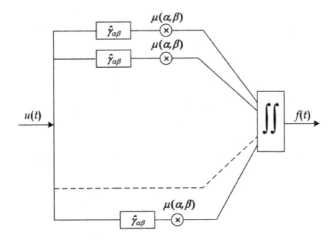

Fig. 3.3

It is clear from the above discussion that the Preisach model is constructed as a superposition of simplest hysteresis loops (i.e., operators) $\hat{\gamma}_{\alpha,\beta}$. These operators can be construed as the main building blocks for the model (3.4). The idea that a complicated operator can be represented as a superposition of simplest operators is not entirely new and was exploited before in mathematics, particularly in functional analysis [52]. For instance, according to the spectral decomposition theory for self-adjoint (Hermitian) operators, any self-adjoint operator can be represented as a superposition of projection operators that are, in a way, the simplest self-adjoint operators. The above analogy shows that the Preisach model (3.4) can be interpreted from the mathematical point of view as a spectral decomposition of complicated hysteresis operator $\hat{\Gamma}$ into the simplest hysteresis operators $\hat{\gamma}_{\alpha,\beta}$. There is also another interesting parallel between the Preisach model and **wavelet transforms** which are currently very popular in the area of signal processing. Indeed, all rectangular loops $\hat{\gamma}_{\alpha,\beta}$ shown in Fig. 3.2 can be obtained by translating and dilating the rectangular loop operator, $\hat{\gamma}_{1,-1}$ (see Fig. 3.4), that can be regarded as the "mother loop" (operator). Thus, the Preisach model can be viewed as a "wavelet operator transform".

It is apparent from the above discussion that the Preisach model has been defined without any reference to a particular origin of hysteresis. This clearly reveals the phenomenological nature of the model and its mathematical generality. This suggests that it can be used for the description of

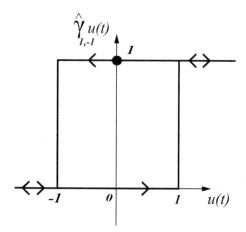

Fig. 3.4

hysteresis of any nature, including hysteresis in economics. The later is the purpose of our subsequent discussion.

The origin of hysteresis in physical systems is very often related to the multiplicity of metastable states in such systems. These metastable states correspond to different local energy minima. In this sense, the origin of hysteresis in physical systems is quite remote from the mathematical structure of the classical Preisach model of hysteresis presented by formula (3.4).

In contrast, the origin of economic hysteresis is of a different nature. As discussed in the previous chapter, this origin is due to the occurrence of microeconomic binary actions such as hiring-firing in the case of hysteresis of cyclical unemployment or buying-selling in the case of trade hysteresis. Each of these binary actions are usually triggered at different values α and β of input such as interest rate, price, assessed risk in the market, etc. It is remarkable that the aforementioned origin of economic hysteresis is intimately related to and reflected in the mathematical structure of the classical Preisach model of macroeconomic hysteresis presented by formula (3.4).

Indeed, the above asymmetric economic binary actions are represented in the mathematical structure of the classical Preisach model by rectangular loops $\hat{\gamma}_{\alpha,\beta}$, while the function $\mu(\alpha, \beta)$ reflects the scale of the above binary actions. In this sense, $\mu(\alpha, \beta)\hat{\gamma}_{\alpha,\beta}$ can be viewed as models of microeconomic hysteresis. It is the task of microeconomics to develop the techniques for the determination of trigger values α and β (see Sec. 2.2 of the previous chapter), as well as the expressions for the scalar function $\mu(\alpha, \beta)$.

On the macroeconomic level, the main task is to understand the consequences of aggregation of numerous binary actions. Mathematically, this aggregation is tantamount to summation. This summation is performed over a huge number of heterogeneous firms whose microeconomic hysteresis is described by $\mu(\alpha, \beta)\hat{\gamma}_{\alpha, \beta}u(t)$ with different trigger values of α and β. Since the summation is usually performed over a huge number of firms, contributions of individual firms to macroeconomic hysteresis are relatively quite small. This implies that the above summation can be with high accuracy replaced by integration. Accordingly, formula (3.4) emerges as the Preisach model of macroeconomic hysteresis. It is clear from the above discussion that the mathematical structure of the Preisach model is directly related to the **origin** of macroeconomic hysteresis. This brings credence to the Preisach approach for the modeling of macroeconomic activities.

It must be noted that the integration in formula (3.4) implies that the aggregation is performed over an infinite number of heterogeneous firms with continuous distributions of trigger values α and β. In reality, a very large but finite number of such firms with discrete sets of trigger values α and β are involved in the aggregation process. The latter can be accounted for by using the following formula for $\mu(\alpha, \beta)$:

$$\mu(\alpha, \beta) = \sum_k \nu(\alpha, \beta)\delta(\alpha - \alpha_k)\delta(\beta - \beta_k), \qquad (3.5)$$

where δ is the traditional notation for the Dirac delta function, while the summation is performed over all firms involved in the aggregation.

By substituting the last expression into formula (3.4), we arrive at:

$$f(t) = \sum_k \nu(\alpha_k, \beta_k)\hat{\gamma}_{\alpha_k \beta_k}u(t). \qquad (3.6)$$

In this way, the aggregation in formula (3.4) is reduced to the summation in the above expression. Formula (3.6) can be also viewed as the "summation" form of the Preisach model. It is also apparent that the summation and the integration forms of the Preisach model are mathematically equivalent under condition (3.5). In our subsequent discussions, we shall use the integration form of the Preisach model for the analysis of macroeconomic aggregation.

Having defined the Preisach model by formula (3.4), the question of how this model works must be posed. It turns our that this model has unique properties of **detecting extremum values of the input** $u(t)$**, storing these values in its structure and choosing the appropriate future**

branches of macroeconomic hysteresis according to the accumulated history of past input extrema. In other words, the Preisach model reveals that macroeconomic aggregation **elevates weak microeconomic hysteresis to the level of strong history-dependent multibranch hysteresis.** It is not immediately apparent from formula (3.4) that the Preisach model has the above properties. To demonstrate how these properties emerge, it requires the development of a special diagram technique. This technique will constitute the mathematical foundation of the subsequent analysis of macroeconomic aggregation of microeconomic hysteresis. This diagram technique is discussed in the next section. The same diagram technique will be used in the next chapter to study the macroeconomic hysteresis resulting from the aggregation of microeconomic hysteresis represented by hysteresis loops which are more realistic and more complex than the rectangular loops $\hat{\gamma}_{\alpha,\beta}$.

3.2   Diagram Technique

The mathematical analysis of the Preisach model of macroeconomic aggregation of microeconomic hysteresis is significantly facilitated by the geometric interpretation of this model. This interpretation is based on the following simple fact. There is one-to-one correspondence between rectangular loops $\hat{\gamma}_{\alpha,\beta}$ and points (α, β) of the half-plane $\alpha > \beta$ (see Fig. 3.5). In other words, each point on the half-plane $\alpha > \beta$ can be identified with only one rectangular loop $\hat{\gamma}_{\alpha,\beta}$ whose trigger values α and β are respectively equal to the α and β coordinate of the point. It is clear that this identification is possible because both rectangular loops $\hat{\gamma}_{\alpha,\beta}$ and the points of the half-plane $\alpha > \beta$ are uniquely defined by pairs of numbers α and β.

Consider a right triangle T shown in Fig. 3.5. Its hypotenuse is a part of the line $\alpha = \beta$, while the vertex of its right angle has the coordinates α_0 and zero. In our discussion, this triangle will be called the limiting triangle and the case when $\mu(\alpha, \beta)$ is a finite function with support within T will be discussed. This means that the function $\mu(\alpha, \beta)$ is equal to zero outside the triangle T. The latter is consistent with the fact that the aggregation is performed over firms with finite trigger values α and β.

The triangle T is in the first quadrant of the (α, β) plane, because in economics the forcing input $u(t)$ (such as price, interest rate, risk in the market, etc.) is usually positive. The latter implies that only rectangular loops $\hat{\gamma}_{\alpha,\beta}$ with positive trigger values α and β can be affected by the time variations of positive forcing inputs. In rare cases when $u(t)$ may assume

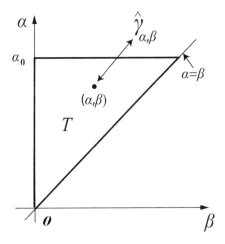

Fig. 3.5

negative values, the triangle T can be extended to the second and third quadrants. However, this will not affect our subsequent discussions.

To start the discussion, it is first assumed that the input $u(t)$ has zero value at some instant of time t_0 and the outputs of all rectangular loops $\hat{\gamma}_{\alpha,\beta}$ which correspond to points of the triangle T are equal to zero. Next, we assume that the input $u(t)$ is monotonically increased until it reaches at time t_1 some maximum value u_1. During this monotonic increase of $u(t)$, **all rectangular loops whose trigger values α less than the current input value $u(t)$ are being switched to the upward position.** This means that their outputs become equal to one. Geometrically, this leads to the subdivision of the triangle T into two sets: $S^+(t)$ consisting of points (α, β) for which the outputs of corresponding rectangular loops $\hat{\gamma}_{\alpha,\beta}$ are equal to one, and the set $S^0(t)$ consisting of points (α, β) such that the outputs of the corresponding rectangular loops $\hat{\gamma}_{\alpha,\beta}$ are still equal to zero. This subdivision is produced by the line $\alpha = u(t)$ (see Fig. 3.6) moving upwards as the input is being increased. This upward motion is terminated as soon as the input reaches the maximum value u_1. This leads to the subdivision of the triangle T into two sets $S^+(t_1)$ and $S^0(t_1)$, which is shown in Fig. 3.7.

Next, we assume that the input is monotonically decreased until it reaches at time t_2 some minimum value u_2. **As the input is being decreased, all rectangular loops $\hat{\gamma}_{\alpha,\beta}$, whose trigger values β are above the current value $u(t)$ of the input, are being switched downward.**

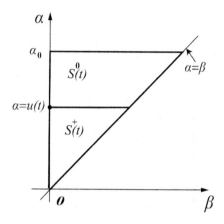

Fig. 3.6

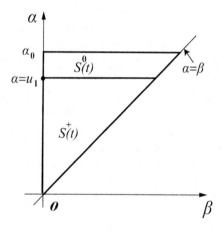

Fig. 3.7

This means that their outputs are equal to zero. This changes the previous subdivision of T into two sets $S^+(t)$ and $S^0(t)$. Indeed, the interface $L(t)$ between $S^+(t)$ and $S^0(t)$ has now two links, the horizontal and vertical ones. This is illustrated by Fig. 3.8. During the above monotonic decrease of the input $u(t)$, the vertical link moves from right to left, and its motion is specified by the equation $\beta = u(t)$ as shown in Fig. 3.8. The above motion of the vertical link is terminated when the input reaches its minimum value u_2. The subdivision of the triangle T for this particular instant of time t_2 is

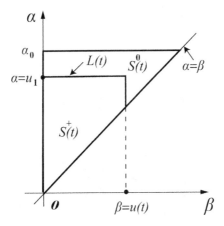

Fig. 3.8

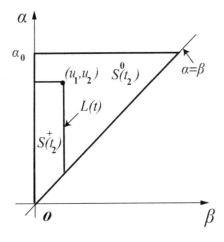

Fig. 3.9

shown in Fig. 3.9. The vertex of the interface $L(t)$ at the above instant of time has the coordinates $\alpha = u_1$ and $\beta = u_2$.

Now, we assume that the input $u(t)$ is monotonically increased again until it reaches some maximum value u_3 at time t_3 which is less than u_1. Geometrically, this increase results in the formation of a new horizontal link of $L(t)$ which moves upwards. This upward motion is terminated at time t_3 when the maximum u_3 is reached. This is shown in Fig. 3.10.

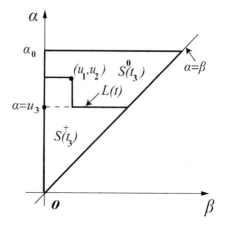

Fig. 3.10

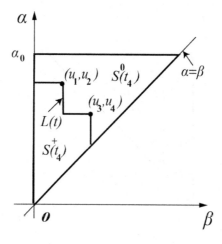

Fig. 3.11

Next, we assume that the input is monotonically decreased again until it reaches at some time t_4 its minimum value u_4 which is above u_2. Geometrically, this input variation results in the formation of a new vertical link that moves from right to left. This motion is terminated at the instant of time t_4 when the input reaches its minimum value u_4. As a result, a new vertex of the interface $L(t)$ is formed. This vertex has the coordinates $\alpha = u_3$ and $\beta = u_4$. This is illustrated in Fig. 3.11.

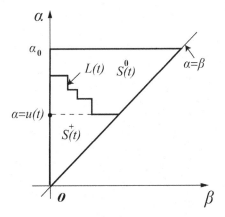

Fig. 3.12

By generalizing the previous analysis, the following conclusion can be reached. At any instant of time t, the triangle T is subdivided into two sets: the set $S^+(t)$ consisting of points (α, β), for which the outputs of corresponding rectangular loops $\hat{\gamma}_{\alpha,\beta}$ are equal to one, and the set $S^0(t)$ consisting of points (α, β), for which the outputs of corresponding rectangular loops are equal to zero. **The interface $L(t)$ between the sets $S^+(t)$ and $S^0(t)$ is a staircase line whose vertices have α and β coordinates coinciding respectively with local maxima and minima of input $u(t)$ at past instants of time.** The final link of interface $L(t)$ is attached to the line $\alpha = \beta$ and it moves when the input is changed. This link is a horizontal one and it moves upwards as the input $u(t)$ is monotonically increased (see Fig. 3.12). On the other hand, the final link of the interface $L(t)$ is a vertical one and it moves from right to left as the input $u(t)$ is monotonically decreased (see Fig. 3.13).

The previous discussion implies that at any instant of time the integral in formula (3.4) can be subdivided into two integrals over sets $S^+(t)$ and $S^0(t)$, respectively:

$$f(t) = \hat{\Gamma}u(t) = \iint\limits_{S^+(t)} \mu(\alpha,\beta)\hat{\gamma}_{\alpha\beta}u(t)d\alpha d\beta \;+\; \iint\limits_{S^0(t)} \mu(\alpha,\beta)\hat{\gamma}_{\alpha\beta}u(t)d\alpha d\beta.$$

$$(3.7)$$

Since,

$$\hat{\gamma}_{\alpha\beta}u(t) = 1, \text{ if } (\alpha,\beta) \in S^+(t) \tag{3.8}$$

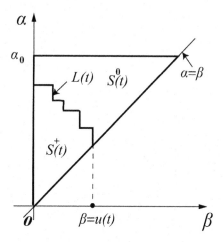

Fig. 3.13

and

$$\hat{\gamma}_{\alpha\beta}u(t) = 0, \text{ if } (\alpha, \beta) \in S^0(t),\tag{3.9}$$

from formula (3.7) we find:

$$f(t) = \iint\limits_{S^+(t)} \mu(\alpha, \beta)d\alpha d\beta.\tag{3.10}$$

From the last expression, it follows that an instantaneous value of output of the Preisach model depends on a particular subdivision of the triangle T into sets $S^+(t)$ and $S^0(t)$. This subdivision is determined by a particular shape of the staircase interface $L(t)$ producing the above subdivision. This shape, in turn, depends on the past extremum values of input, because these extremum values are the coordinates of the protruding vertices of $L(t)$. **This implies that the past extremum values of input shape the geometry of the staircase interface $L(t)$, and in this way they leave their mark upon the future output values.**

To make the above points perfectly clear, consider two inputs $u_1(t)$ and $u_2(t)$ with different past histories for $t < t'$. This means that they have different local extrema for $t < t'$. It is next assumed that these two inputs coincide for $t > t'$. Then according to formula (3.10), the outputs $f_1(t)$ and $f_2(t)$ corresponding to the above inputs are given by the formulas:

$$f_1(t) = \iint\limits_{S_1^+(t)} \mu(\alpha, \beta)d\alpha d\beta,\tag{3.11}$$

$$f_2(t) = \iint\limits_{S_2^+(t)} \mu(\alpha, \beta) d\alpha d\beta, \tag{3.12}$$

where $S_1^+(t)$ and $S_2^+(t)$ are the sets of points (α, β) for which the outputs of rectangular loops $\hat{\gamma}_{\alpha,\beta}$ corresponding to the above points are equal to one. The sets $S_1^+(t)$ and $S_2^+(t)$ correspond to two different subdivisions of T associated with different inputs $u_1(t)$ and $u_2(t)$.

The above two subdivisions are different because they correspond to two different histories of input variations with different past input extrema. These past time input variations result in different geometries of corresponding interfaces $L_1(t)$ and $L_2(t)$. This implies that the sets $S_1^+(t)$ and $S_2^+(t)$ are different as well. Thus, from formulas (3.11) and (3.12) we conclude that

$$f_1(t) \neq f_2(t) \text{ for } t > t'. \tag{3.13}$$

It is clear that the last inequality holds even if the outputs $f_1(t')$ and $f_1(t')$ are somehow the same at t'. The above discussion clearly suggests that the Preisach model (3.4) is endowed with the memory of past input extrema, which affects the future output values.

The above discussion clearly reveals the mechanism of memory formation in the Preisach model. Namely, the memory is formed as a result of two different ways for the modification of the staircase interface $L(t)$. Indeed, for a monotonically increasing input $u(t)$, a horizontal final link of $L(t)$ is formed, which moves upwards. On the other hand, for a monotonically decreasing input $u(t)$, a vertical final link is formed, which moves from right to left. These two different ways of modifications of $L(t)$ result in the formation of a staircase interface, whose protruding vertices have α and β coordinates equal to past maxima and minima, respectively.

Remarkably, the above mechanism of memory formation is also responsible for branching. To demonstrate this, consider the input variations which result in the staircase interface shown in Fig. 3.11. At first, when the input is monotonically increased from zero to u_1, the output is monotonically increased, as well. This is true, because the monotonic increase of input results in the continuous upwards extension of the set $S^+(t)$, which according to formula (3.10) leads to the monotonic increase of output $f(t)$. By plotting f vs. u at identical instants of time, we end up with the first branch shown in Fig. 3.14. After achieving its maximum u_1, the input is monotonically decreased achieving its minimum value u_2. This monotonic decrease of input results in the continuous reduction of the set $S^+(t)$, which

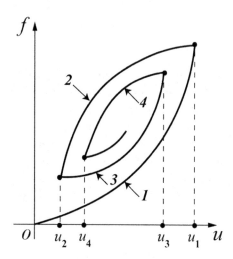

Fig. 3.14

according to formula (3.10) leads to the monotonic decrease of output $f(t)$. By plotting again f vs. u at the identical instants of time, we end up with the second branch shown in Fig. 3.14. This branch is above the first branch. This is because according to Fig. 3.9 a monotonic decrease of input $u(t)$ immediately after the instant of time t_1 when the maximum u_1 was achieved results only in the **partial reduction** of the previous extension of $S^+(t)$, which occurred for the equal monotonic increase of input $u(t)$ just before the time instant t_1. By using the same line of reasoning, it can be established that subsequent monotonic increases of input $u(t)$ followed by its monotonic decrease results in the formation of branches 3 and 4, respectively, as shown in Fig. 3.14.

Finally, as a summary of this section, it can be concluded that **the Preisach model detects extremum values of input and stores them in the staircase geometry of interface $L(t)$. Furthermore, this model describes multi-branch hysteresis with the property that new branches are formed after each input extrema. The output values along these branches are controlled by the values of past input extrema and instantaneous values of input. This implies that the Preisach model describes rate-independent multi-branch hysteresis which is endowed with a discrete memory structure consisting of past extremum values of input.**

3.3 Basic Properties of Macroeconomic Hysteresis

It is clear from the discussion presented in the previous sections that the Preisach model can be viewed as a model of aggregation of microeconomic hysteresis represented by heterogeneous rectangular loops. This aggregation elevates weak (Markovian) microeconomic hysteresis of rectangular loops to the level of strong (non-Markovian) macroeconomic hysteresis. The latter hysteresis manifests itself as history dependent branching controlled not only by the input time variations but by the past extremum values of input as well. This suggests that the past input extrema have long-lasting economic consequences. They are also exogenous in nature. Consequently, past input extrema can be identified with past economic **shocks**. It turns out that not all past input extrema may be viewed as shocks at any given instant of time t. In other words, the effect of some past shocks can be eliminated by sufficiently large future shocks. This elimination is based on the **erasure property** of aggregation described by the Preisach model.

To make this property clear, consider a particular input history that is characterized by a finite decreasing sequence $\{u_1, u_3, u_5, u_7\}$ of local input maxima and by a finite increasing sequence $\{u_2, u_4, u_6\}$ of local input minima. A typical (α, β)-diagram for this kind of history is shown in Fig. 3.15. Now, we assume that the input $u(t)$ is monotonically increased until it reaches some maximum value u_9 that is above u_3. This monotonic increase of input $u(t)$ results in the formation of the last horizontal link of $L(t)$ that moves upwards until the maximum value u_9 is reached. This results in the modified (α, β)-diagram shown in Fig. 3.16. It is evident from this diagram that all vertices of the interface $L(t)$ whose α-coordinates were below u_9 have been erased. It is also clear that this erasure of vertices is equivalent to the erasing of memory associated with these vertices. Namely, the past input maxima and minima that were respectively equal to the α- and β-coordinates of the erased vertices have been erased from the memory of the Preisach model.

We have illustrated the erasure property for monotonically increasing input. However, it is obvious that the erasure of vertices may occur in a similar manner for monotonically decreasing inputs as well. Indeed, let us go back to the (α, β)-diagram shown in Fig. 3.15 and suppose that the input is monotonically decreased until it reaches some minimum value u_8 that is below u_2. This monotonic decrease of input results in the formation of the last vertical link of $L(t)$ that moves leftward until the minimum value u_8 is achieved. This leads to the modified (α, β)-diagram shown in Fig. 3.17.

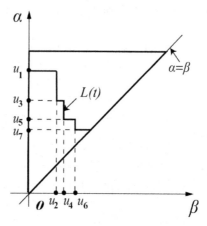

Fig. 3.15

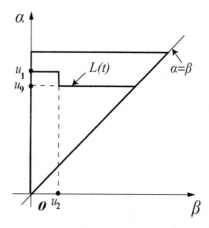

Fig. 3.16

It is clear from this diagram that all vertices of the interface $L(t)$ whose β-coordinates were above u_8 have been erased. This results in the erasure of memory associated with the above vertices. Thus, the following property of the Preisach aggregation model is valid.

ERASURE PROPERTY: Each new input maximum erases the vertices of interface $L(t)$ whose α-coordinates are below this maximum, and each new input minimum erases the vertices whose β-coordinates are above this minimum.

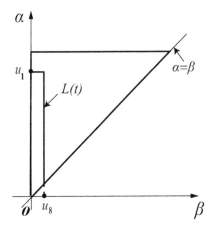

Fig. 3.17

The erasure property is asserted above in purely geometric terms. This makes the origin of this property quite transparent. However, the same property can also be stated in analytical terms. The analytical formulation complements the geometric one, because it is directly stated in terms of time input variations.

To arrive at the analytical statement of the erasure property, consider some general type of time input variations shown in Fig. 3.18 for a time interval $t_0 < t < t'$. Our goal is to specify explicitly the past input extrema that will be stored by the Preisach aggregation model at time t'. Consider the global maximum of the input at the time interval $t_0 < t < t'$. We shall use the notation M_1 for this maximum and t_1^+ for the instant of time at which this maximum was reached. Then:

$$M_1 = u(t_1^+) = \max_{t_0 < t < t'} u(t). \qquad (3.14)$$

It is clear from our previous discussion that all previous input extrema, which occurred during the time interval $t_0 < t < t_1^+$ were erased by this maximum.[1]

Now, consider the global minimum of the input for the time interval $t_1^+ < t < t'$. We shall use the notation m_1 for this minimum and t_1^- for the

---

[1]It is tacitly assumed that M_1 is larger than all previous maxima occurring before t_0. This implies that the entire input history before t_0 has been erased by this maximum.

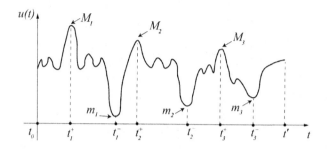

Fig. 3.18

time instant it was reached:

$$m_1 = u(t_1^-) = \min_{t_1^+ < t < t'} u(t). \tag{3.15}$$

It is apparent from our previous discussion that all intermediate input extrema that occurred between t_1^+ and t_1^- were erased by the minimum m_1.

Next, consider the global maximum of the input for the time interval $t_1^- < t < t'$ and introduce the notations M_2 and t_2^+ for this maximum and the time it occurred, respectively. Then:

$$M_2 = u(t_2^+) = \max_{t_1^- < t < t'} u(t). \tag{3.16}$$

It is obvious that this maximum erased all intermediate input extrema that occurred between t_1^- and t_2^+.

Similarly, we consider the global minimum of input at the time interval $t_2^+ < t < t'$ and use the notations m_2 and t_2^- for this minimum and the time it was achieved, respectively. Then:

$$m_2 = u(t_2^-) = \min_{t_2^+ < t < t'} u(t). \tag{3.17}$$

It is clear that all intermediate input extrema, that occurred between t_2^+ and t_2^-, were erased by this minimum.

By continuing the above line of reasoning, we can inductively introduce the global maxima M_k and global minima m_k by the formulas:

$$M_k = u(t_k^+) = \max_{t_{k-1}^- < t < t'} u(t), \tag{3.18}$$

and

$$m_k = u(t_k^-) = \min_{t_k^+ < t < t'} u(t). \tag{3.19}$$

It is natural to say that M_k and m_k, $(k = 1, 2, \ldots, N)$, form an alternating sequence $\{M_1, m_1, M_2, m_2, \ldots, M_k, m_k, \ldots\}$ of **dominant** input maxima and minima.

It is evident from the above analysis that α- and β-coordinates of vertices of the interface $L(t')$ are equal to M_k and m_k, respectively. It is also clear that this sequence of alternating dominant extrema is modified with time. This means that new dominant extrema can be introduced as a result of the subsequent time variations of input, while some previous dominant extrema may be erased. In other words, M_k and m_k are functions of t' as it is clearly suggested by their definitions (3.18) and (3.19), respectively.

Now, the erasure property can be stated in the following form:

ERASURE PROPERTY: Only the sequence of alternating dominant input extrema are stored by the Preisach aggregation model. All other input extrema are erased.

Next, we consider the economic interpretation of the above Erasure Property. As previously discussed, the input extrema can be identified with shocks. Consequently, the Erasure Property of macroeconomic aggregation of microeconomic hysteresis implies **that not all shocks affect the future branching of macroeconomic hysteresis**. In other words, **the persistence and protracted effects of some past shocks can be eliminated by larger future shocks**. The Erasure Property of macroeconomic hysteresis clearly identifies the specific past shocks whose long-lasting effects will still exist at a given instant of time t'. Namely, these shocks correspond to the alternating sequence of past dominant input maxima and minima (see formulas (3.14)–(3.19)). These shocks can be viewed as **dominant** shocks at time t'.

The Erasure Property of macroeconomic hysteresis is quite natural from the economics point of view. This is because the dominant shocks may usually result in appreciable and irreversible structural changes in industry and society. These changes may render the structural changes caused by past intermediate shocks to be irrelevant as far as the future development of the economy is concerned.

The fact that not all past input shocks (i.e., past input extrema) may have persistent economic effects has been recognized by Baldwin and Krugman (see [9] and [11]). For instance, it is stated in [9] that:

"This paper shows that in a simple industrial organization model, large exchange rate shocks can have persistent real effects, while small shocks cannot."

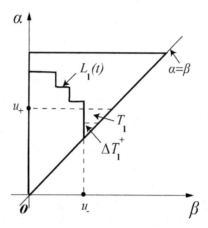

Fig. 3.19

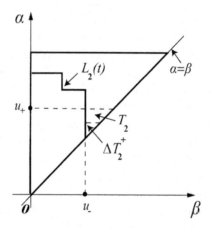

Fig. 3.20

Similarly, it is stated in [11] that:

"*This paper presents a theoretical basis for the argument that large exchange rate shocks - such as the 1980's dollar cycle - may have persistent effects on trade flows and the equilibrium exchange rate itself.*"

It is apparent that the above reference statements are consistent with the Erasure Property.

Next, we consider another characteristic property of the Preisach aggregation model which is valid for periodic (i.e., cyclic) input variations.

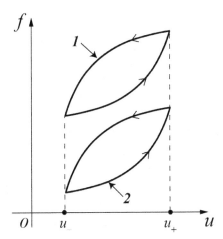

Fig. 3.21

These cyclic input variations result in **macroeconomic** hysteresis loops which have special properties. To be specific, let $u_1(t)$ and $u_2(t)$ be two inputs that may have different past histories (i.e., different alternating dominant extrema). However, starting from some instant of time $\tilde{t}$, these inputs vary back and forth between the **same** two consecutive extremum values u_+ and u_-. It is easy to see that these periodic input variations results in macroeconomic hysteresis loops. Indeed, let Figs. 3.19 and 3.20 represent (α, β)-diagrams corresponding to time variations of inputs $u_1(t)$ and $u_2(t)$, respectively. As these inputs vary back and forth between u_+ and u_-, the last links of staircase interfaces $L_1(t)$ and $L_2(t)$ move the same way within the identical triangles T_1 and T_2. This results in periodic variations of shapes for $L_1(t)$ and $L_2(t)$, which produce periodic variations of outputs $f_1(t)$ and $f_2(t)$, respectively. This means that some hysteresis loops are traced in the (f, u)-diagram for both inputs (see Fig. 3.21). The positions of these loops with respect to the f-axis are different. This is because the above two inputs have different past histories, which lead to different shapes for staircase interfaces $L_1(t)$ and $L_2(t)$. The latter implies that the sets $S_1^+(t)$ and $S_2^+(t)$ are also different and, according to formulas (3.11) and (3.12), this means that $f_1(t) \neq f_2(t)$. However, it can be proved that the above two hysteresis loops are **congruent**. It means that the coincidence of these loops can be achieved by the appropriate translation of these loops along the f-axis.

The proof of congruency of the above loops is equivalent to showing that any equal increments of inputs $u_1(t)$ and $u_2(t)$ result in equal increments of outputs $f_1(t)$ and $f_2(t)$, respectively. To this end, let us assume that after achieving the same minimum value u_- both inputs are increased by the same amount:

$$\Delta u_1 = \Delta u_2 = \Delta u. \tag{3.20}$$

As a result of these increases, the identical triangles ΔT_1^+ and ΔT_2^+ are added to the sets $S_1^+(t)$ and $S_2^+(t)$, and subtracted from the sets $S_1^0(t)$ and $S_2^0(t)$ (see Figs. 3.19 and 3.20). Now, by using formula (3.10), we find that the corresponding output increments are given by the following equations:

$$\Delta f_1^+ = \iint\limits_{\Delta T_1^+} \mu(\alpha, \beta) d\alpha d\beta, \tag{3.21}$$

and

$$\Delta f_2^+ = \iint\limits_{\Delta T_2^+} \mu(\alpha, \beta) d\alpha d\beta. \tag{3.22}$$

Since,

$$\Delta T_1^+ = \Delta T_2^+, \tag{3.23}$$

we find that

$$\Delta f_1^+ = \Delta f_2^+. \tag{3.24}$$

The last equality has been proved for the case when inputs $u_1(t)$ and $u_2(t)$ are monotonically increased by the same amount after achieving the same minimum value u_-. Consequently, this equality means the **congruency for ascending branches of the above minor loops.** By using the same line of reasoning, it can be proved that an equality similar to (3.24) holds when the inputs $u_1(t)$ and $u_2(t)$ are monotonically decreased by the same amount Δu after achieving the maximum value u_+. This means that the **descending branches of the above hysteresis loops are congruent as well.** Indeed, as a result of the above monotonic decreases of inputs $u_1(t)$ and $u_2(t)$, the identical triangles ΔT_1^- and ΔT_2^- are subtracted from the sets $S_1^+(t)$ and $S_2^+(t)$ (see Figs. 3.22 and 3.23). According to formula (3.10), this implies that the corresponding output increments are given by the following equations:

$$\Delta f_1^- = - \iint\limits_{\Delta T_1^-} \mu(\alpha, \beta) d\alpha d\beta, \tag{3.25}$$

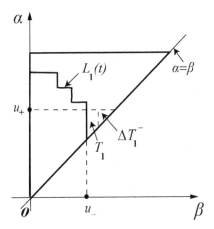

Fig. 3.22

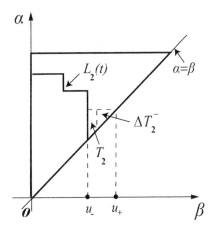

Fig. 3.23

and

$$\Delta f_2^- = - \iint\limits_{\Delta T_2^-} \mu(\alpha, \beta) d\alpha d\beta. \qquad (3.26)$$

Since, ΔT_1^- and ΔT_2^- are identical, the latter implies that

$$\Delta f_1^- = \Delta f_2^-. \qquad (3.27)$$

Thus, the following important property of the Preisach aggregation model has been established.

CONGRUENCY PROPERTY: All macroeconomic hysteresis loops corresponding to cyclic (back-and-forth) variations of input between the same two consecutive input extrema are congruent.

It has been proven (see Mayergoyz [70] and [73]) that the Erasure Property and the Congruency Property are the characteristic properties of the classical Preisach model in the sense that the following theorem is valid.

REPRESENTATION THEOREM: The Erasure Property and the Congruency Property constitute the necessary and sufficient conditions for the representation of an actual multi-branch hysteresis nonlinearity by the Preisach model.

In natural sciences and engineering applications, the stated theorem clearly establishes the limits of applicability of the classical Preisach model, and these limits are experimentally verifiable. Within these limits, the Preisach model has predictive powers for history-dependent branching. In the case of economics, the direct empirical macroeconomic verification of the Congruency Property may be very difficult.

The above Congruency Property is related to the rectangular loop representation of microeconomic hysteresis. It is shown in the next chapter that if the above representation is not accurate, then the Congruency Property is replaced by another more general property of macroeconomic hysteresis loops.

The Congruency Property is quite interesting from the economic point of view. It is clear from this property that the shape of hysteresis loops is completely determined by the last two input extrema, and it does not depend on the past input extrema. In other words, **the last two shocks completely control the shape of macroeconomic hysteresis loops. This shape is independent of previous dominant shocks.**

It is clear from the proof of the Congruency Property, that the shape of the ascending branch of a macroeconomic hysteresis loop depends only on the last input minimum, and it does not depend on other past input extrema. This is evident from Figs. 3.19 and 3.20 as well as from formulas (3.21) and (3.22). Similarly, the shape of the descending branch of macroeconomic hysteresis depends only on the last input maxima, and it does not depend on other past input extrema. This is evident from Figs. 3.22 and 3.23, as well as from formulas (3.25) and (3.26). **In economic terms, this means that the shape of future branches of macroeconomic hysteresis is controlled by the last shocks and it does not depend**

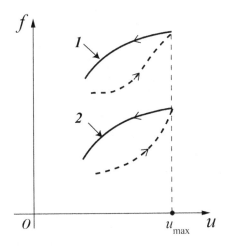

Fig. 3.24

on previous shocks. This is illustrated by Fig. 3.24. In this figure, two different ascending branches corresponding to two different inputs $u_1(t)$ and $u_2(t)$ are shown. As soon as these inputs reach the same maximum value $u_{\max}$ and then are monotonically decreased, new descending branches 1 and 2 are respectively formed. These two descending branches are **congruent,** i.e., they have the same shape. In other words, for these branches, equal increments of inputs $u_1(t)$ and $u_2(t)$ result in equal increments of corresponding outputs $f_1(t)$ and $f_2(t)$. This implies that the geometry of these newly formed branches is controlled by the last shock related to the last maximum $u_{\max}$. **The previous shocks may control the values of outputs $f_1(t)$ and $f_2(t)$ but not their increments, which are controlled by the last shock.**

It turns out that the Congruency Property has another very important implication in economics. To demonstrate this, consider two unemployment cycles represented by two hysteresis loops shown in Fig. 3.25. Here, outputs $f_1(t)$ and $f_2(t)$ can be viewed as cyclical unemployment rates, whereas inputs $u_1(t)$ and $u_2(t)$ can be viewed as the interest rate. Then the lengths of vertical chords of hysteresis loops can be interpreted as a measure of economic recovery. Indeed, **these vertical chords represent a measure of persisting unemployment, which is a direct consequence of macroeconomic hysteresis branching.** Due to the Congruency Property, these vertical chords are the same for all loops corresponding to the

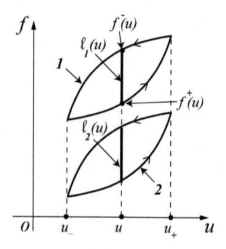

Fig. 3.25

same two last consecutive input extremum values u_- and u_+:

$$\ell_1(u) = \ell_2(u). \tag{3.28}$$

This means that the degree of recovery dependence on the past is controlled only by the last two shocks, while all other past shocks have no protracted effects on recovery. In this respect, the vertical chords represent the **universal** measure of economic recovery. Remarkably, this universality exists despite the fact that the output values corresponding to u_- and u_+ **are affected** by past dominant shocks.

It is interesting to find the expression for vertical chords in terms of microeconomic data represented by $\mu(\alpha, \beta)$. This can be accomplished by using Figs. 3.26, 3.27 and 3.28. According to Fig. 3.25, we find:

$$\ell_1(u) = f^-(u) - f^+(u). \tag{3.29}$$

The last expression can be written in the following mathematically equivalent form:

$$\ell_1(u) = \left[f^-(u) - f(u_+) \right] + \left[f(u_+) - f^+(u) \right]. \tag{3.30}$$

According to the (α, β)-diagram shown in Fig. 3.26, the following formula is valid

$$f(u_+) - f^+(u) = \iint\limits_{A_1} \mu(\alpha, \beta) d\alpha d\beta. \tag{3.31}$$

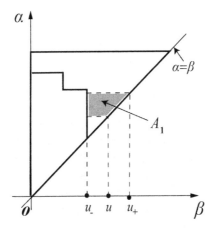

Fig. 3.26

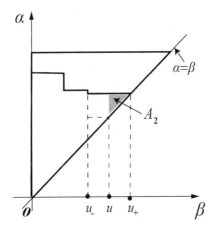

Fig. 3.27

On the other hand, from Fig. 3.27 we find

$$f^-(u) - f(u_+) = -\iint\limits_{A_2} \mu(\alpha,\beta)d\alpha d\beta. \tag{3.32}$$

By substituting formulas (3.31) and (3.32) into equation (3.30), we obtain

$$\ell_1(u) = \iint\limits_{A_1} \mu(\alpha,\beta)d\alpha d\beta - \iint\limits_{A_2} \mu(\alpha,\beta)d\alpha d\beta. \tag{3.33}$$

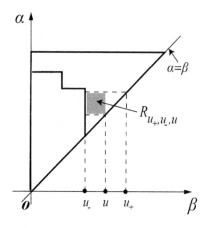

Fig. 3.28

From Figs. 3.26, 3.27 and 3.28, it follows that

$$\iint_{A_1} \mu(\alpha,\beta)d\alpha d\beta - \iint_{A_2} \mu(\alpha,\beta)d\alpha d\beta = \iint_{R_{u_+,u_-,u}} \mu(\alpha,\beta)d\alpha d\beta. \qquad (3.34)$$

Using formulas 3.33 and 3.34, we arrive at the following final result:

$$\ell_1(u) = \iint_{R_{u_+,u_-,u}} \mu(\alpha,\beta)d\alpha d\beta. \qquad (3.35)$$

It is clear from the last formula that vertical chords of macroeconomic hysteresis loops can be determined if microeconomic data on $\mu(\alpha,\beta)$ is available. By using these data and formula 3.35, **the unemployment persistence for cyclical unemployment may be predicted.**

There is another remarkable feature of macroeconomic hysteresis, which can be stated as follows:

Initial slopes of newly formed branches of macroeconomic hysteresis are equal to zero.

The proof of this property is based on the (α,β)-diagram shown in Fig. 3.29. According to this figure, a new ascending hysteresis branch is formed due to the formation and upward motion of the last horizontal link of the staircase interface $L(t)$ caused by monotonically increasing input. During this monotonic increase, the output $f(t)$ can be represented by the following formula:

$$f(u,u_-) = \iint_{T_{u,u_-}} \mu(\alpha,\beta)d\alpha d\beta + \iint_{A} \mu(\alpha,\beta)d\alpha d\beta, \qquad (3.36)$$

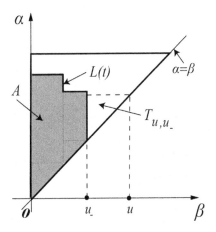

Fig. 3.29

where T_{u,u_-} is a triangle formed as a result of the initial stage of the monotonic increase of input from u_- to u, while the shaded region A remains constant during this initial stage of input variation. The latter implies that

$$\iint_A \mu(\alpha, \beta) d\alpha d\beta = C = \text{const.} \tag{3.37}$$

Consequently,

$$f(u, u_-) = \iint_{T_{u,u_-}} \mu(\alpha, \beta) d\alpha d\beta + C. \tag{3.38}$$

The integral over triangle T_{u,u_-} can be represented as the following double integral:

$$\iint_{T_{u,u_-}} \mu(\alpha, \beta) d\alpha d\beta = \int_{u_-}^u \left(\int_{u_-}^\alpha \mu(\alpha, \beta) d\beta \right) d\alpha, \tag{3.39}$$

which according to equation 3.38 leads to the following formula:

$$f(u, u_-) = \int_{u_-}^u \left(\int_{u_-}^\alpha \mu(\alpha, \beta) d\beta \right) d\alpha + C. \tag{3.40}$$

The slope of the newly formed ascending branch is equal to the derivative of $f(u, u_-)$ with respect to u. By performing the differentiation in formula (3.40), we find:

$$\frac{df}{du}(u, u_-) = \int_{u_-}^u \mu(\alpha, \beta) d\beta. \tag{3.41}$$

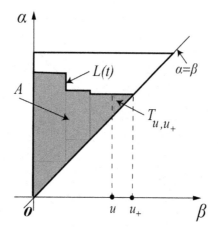

Fig. 3.30

Now, it is clear that the initial slope of the ascending branch is equal to zero, because

$$\lim_{u \to u_-} \frac{df}{du}(u, u_-) = \lim_{u \to u_-} \int_{u_-}^{u} \mu(\alpha, \beta)d\beta = 0. \qquad (3.42)$$

The proof that the initial slope of a newly formed descending branch is equal to zero can be performed by using the (α, β)-diagram shown in Fig. 3.30. According to this figure, we find that

$$f(u, u_+) = -\iint_{T_{u, u_+}} \mu(\alpha, \beta)d\alpha d\beta + \iint_{A} \mu(\alpha, \beta)d\alpha d\beta. \qquad (3.43)$$

Here, A is the shaded area, corresponding to the set S^+ immediately before the monotonic decrease of input from its maximum value u_+ to u.

By using the last formula and the same line of reasoning as before, it can be proved that

$$\lim_{u_+ \to u} \frac{df}{du}(u, u_+) = 0. \qquad (3.44)$$

Small slopes of newly formed branches may persist for appreciable initial parts of these branches. This is true because initial slope increases are controlled by the number of firms whose microeconomic hysteresis is described by narrow rectangular loops. These numbers tend to be small because, as discussed in Sec. 2.2, the broadening of the band of inaction, which is equal to $\alpha - \beta$, may be beneficial for efficient firm operations in the case of uncertain economic environments.

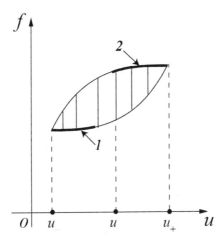

Fig. 3.31

In the case of branches corresponding to economic recovery, these almost flat and protracted initial parts of hysteresis branches **may lead to lingering high unemployment rates, which is the manifestation of recovery sluggishness.** Indeed, it is clear from Fig. 3.31 that the almost flat sections of initial parts of hysteresis branches may lead to the initial protracted increase in lengths of vertical chords. These vertical chord lengths represent the difference in unemployment rates occurring for the same value of input during a recession (curve 1) and a subsequent recovery (curve 2). It is evident that due to persisting "flatness" of the initial part of the recovery curve 2, there exists a sustained unemployment upturn that may last over appreciable initial parts of the recovery. In other words, **the almost flat initial part of the recovery curve reflects high and almost constant unemployment during the protracted initial stage of recovery, which may mask the onset of recovery. Similarly, the persisting flatness of the initial part of the recession curve 1 may mask the onset of a recession.**

We conclude this section with the following remark. We have established the history dependent branching property, the Erasure Property, the Congruency Property, the Property of Equal Vertical Chords and the Zero Initial Slope Property of macroeconomic hysteresis by using the classical Preisach aggregation model. In this model, microeconomic hysteresis is represented by simple rectangular hysteresis loops. This may lead to the point of view that the above properties are the consequences of rectangular loop representation of microeconomic hysteresis. However, in the next chapter the history dependent branching property, the Erasure Property and the Property of Equal Vertical Chords are established for generalized aggregation models. In these models, microeconomic hysteresis is represented by more realistic and more complex hysteresis loops. This suggests that the above properties are **insensitive** to the structure of the underlying microeconomic hysteresis, and that their **true origin may be due to the aggregation process itself**.

3.4 Alternative Forms of the Preisach Model of Macroeconomic Hysteresis

We begin this section with an interesting discussion of an alternative mathematical form of the Preisach model (3.4) of macroeconomic hysteresis. This form reveals that the Preisach model has a reversible component. This fact may be surprising because the Preisach model of macroeconomic hysteresis is the aggregation of various cases of microeconomic hysteresis described by heterogeneous rectangular loops $\hat{\gamma}_{\alpha\beta}$ shown in Fig. 3.3. As it is evident from this figure, these hysteresis loops do not contain locally reversible nonconstant components. Indeed, these hysteresis loops describe locally irreversible jumps from zero to one and from one to zero at the trigger values α and β, respectively. In other words, these rectangular hysteresis loops do not contain non-constant continuous reversible output variations. For this reason, **the emergence of locally reversible nonconstant components of macroeconomic hysteresis can be viewed as the effect of aggregation**.

To demonstrate the emergence of the reversible component, we represent equation (3.4) in the form.

$$f(t) = \iint\limits_{T} \mu(\alpha, \beta)\hat{\gamma}_{\alpha\beta}u(t)d\alpha d\beta, \qquad (3.45)$$

where T is the limiting triangle outside of which $\mu(\alpha, \beta)$ is equal to zero (see the discussion at the beginning of Sec. 3.2).

It is clear that for any value of input $u(t)$, the triangle T can be always subdivided into three sets: two triangles $T^+_{u(t)}$ and $T^0_{u(t)}$, and rectangle $R_{u(t)}$. This is shown in Figs. 3.32 and 3.33. These sets are defined by the formulas:

$$(\alpha, \beta) \in T^+_{u(t)} \text{ if } 0 < \beta < \alpha \le u(t), \qquad (3.46)$$

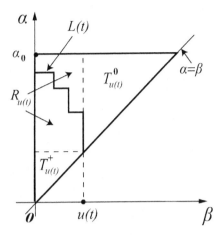

Fig. 3.32

$$\left(\alpha, \beta\right) \; \in \; R_{u(t)} \text{ if } 0 < \beta < u(t) \text{ and } u(t) < \alpha < \alpha_0, \qquad (3.47)$$

$$\left(\alpha, \beta\right) \; \in \; T^0_{u(t)} \text{ if } u(t) < \beta < \alpha_0. \qquad (3.48)$$

By using the above subdivision, we can represent equation (3.45) as follows:

$$f(t) = \iint\limits_{T^+_{u(t)}} \mu(\alpha, \beta)\hat{\gamma}_{\alpha\beta}u(t)d\alpha d\beta \; + \; \iint\limits_{R_{u(t)}} \mu(\alpha, \beta)\hat{\gamma}_{\alpha\beta}u(t)d\alpha d\beta$$

$$+ \iint\limits_{T^0_{u(t)}} \mu(\alpha, \beta)\hat{\gamma}_{\alpha\beta}u(t)d\alpha d\beta. \qquad (3.49)$$

Since, $u(t) > \alpha$ for any point (α, β) belonging to the triangle $T^+_{u(t)}$, we find that

$$\hat{\gamma}_{\alpha\beta}u(t) \; = \; 1, \qquad (3.50)$$

and

$$\iint\limits_{T^+_{u(t)}} \mu(\alpha, \beta)\hat{\gamma}_{\alpha\beta}u(t)d\alpha d\beta \; = \; \iint\limits_{T^+_{u(t)}} \mu(\alpha, \beta)d\alpha d\beta. \qquad (3.51)$$

Similarly, since $u(t) < \beta$ for any point (α, β) belonging to the triangle $T^0_{u(t)}$, we find that

$$\hat{\gamma}_{\alpha\beta}u(t) \; = \; 0, \qquad (3.52)$$

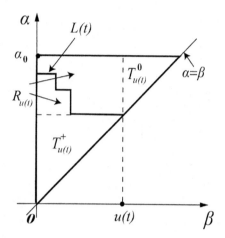

Fig. 3.33

and

$$\iint\limits_{T^0_{u(t)}} \mu(\alpha, \beta)\hat{\gamma}_{\alpha\beta} u(t) d\alpha d\beta = 0. \qquad (3.53)$$

By substituting formulas (3.51) and (3.53) into (3.49), we obtain:

$$f(t) = \iint\limits_{R_{u(t)}} \mu(\alpha, \beta)\hat{\gamma}_{\alpha\beta} u(t) d\alpha d\beta + \iint\limits_{T^+_{u(t)}} \mu(\alpha, \beta) d\alpha d\beta. \qquad (3.54)$$

By introducing the notation

$$\tilde{f}\big(u(t)\big) = \iint\limits_{T^+_{u(t)}} \mu(\alpha, \beta) d\alpha d\beta. \qquad (3.55)$$

the last formula can be written as follows:

$$f(t) = \iint\limits_{R_{u(t)}} \mu(\alpha, \beta)\hat{\gamma}_{\alpha\beta} u(t) d\alpha d\beta + \tilde{f}\big(u(t)\big). \qquad (3.56)$$

The last expression is mathematically equivalent to formula (3.45). How-ever, this expression can be construed as the decomposition of macroe-conomic hysteresis described by the Preisach aggregation model into irre-versible and reversible components. Indeed, the first term in the right-hand side of equation (3.56) can be viewed as the **irreversible** component. This is true, because the staircase interface belongs to the rectangle $R_{u(t)}$ for

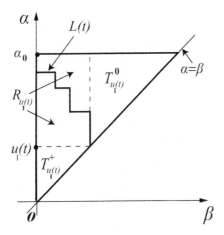

Fig. 3.34

any values of input $u(t)$. The shape of this interface $L(t)$ is controlled by the dominant past input extrema (i.e., dominant past shocks), and this shape of $L(t)$ is the source of irreversibility. On the other hand, the second term $\tilde{f}(u(t))$ in the right-hand side of equation (3.56) can be viewed as a fully **reversible** component of macroeconomic hysteresis. This can be demonstrated by using Figs. 3.34 and 3.35. These figures represent the change in (α, β)-diagrams for monotonic input increase from $u_1(t)$ to $u_2(t)$. This monotonic input increase results in the upward movement of the last horizontal link of $L(t)$ until the value $u_2(t)$ is achieved. This leads to the transition from the diagram shown in Fig. 3.34 to the diagram shown in Fig. 3.35. The subsequent monotonic decrease of input from $u_2(t)$ to $u_1(t)$ results in the formation of the last vertical link of $L(t)$ and its leftward movement until the value $u_1(t)$ is achieved. This leads to the transition from the diagram shown in Fig. 3.35 to the diagram shown in Fig. 3.34. In other words, the monotonic increase of input results in the addition of the shaded region A to $T^+_{u_1(t)}$, which means that

$$T^+_{u_2(t)} = T^+_{u_1(t)} + A. \qquad (3.57)$$

However, the subsequent monotonic decrease of input to $u_1(t)$ results in the removal of the same shaded region A from triangle $T^+_{u_2(t)}$ leading to the initial diagram shown in Fig. 3.34. This ensures the same value of $\tilde{f}(u(t_1))$ as before. The latter implies that $\tilde{f}(u(t))$ is a fully reversible component of macroeconomic hysteresis described by the classical Preisach model.

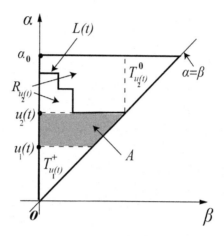

Fig. 3.35

If we are interested only in irreversible effects of macroeconomic hysteresis, then the reversible part $\tilde{f}\big(u(t)\big)$ can be omitted in formula (3.56). This leads to the following alternative form of the Preisach model of macroeconomic hysteresis

$$f(t) = \iint\limits_{R_{u(t)}} \mu(\alpha,\beta)\hat{\gamma}_{\alpha\beta}u(t)d\alpha d\beta. \tag{3.58}$$

The above formula accounts only for purely irreversible effects of macroeconomic hysteresis. A similar approach will be used in the next chapter in the study of generalized aggregation models of macroeconomic hysteresis.

Now, we consider another alternative form of the Preisach model (3.45) of macroeconomic hysteresis. This is an algebraic form in which the output $f(t)$ is explicitly expressed in terms of the function $\Im(\alpha',\beta')$ defined by the following formula:

$$\Im(\alpha',\beta') = \iint\limits_{T(\alpha',\beta')} \mu(\alpha,\beta)d\alpha d\beta. \tag{3.59}$$

Here, $T(\alpha',\beta')$ is a right-angle triangle shown in Fig. 3.36.

Next, consider a general (α,β)-diagram corresponding to monotonically decreasing input $u(t)$. This diagram is shown in Fig. 3.37. Our immediate goal is to find the expression for output $f(t)$ corresponding to this figure in terms of function $\Im$.

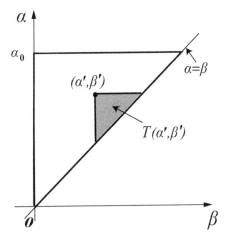

Fig. 3.36

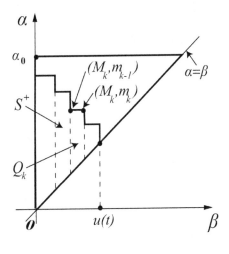

Fig. 3.37

According to formula (3.10), the output $f(t)$ is given by the following integral

$$f(t) = \iint\limits_{S^+_{u(t)}} \mu(\alpha, \beta) d\alpha d\beta. \tag{3.60}$$

It is clear from Fig. 3.37, that the set $S^+(t)$ can be subdivided into $n(t)$ trapezoids Q_k. Consequently,

$$f(t) = \sum_{k=1}^{n(t)} \iint_{Q_k(t)} \mu(\alpha, \beta)d\alpha d\beta. \tag{3.61}$$

It is clear that the number of these trapezoids $n(t)$ and their geometry may change with time. For this reason, n and Q_k are written in formula (3.61) as functions of time.

Each trapezoid Q_k can be represented as the difference of two triangles $T(M_k, m_{k-1})$ and $T(M_k, m_k)$:

$$Q_k(t) = T(M_k, m_{k-1}) - T(M_k, m_k). \tag{3.62}$$

This implies that

$$\iint_{Q_k(t)} \mu(\alpha, \beta)d\alpha d\beta = \iint_{T(M_k, m_{k-1})} \mu(\alpha, \beta)d\alpha d\beta - \iint_{T(M_k, m_k)} \mu(\alpha, \beta)d\alpha d\beta. \tag{3.63}$$

According to formula (3.59), we have:

$$\iint_{T(M_k, m_{k-1})} \mu(\alpha, \beta)d\alpha d\beta = \Im(M_k, m_{k-1}). \tag{3.64}$$

$$\iint_{T(M_k, m_k)} \mu(\alpha, \beta)d\alpha d\beta = \Im(M_k, m_k). \tag{3.65}$$

By substituting the last two formulas into equation (3.63), we obtain

$$\iint_{Q_k(t)} \mu(\alpha, \beta)d\alpha d\beta = \Im(M_k, m_{k-1}) - \Im(M_k, m_k). \tag{3.66}$$

Now, from formulas (3.61) and (3.66) we find:

$$f(t) = \sum_{k=1}^{n(t)} \left[\Im(M_k, m_{k-1}) - \Im(M_k, m_k) \right]. \tag{3.67}$$

It is clear from Fig. 3.37 that

$$m_n = u(t). \tag{3.68}$$

By using this fact, formula (3.66) can be modified as follows:

$$f(t) = \sum_{k=1}^{n(t)-1} \left[\Im(M_k, m_{k-1}) - \Im(M_k, m_k) \right] + \Im(M_n, m_{n-1}) - \Im(M_n, u(t)).$$

$$\tag{3.69}$$

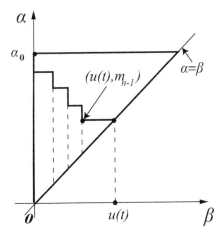

Fig. 3.38

The last formula is the alternative algebraic form of the classical Preisach model of macroeconomic hysteresis explicitly expressed in terms of the function $\Im$. However, the last formula has been derived for monotonically decreasing input $u(t)$, when the last link of interface $L(t)$ is a vertical one. In the case when the input $u(t)$ is being monotonically increased, the last link of $L(t)$ is a horizontal one and the (α, β)-diagram shown in Fig. 3.37 should be modified. The modified diagram is shown in Fig. 3.38. This diagram can be viewed as a proper amendment of the diagram shown in Fig. 3.37. The main change is that the last trapezoid Q_n shown in diagram Fig 3.37 is replaced by the triangle $T(u(t), m_{n-1})$ shown in Fig. 3.38. This leads to the following modification of formula (3.61):

$$f(t) = \sum_{k=1}^{n(t)-1} \iint_{Q_k(t)} \mu(\alpha, \beta) d\alpha d\beta \;+\; \iint_{T(u(t), m_{n-1})} \mu(\alpha, \beta) d\alpha d\beta. \qquad (3.70)$$

According to equation (3.59), we have

$$\iint_{T(u(t), m_{n-1})} \mu(\alpha, \beta) d\alpha d\beta \;=\; \Im\big(u(t), m_{n-1}\big). \qquad (3.71)$$

By substituting formulas (3.66) and (3.71) into equation (3.70), we find:

$$f(t) = \sum_{k=1}^{n(t)-1} \Big[\Im(M_k, m_{k-1}) - \Im(M_k, m_k) \Big] + \Im\big(u(t), m_{n-1}\big). \qquad (3.72)$$

Formulas (3.69) and (3.72) provide the complete reduction of the integral form of the classical Preisach model of macroeconomic hysteresis to the equivalent algebraic form. The above formulas may provide the **prediction power** of history-dependent branching of macroeconomic hysteresis. Indeed, the last input-dependent terms in formulas (3.69) and (3.72) may predict the future descending and ascending branches, respectively. Of course, these predictions are only possible if the function $\Im$ is known. However, according to formula (3.59), the function $\Im$ can be precomputed and used for macroeconomic hysteresis branching predictions only if the information concerning $\mu(\alpha, \beta)$ is available. The latter implies that sufficient information about the underlying microeconomic hysteresis must be known. The accuracy of branching predictions can be negatively affected by somewhat simplistic rectangular loop representation of microeconomic hysteresis. Furthermore, the Preisach model does not account for continuous structural evolution of the economy and its effects on macroeconomic hysteresis. It turns out that the last two limitations of the classical Preisach model of macroeconomic hysteresis can be relaxed by using generalized hysteresis models discussed in the next chapter.

We conclude this section by discussing the algebraic form for the irreversible component of the Preisach model of macroeconomic hysteresis represented by formula (3.58). This algebraic form is given in terms of function $G(\alpha', \beta')$ specified by the following equation:

$$G(\alpha', \beta') = \iint\limits_{R(\alpha',\beta')} \mu(\alpha, \beta)d\alpha d\beta, \qquad (3.73)$$

where $R(\alpha', \beta')$ is a rectangle shown in Fig. 3.39.

Next, consider a general (α, β)-diagram corresponding to monotonically increasing $u(t)$. This diagram for the model (3.58) is shown in Fig. 3.40. Our goal is to find the expression for output $f(t)$. According to this figure and formula (3.58), this output is given by the following expression:

$$f(t) = \iint\limits_{S_{u(t)}^+} \mu(\alpha, \beta)d\alpha d\beta. \qquad (3.74)$$

It is clear that the set $S_{u(t)}^+$ can be subdivided into $n(t)$ rectangles R_k. Consequently,

$$f(t) = \sum_{k=1}^{n(t)} \iint\limits_{R_k} \mu(\alpha, \beta)d\alpha d\beta. \qquad (3.75)$$

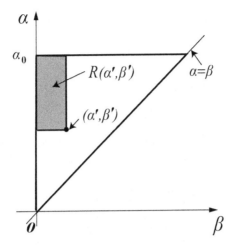

Fig. 3.39

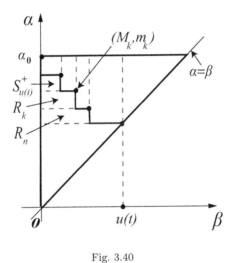

Fig. 3.40

Each rectangle R_k for $k \neq n$ can be represented as a difference of two rectangles:

$$R_k = R(M_k, m_k) - R(M_{k+1}, m_k). \tag{3.76}$$

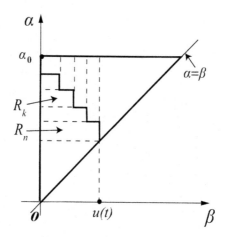

Fig. 3.41

Then, according to formula (3.73), we find that:

$$\iint\limits_{R_k} \mu(\alpha, \beta)d\alpha d\beta = G(M_{k+1}, m_k) - G(M_k, m_k). \tag{3.77}$$

It is also apparent that for rectangle R_n, we have:

$$R_n = R\big(u(t), m_n\big) - R(M_n, m_n), \tag{3.78}$$

which implies that

$$\iint\limits_{R_n} \mu(\alpha, \beta)d\alpha d\beta = G\big(u(t), m_n\big) - G(M_n, m_n). \tag{3.79}$$

By substituting formulas (3.77) and (3.79) into (3.75), we find:

$$f(t) = \sum_{k=1}^{n(t)-1} \Big[G(M_{k+1}, m_k) - G(M_k, m_k)\Big] + \Big[G\big(u(t), m_n\big) - G(M_n, m_n)\Big].$$
$$\tag{3.80}$$

The last formula was derived for monotonically increasing input $u(t)$. By using the same line of reasoning as well as the (α, β)-diagram shown in Fig. 3.41, the following algebraic expressions can be derived for the case of monotonically decreasing input:

$$f(t) = \sum_{k=1}^{n(t)-1} \Big[G(M_{k+1}, m_k) - G(M_k, m_k)\Big] + \Big[G\big(u(t), u(t)\big) - G\big(M_n, u(t)\big)\Big].$$
$$\tag{3.81}$$

The derived algebraic expressions (3.69) and (3.72), as well as (3.80) and (3.81) are very convenient for numerical implementation of the Preisach model of macroeconomic hysteresis. Indeed, as soon as functions $\Im$ and G are precomputed by using their definitions (3.59) and (3.73), respectively, the above algebraic expressions can be used for any shape of interface $L(t)$, i.e., for any sequences of global dominant extrema M_k and m_k. As discussed before, they can also be used (with some limitations) for the prediction of future branches of macroeconomic hysteresis.

Chapter 4

Generalized Aggregation Models of Macroeconomic Hysteresis

4.1 Definition of the Generalized Aggregation Model

In the case of the Preisach model discussed in the previous chapter, macroeconomic hysteresis has been constructed as the aggregation of heterogeneous rectangular loops describing microeconomic hysteresis. Such loops represent the idealization of microeconomic hysteresis. Indeed, they describe this hysteresis in terms of only two possible outcomes for such actions as buying-selling, hiring-firing, investing-disinvesting, etc. A more realistic way to describe microeconomic hysteresis is to use a loop shown in Fig. 4.1. For this loop, α and β are "up" and "down" switching triggers between the ascending branch $f_{\alpha\beta}^+(u)$ and descending branch $f_{\alpha\beta}^-(u)$, respectively. It is clear that the hysteresis loops of the type shown in Fig. 4.1 are generalizations of rectangular loops. The essence of this generalization is the replacement of the range of inactivity between α and β by the range of gradual and locally reversible activity. In other words, the hysteresis loop shown in Fig. 4.1 has a salient feature of representing two locally reversible parts of microeconomic hysteresis by nonconstant monotonic functions $f_{\alpha\beta}^+(u)$ and $f_{\alpha\beta}^-(u)$ for input variations within the following ranges, respectively:

$$0 < u < \alpha, \tag{4.1}$$

and

$$\beta < u < \infty. \tag{4.2}$$

This feature presents the opportunity to account for locally reversible actions of individual firms. In the case of employment, for instance, the rectangular hysteresis loops $\hat{\gamma}_{\alpha\beta}$ may only describe locally irreversible changes in employment occurring at input values α and β, while all other employment changes are neglected. Whereas, hysteresis loops of the type shown in

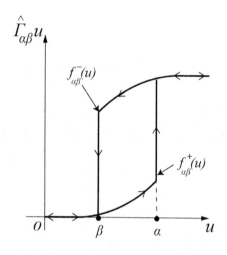

Fig. 4.1

Fig. 4.1 can model a broader array of locally reversible employer-employee actions occurring in response to changing economic conditions. For this reason, these types of heterogeneous microeconomic hysteresis loops may lead through aggregation to a more realistic approach to the modelling of macroeconomic hysteresis.

In the economic literature, the input variation range

$$\beta < u(t) < \alpha \qquad (4.3)$$

is usually called the band of inaction. Such a terminology is quite natural, when microeconomic hysteresis is described by rectangular loops. However, in the case when microeconomic hysteresis is described by loops of the type shown in Fig. 4.1, this terminology may be misleading. It is probably better to call the range (4.3) of input variations as the **irreversibility band**. Indeed, for this range there are nonzero vertical chords between ascending $f_{\alpha\beta}^{+}(u)$ and descending $f_{\alpha\beta}^{-}(u)$ branches (see Fig. 4.2). The lengths of these chords can be viewed as a measure of irreversibility. Such vertical chords do not exist for ranges of input variations described by formulas (4.1) and (4.2). This is the reason why the above irreversibility is revealed when the entire hysteresis loop is traversed.

To properly ascertain the structure of microeconomic hysteresis belongs to the field of microeconomics. In this respect, it is worthwhile to point out that some interesting results in this direction can be obtained by using the physical Random Field Ising Model (RFIM). This model has been applied

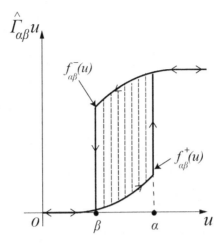

Fig. 4.2

to account for the interaction between individual firms. This approach is discussed in the very interesting paper of Bouchard [27]. A conceptually similar discussion on the origin and nature of hysteresis loops in magnetics in connection with Barkhausen jumps is presented in publications of Sethna and Dahmen and their collaborators (see [34] and [88]). It is demonstrated by Bouchard, Sethna and Dahmen that the RFIM may lead to hysteresis loops which are not perfectly rectangular and are similar in shape to hysteresis loops of the type shown in Fig. 4.1.

It is remarkable that nonrectangular loops similar to the one shown in Fig. 4.1 can be mathematically represented in terms of rectangular loops $\hat{\gamma}_{\alpha\beta}$. This issue has been briefly touched upon in Sec. 2.2. To make our discussion in this chapter self-contained, the above rectangular loops representation will be considered here again in more detail. This representation is given by the following formula:

$$\hat{\Gamma}_{\alpha\beta}(u) = \left(f_{\alpha\beta}^{-}(u) - f_{\alpha\beta}^{+}(u) \right)\hat{\gamma}_{\alpha\beta}u + f_{\alpha\beta}^{+}(u). \tag{4.4}$$

The mathematical proof of this representation proceeds as follows. If the input is monotonically increased from zero to α, then

$$\hat{\gamma}_{\alpha\beta}u(t) = 0. \tag{4.5}$$

The last formula is also valid if the variations of input start from some value between zero and β and then remain within the range specified by formula (4.1).

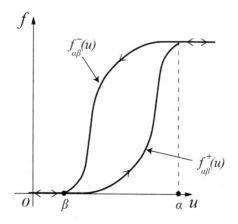

Fig. 4.3

From the last equation and formula (4.4), we find:

$$\hat{\Gamma}_{\alpha\beta}(u)(t) = f^+_{\alpha\beta}\big(u(t)\big). \tag{4.6}$$

This means that the ascending branch is traced for the case of above input variations.

On the other hand, if the input variations start from some value larger than α and then remain within the range defined by formula (4.2), then

$$\hat{\gamma}_{\alpha\beta}u(t) = 1. \tag{4.7}$$

In particular, the last equation is also valid if the input is monotonically decreased from some value above α to β.

From the above formula and equation (4.4), we conclude that

$$\hat{\Gamma}_{\alpha\beta}(u)(t) = f^-_{\alpha\beta}\big(u(t)\big). \tag{4.8}$$

This implies that the descending branch is traced. Thus, expressions (4.6) and (4.8) imply the validity of the rectangular loop representation (4.4).

It is worthwhile to stress that formula (4.4) is quite general, and it can be used for the rectangular loop representation of various hysteresis loops. For instance, such a representation is also valid for the loop shown in Fig. 4.3. This fact can be proved by using the same line of reasoning as presented above. Hysteresis loops of the type shown in Fig. 4.3 may describe not abrupt but rather incremental investments occurring gradually.

It is important to point out that the right-hand side of formula (4.4) can be viewed as the decomposition of hysteresis loops into irreversible and reversible components. Indeed, it is clear that the first term in the right-hand side of that formula corresponds to irreversible components, while the second term corresponds to reversible components.

Finally, the rectangular loop representation (4.4) of microeconomic hysteresis will be very instrumental for the analysis of macroeconomic hysteresis models obtained as the aggregation of heterogeneous hysteresis loops of the type shown in Figs. 4.1 or 4.3. This is because the representation (4.4) makes it possible to use the diagram technique developed in Sec. 3.2 in the analysis of the above macroeconomic hysteresis.

Next, we proceed to the definition of the generalized aggregation model of macroeconomic hysteresis. This model is constructed by aggregating heterogeneous hysteresis loops of the type shown in Figs. 4.1 or 4.3. As in the case of the classical Preisach model, this aggregation can be mathematically accomplished by performing the following integration:

$$f(t) = \iint\limits_{\alpha \geq \beta} \hat{\Gamma}_{\alpha\beta} u(t) d\alpha d\beta. \tag{4.9}$$

By using the rectangular loop representation (4.4) for $\hat{\Gamma}_{\alpha\beta} u(t)$ and by introducing the notation

$$\mu\big(\alpha, \beta, u(t)\big) = f_{\alpha\beta}^-\big(u(t)\big) - f_{\alpha\beta}^+\big(u(t)\big), \tag{4.10}$$

we arrive at the formula:

$$f(t) = \iint\limits_{\alpha \geq \beta} \mu\big(\alpha, \beta, u(t)\big) \hat{\gamma}_{\alpha\beta} u(t) d\alpha d\beta + \iint\limits_{\alpha \geq \beta} f_{\alpha\beta}^+\big(u(t)\big) d\alpha d\beta. \tag{4.11}$$

As in Sec. 3.2, consider a right triangle T shown in Fig. 4.4. This is the smallest right triangle outside of which the function $\mu\big(\alpha, \beta, u(t)\big)$ is equal to zero for any value $u(t)$. In other words, each hysteresis loop $\hat{\Gamma}_{\alpha\beta} u$ can be identified with the specific point (α, β) inside the triangle T, and there are no such points with this property outside T. This implies that the integration in formula (4.11) can be performed over T. This leads to the expression:

$$f(t) = \iint\limits_{T} \mu\big(\alpha, \beta, u(t)\big) \hat{\gamma}_{\alpha\beta} u(t) d\alpha d\beta + \iint\limits_{T} f_{\alpha\beta}^+\big(u(t)\big) d\alpha d\beta. \tag{4.12}$$

It is apparent that the second term in the right-hand side of the last formula is a single-valued function of $u(t)$. For this reason, it can be viewed as a fully reversible part of $f(t)$. By introducing the notation

$$g\big(u(t)\big) = \iint\limits_{T} f_{\alpha\beta}^+\big(u(t)\big) d\alpha d\beta, \tag{4.13}$$

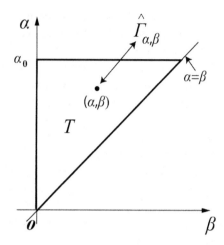

Fig. 4.4

the formula (4.12) can be written in the more concise form

$$f(t) = \iint\limits_{T} \mu\big(\alpha, \beta, u(t)\big)\hat{\gamma}_{\alpha\beta}u(t)d\alpha d\beta + g\big(u(t)\big). \qquad (4.14)$$

This formula (as well as formula (4.12) can be viewed as a **generalized** aggregation model of macroeconomic hysteresis. Indeed, there are three reasons to view this model as a generalization of the classical Preisach model (3.4) of macroeconomic hysteresis. First, the model (4.14) is the aggregation of more general microeconomic hysteresis loops than rectangular loops used in the classical Preisach model. Second, the function μ in formula (4.14) depends on the current value of input, while there is no such dependence in the classical Preisach model. Third, in model (4.14), there is a fully reversible term $g\big(u(t)\big)$, which is **inherited** from the structure of microeconomic hysteresis (see formula (4.14)).

It turns out that the function $\mu\big(\alpha, \beta, u(t)\big)$ has some properties which lead to further modification of formula (4.14). Indeed, it is clear from Fig. 4.1 that ascending $f^{+}_{\alpha\beta}(u)$ and descending $f^{-}_{\alpha\beta}(u)$ branches coincide, if

$$u(t) > \alpha. \qquad (4.15)$$

This means that under condition (4.15)

$$f^{-}_{\alpha\beta}\big(u(t)\big) = f^{+}_{\alpha\beta}\big(u(t)\big). \qquad (4.16)$$

Consequently, according to formula (4.10), we find that

$$\mu\big(\alpha, \beta, u(t)\big) = 0, \text{ if } u(t) > \alpha. \qquad (4.17)$$

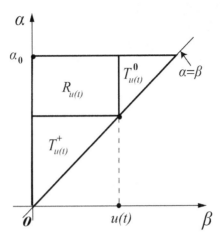

Fig. 4.5

Similarly, it is clear from Fig. 4.1 that ascending $f_{\alpha\beta}^+(u)$ and descending $f_{\alpha\beta}^-(u)$ branches coincide, if

$$u(t) < \beta. \tag{4.18}$$

The latter implies that under condition (4.18)

$$f_{\alpha\beta}^-\big(u(t)\big) = f_{\alpha\beta}^+\big(u(t)\big). \tag{4.19}$$

Consequently, according to formula (4.10), we find that

$$\mu\big(\alpha, \beta, u(t)\big) = 0, \text{ if } u(t) < \beta. \tag{4.20}$$

By using equalities (4.17) and (4.20), formula (4.14) can be modified as follows. We subdivide the triangle T into three regions: $T_{u(t)}^+$, $T_{u(t)}^0$ and $R_{u(t)}$ as shown in Fig. 4.5. These regions are defined by the following formulas:

$$(\alpha, \beta) \in T_{u(t)}^+, \text{ if } 0 < \beta < \alpha < u(t), \tag{4.21}$$

$$(\alpha, \beta) \in T_{u(t)}^0, \text{ if } u(t) < \beta < \alpha_0, \tag{4.22}$$

$$(\alpha, \beta) \in R_{u(t)}, \text{ if } 0 < \beta < u(t) \text{ and } u(t) < \alpha < \alpha_0, \tag{4.23}$$

It is clear from formulas (4.17) and (4.21) that

$$\mu\big(\alpha, \beta, u(t)\big) = 0, \text{ if } (\alpha, \beta) \in T_{u(t)}^+. \tag{4.24}$$

Similarly, it is apparent from formulas (4.20) and (4.22) that

$$\mu(\alpha, \beta, u(t)) = 0, \text{ if } (\alpha, \beta) \in T_{u(t)}^0. \tag{4.25}$$

Now, form Fig. 4.5 and formula (4.14) we find that:

$$f(t) = \iint\limits_{R_{u(t)}} \mu(\alpha, \beta, u(t))\hat{\gamma}_{\alpha\beta}u(t)d\alpha d\beta + \iint\limits_{T_{u(t)}^+} \mu(\alpha, \beta, u(t))\hat{\gamma}_{\alpha\beta}u(t)d\alpha d\beta$$

$$+ \iint\limits_{T_{u(t)}^0} \mu(\alpha, \beta, u(t))\hat{\gamma}_{\alpha\beta}u(t)d\alpha d\beta + g(u(t)). \tag{4.26}$$

According to formulas (4.24) and (4.25), we find respectively that

$$\iint\limits_{T_{u(t)}^+} \mu(\alpha, \beta, u(t))\hat{\gamma}_{\alpha\beta}u(t)d\alpha d\beta = 0, \tag{4.27}$$

and

$$\iint\limits_{T_{u(t)}^0} \mu(\alpha, \beta, u(t))\hat{\gamma}_{\alpha\beta}u(t)d\alpha d\beta = 0. \tag{4.28}$$

From the last two expressions and formula (4.26) we derive that

$$f(t) = \iint\limits_{R_{u(t)}} \mu(\alpha, \beta, u(t))\hat{\gamma}_{\alpha\beta}u(t)d\alpha d\beta + g(u(t)). \tag{4.29}$$

If we are interested only in irreversible effects of macroeconomic hysteresis, then the reversible part $g(u(t))$ can be omitted from formula (4.29). This leads to the following form of the generalized model of macroeconomic hysteresis:

$$f(t) = \iint\limits_{R_{u(t)}} \mu(\alpha, \beta, u(t))\hat{\gamma}_{\alpha\beta}u(t)d\alpha d\beta. \tag{4.30}$$

It was shown in Sec. 3.4 that if we are interested only in the irreversible component of macroeconomic hysteresis described by the Preisach model, then this component is given by the formula (see (3.56)):

$$f(t) = \iint\limits_{R_{u(t)}} \mu(\alpha, \beta)\hat{\gamma}_{\alpha\beta}u(t)d\alpha d\beta. \tag{4.31}$$

It is apparent from formulas (4.30) and (4.31) that the only mathematical difference between the generalized and classical Preisach models is the dependence of the μ-function on input $u(t)$ in the generalized model.

This allows for another interpretation of formula (4.30) as the aggregation of microeconomic hysteresis described by rectangular loops **whose heights depend on** $u(t)$. One possible reason for such a dependence may be that the switching triggers α and β of microeconomic rectangular hysteresis loops may not remain constant as a result of changing economic conditions. These triggers may be shifted as the economy evolves. These shifts may be expressed as follows:

$$\alpha' = \alpha - g_1\big(u(t)\big), \ \beta' = \beta - g_2\big(u(t)\big). \tag{4.32}$$

It belongs to the area of microeconomics to ascertain the relevant expressions for functions $g_1(u)$ and $g_2(u)$. It is clear that these expressions must be such that the inequality

$$\beta' < \alpha' \tag{4.33}$$

holds.

By using formulas in equation (4.32), the Preisach model (4.31) can be written as follows:

$$f(t) = \iint\limits_{R_{u(t)}} \mu\big(\alpha, \beta\big)\hat{\gamma}_{\alpha - g_1(u(t)), \beta - g_2(u(t))} u(t) d\alpha d\beta. \tag{4.34}$$

Next, by considering formulas in (4.32) as a change of variables from α and β to α' and β', the last equation can be represented in the form:

$$f(t) = \iint\limits_{R'_{u(t)}} \mu\big(\alpha' + g_1(u(t)), \beta' + g_2(u(t))\big)\hat{\gamma}_{\alpha'\beta'} u(t) d\alpha' d\beta', \tag{4.35}$$

where $R'_{u(t)}$ is defined as follows:

$$(\alpha', \beta') \in R'_{u(t)}, \text{ if } 0 < \beta' < u(t) \text{ and } u(t) < \alpha < \alpha'. \tag{4.36}$$

By introducing the new notation

$$\tilde{\mu}\big(\alpha', \beta', u(t)\big) = \mu\big(\alpha' + g_1(u(t)), \beta' + g_2(u(t))\big), \tag{4.37}$$

formula (4.35) can be written as follows

$$f(t) = \iint\limits_{R'_{u(t)}} \tilde{\mu}\big(\alpha', \beta', u(t)\big)\hat{\gamma}_{\alpha'\beta'} u(t) d\alpha' d\beta', \tag{4.38}$$

which is mathematically identical to the expression (4.30) for the generalized macroeconomic hysteresis model. This clearly suggests that when changes in economic conditions result in trigger shifts in microeconomic hysteresis loops, then macroeconomic hysteresis may be represented by the generalized model (4.30). The latter reveals another usefulness of the model (4.30) for the analysis of macroeconomic hysteresis.

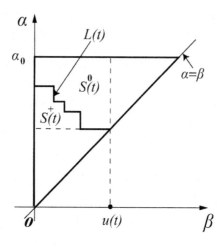

Fig. 4.6

4.2 Basic Properties of the Generalized Model of Macroeconomic Hysteresis

The mathematical analysis of the generalized model (4.30) of macroeconomic hysteresis is based on the diagram technique discussed in Sec. 3.2. According to this technique, at any instant of time the rectangle $R_{u(t)}$ is subdivided into two regions: the region $S^+(t)$ consisting of points (α, β), for which the outputs of corresponding rectangular loops are equal to one, and the region $S^0(t)$ consisting of points (α, β) for which the outputs of corresponding rectangular loops are equal to zero. The interface $L(t)$ between the regions $S^+(t)$ and $S^0(t)$ is a staircase line whose vertices have α and β coordinates coinciding respectively with local maxima and minima of input $u(t)$ assumed in the past instants of time. The final link of interface $L(t)$ is always attached to the line $\alpha = \beta$, and it moves as the input is changed with time. This link is a horizontal one and it moves upwards when the input is monotonically increased in time. On the other hand, the final link of the interface $L(t)$ is a vertical one and it moves leftwards as the input is monotonically decreased with time. This is illustrated by Figs. 4.6 and 4.7, respectively.

In Sec. 3.2, the stated facts were established for the case of the classical Preisach model, where the integration is performed over the limiting triangle T, whose boundary does not change with time. The situation is quite different in the case of the generalized model (4.30) of macroeconomic

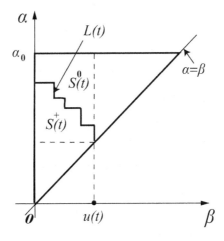

Fig. 4.7

hysteresis. In this model, the integration is performed over the rectangle $R_{u(t)}$, whose boundary is changed with time as a result of time variations of input $u(t)$. Nevertheless, the diagrams shown in Figs. 4.6 and 4.7 can be justified for model (4.30). This justification is based on the same rules of movement of the final link of the interface $L(t)$ which are also valid for model (4.30). This is illustrated by Figs. 4.8, 4.9, 4.10, 4.11 and 4.12. Indeed, let us assume that the input $u(t)$ has zero value at some time t_0 and the output of all rectangular loops $\hat{\gamma}_{\alpha\beta}$ are equal to zero. Next, we assume that the input $u(t)$ is monotonically increased in time until it reaches at time t_1 its maximum value u_1. The corresponding diagram is shown in Fig. 4.8. Next, we assume that the input is subsequently monotonically decreased in time until it reaches its minimum value u_2 at the time instant t_2. The corresponding diagram is shown in Fig. 4.9. Now, we assume that the input $u(t)$ is monotonically increased again until it reaches its maximum value u_3 at the time instant t_3. This leads to the diagram shown in Fig. 4.10. Subsequently, the monotonic decrease of input $u(t)$ until it reaches its minimum value u_4 at time t_4 leads to the diagram shown in Fig. 4.11. Similarly, the subsequent monotonic increase of input $u(t)$ until it reaches its maximum value u_5 at t_5 results in the diagram shown in Fig. 4.12.

The presented discussion clearly reveals that in general the diagram shown in Figs. 4.6 and 4.7 are valid for piecewise monotonic time variations of input.

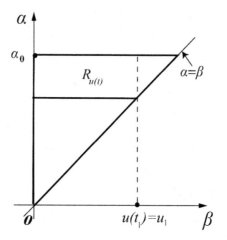

Fig. 4.8

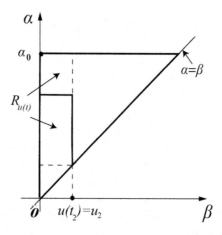

Fig. 4.9

Since

$$\hat{\gamma}_{\alpha\beta} u(t) = 1 \tag{4.39}$$

for all points (α, β) in the region $S^+(t)$, and

$$\hat{\gamma}_{\alpha\beta} u(t) = 0 \tag{4.40}$$

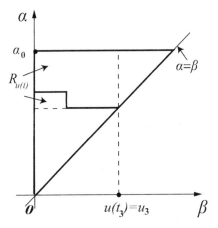

Fig. 4.10

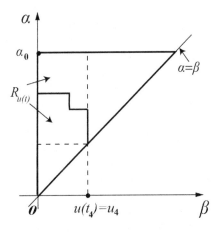

Fig. 4.11

for the points (α, β) in the region $S^0(t)$, formula (4.30) can be reduced to the following expression:

$$f(t) = \iint\limits_{S^+(t)} \mu\big(\alpha, \beta, u(t)\big)\, d\alpha\, d\beta. \tag{4.41}$$

The last expression implies that instantaneous values of $f(t)$ depend on subdivisions of the rectangle $R_{u(t)}$ into regions $S^+(t)$ and $S^0(t)$. Such subdivisions are determined by particular shapes of the staircase interface $L(t)$.

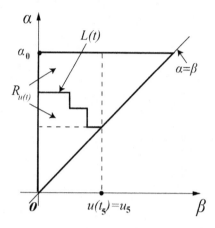

Fig. 4.12

These shapes depend on the past extremum values of input. This is the case because the α- and β-coordinates of the (protruding) vertices of $L(t)$ coincide, respectively, with past maximum and minimum values of input $u(t)$. The latter implies that the past extremum values of input $u(t)$ shape the geometry of the staircase interface $L(t)$, and in this way they leave their mark upon the future values of the output $f(t)$.

The latter discussion clearly reveals the mechanism of discrete memory formation of the generalized model (4.30) of macroeconomic hysteresis. This mechanism is the result of two **different** rules of the modification of interface $L(t)$. Namely, for time-monotonic input increases, horizontal final links of $L(t)$ are formed which move upwards. On the other hand, for time-monotonic decreases of input, vertical links are formed which move leftwards. These two different rules of modification of $L(t)$ result in the formation of the staircase interface whose vertices have α- and β-coordinates equal to past extremum values of input.

Remarkably, the above mechanism of memory formation is also responsible for branching in macroeconomic hysteresis described by the model (4.30). Indeed, two different rules for modifications of interface $L(t)$ for time-monotonic increases and decreases of input results in non-identical (i.e., different) variations of output $f(t)$ before and after any extremum value of input is reached. This leads to the formation of branches (see Fig. 4.13), which, in turn, results in the emergence of irreversibility. It can also be concluded that the aggregation of heterogeneous weak (Markovian) microeconomic hysteresis loops of the type shown in Fig. 4.1 leads

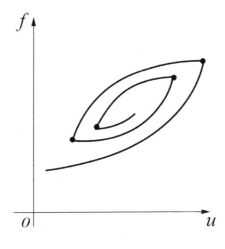

Fig. 4.13

to the emergence of strong (non-Markovian) multibranch macroeconomic hysteresis.

It is also clear that the past input extrema affect future output values and, in this case, they may have lasting economic consequences. Furthermore, these input extrema are exogenous in nature. For these reasons, past input extrema may be viewed as manifestations of economic **shocks**. However, as in the case of the Preisach model, not all past extrema act as shocks at any given time instant t. This is because the effect of certain past shocks can be eliminated by sufficiently large subsequent shocks. This elimination is based on the **erasure property** of the generalized model (4.30) of macroeconomic hysteresis.

To illustrate this property, consider some history of input time variations which results in the diagram shown in Fig. 4.12. Next, consider the time-monotonic input decrease until the minimum value u_6 smaller than u_4 is reached. It is apparent that this will result in the formation of the vertical final link of $L(t)$ and its leftward movement, which will eventually lead to the diagram similar to the one shown in Fig. 4.9. This implies that the vertex whose β-coordinate u_4 is larger than u_6 has been erased. It is apparent that analogous erasure of vertices may occur in the case of time-monotonic increase of input. In other words, it is clear that each new input minimum results in the erasure of the vertices of $L(t)$ whose β-coordinates are above this minimum. Similarly, each new input maximum results in the erasure of the vertices of $L(t)$ whose α-coordinates are below

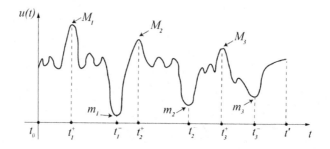

Fig. 4.14

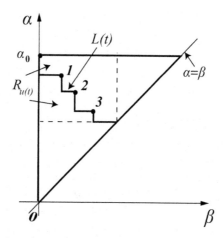

Fig. 4.15

this maximum. The latter is illustrated by Fig. 4.14. According to this figure, only extremum values M_1, m_1, M_2, m_2, M_3 and m_3 will define α- and β-coordinates of the vertices 1, 2 and 3 of the staircase interface $L(t)$ shown in Fig. 4.15 while the effects of other (i.e. intermediate) extrema have been erased.

It is clear from Fig. 4.14 that M_1, m_1, M_2, m_2, M_3 and m_3 form the **alternating sequence of dominant extrema**. As in Sec. 3.3, these extrema can be defined by the formulas

$$M_k = u(t_k^+) = \max_{t_{k-1}^- < t < t'} u(t), \tag{4.42}$$

$$m_k = u(t_k^-) = \min_{t_k^+ < t < t'} u(t). \tag{4.43}$$

It is apparent that the sequence of alternating dominant extrema is modified with time. This implies that new dominant input extrema may emerge as a result of future time variations of input, while some previously dominant input extrema may be erased. This is because M_k and m_k are functions of time t' as suggested by formulas (4.42) and (4.43), respectively.

The above discussion can be summarized as:

ERASURE PROPERTY: Only the sequence of alternating dominant input extrema are stored by the generalized aggregation model (4.30) of macroeconomic hysteresis.

As previously discussed, the input extrema can be viewed as manifestations of economic shocks. The Erasure Property suggests that not all past shocks affect the future branching of macroeconomic hysteresis. This property also clearly identifies the specific past economic shocks whose long-lasting effects may still exist at a given instant of time t'. These shocks correspond to alternative dominant input extrema M_k, m_k ($k = 1, 2, \ldots n$), and they can be viewed as **dominant** shocks at time t'. This is quite natural from the economics point of view, because the dominant shocks usually lead to appreciable and often irreversible structural changes in industry and society. These changes may make the previous structural changes caused by past intermediate shocks to be irrelevant as the future development of economy is concerned.

The stated **ERASURE PROPERTY** is the same as in the case of the classical Preisach model of macroeconomic hysteresis discussed in Sec. 3.3. The Preisach model is based on the aggregation of heterogeneous microeconomic hysteresis described by rectangular hysteresis loops. In this sense, it is quite different from the generalized macroeconomic model (4.30) based on the aggregation of heterogeneous non-rectangular microeconomic hysteresis loops. The fact that these two models have the same **ERASURE PROPERTY** implies that this property is **insensitive** to the structure of the underlying microeconomic hysteresis subject to aggregation. This also suggests that the true origin of the **ERASURE PROPERTY** is the aggregation process itself.

Next we discuss another characteristic property of the generalized model (4.30) of macroeconomic hysteresis. This property is valid for periodic (i.e., cyclic) variations of input. These cyclic input variations result in **macroeconomic** hysteresis loops, which should not be confused with hysteresis loops of the underlying microeconomic hysteresis. The formation of macroeconomic loops for cyclic input variations is evident from the diagram technique discussed above.

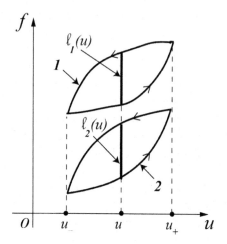

Fig. 4.16

Indeed, cyclic input variations between two consecutive input extremum values u_- and u_+ result in the sequential formation of leftward and upward moving vertical and horizontal links, respectively. As a result, the original diagram structure existing at the beginning of a cycle is restored at the end of the cycle. This implies that cyclic variations of the output lead to the formation of a hysteresis loop. It turns out that macroeconomic hysteresis loops described by the generalized model (4.30) have the following important property.

PROPERTY OF EQUAL VERTICAL CHORDS: All macroeconomic hysteresis loops resulting form cyclic (i.e., back-and-forth) time variations of input between the same two consecutive extremum values have equal vertical chords for the same input values.

This property is illustrated by Fig. 4.16. This figure corresponds to two input time-variations $u_1(t)$ and $u_2(t)$ which have different past histories. However, starting from instants of time $\tilde{t}_1$ and $\tilde{t}_2$, respectively, these inputs vary back-and-forth between the **same** two consecutive extremum values u_- and u_+. These periodic input variations result in two macroeconomic hysteresis loops 1 and 2. These loops are not congruent. The latter is the important difference in comparison with the Preisach model of macroeconomic hysteresis. Nevertheless, the vertical chords $\ell_1(u)$ and $\ell_2(u)$ of these loops, corresponding to the same input values, are equal. Namely,

$$\ell_1(u) = \ell_2(u). \tag{4.44}$$

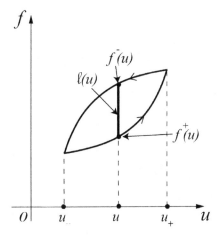

Fig. 4.17

To prove this property, consider a macroeconomic hysteresis loop shown in Fig. 4.17. Let us assume first that the input is monotonically decreased in time from its maximum value u_+ to its minimum value u_- along the descending branch. During this decrease of input, the output assumes the value $f^-(u)$ when the input reaches the value of u. Then, the input is monotonically increased in time from u_- to u_+. The output assumes the value $f^+(u)$ when the input is equal to u. It is clear from Fig. 4.17 that the length of the vertical chord corresponding to u is equal to

$$\ell(u) = f^-(u) - f^+(u). \qquad (4.45)$$

The diagram corresponding to the monotonic in time decrease of the input from u_+ to u_- is shown in Fig. 4.18. Similarly, the diagram corresponding to the monotonic in time increase of the input from u_- to u_+ is shown in Fig. 4.19. It is clear from these diagrams that

$$f^-(u) = \iint\limits_{S'_+(t)} \mu(\alpha, \beta, u) d\alpha d\beta, \qquad (4.46)$$

while

$$f^+(u) = \iint\limits_{S''_+(t)} \mu(\alpha, \beta, u) d\alpha d\beta. \qquad (4.47)$$

From (4.45), (4.46) and (4.47), we find

$$\ell(u) = \iint\limits_{S'_+(t)} \mu(\alpha, \beta, u) d\alpha d\beta - \iint\limits_{S''_+(t)} \mu(\alpha, \beta, u) d\alpha d\beta. \qquad (4.48)$$

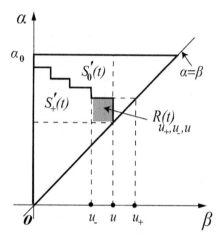

Fig. 4.18

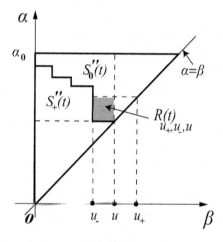

Fig. 4.19

It is also clear from the diagrams shown in Figs. 4.18 and 4.19 that

$$S'_+(t) = S''_+(t) + R_{u_+u_-u}(t), \tag{4.49}$$

where $R_{u_+u_-u}(t)$ is the shaded rectangle in the above figures.

From the last two formulas, we can find that

$$\ell(u) = \iint\limits_{R_{u_+u_-u}(t)} \mu(\alpha, \beta, u) d\alpha d\beta. \tag{4.50}$$

According to the last formula, it is clear that for any u such that $u_- < u < u_+$ the length of the corresponding vertical chord does not depend on a particular past history preceding the formation of the macroeconomic hysteresis loop. This proves that all comparable macroeconomic minor loops, which are the loops with the same reversal input values u_+ and u_-, have equal vertical chords.

The property of equal vertical chords is quite interesting from the economic point of view. To demonstrate this, consider an unemployment cycle represented by a macroeconomic hysteresis loop. In this case, an output $f(t)$ can be viewed as a cyclical unemployment rate. Then the lengths of the vertical chords of the hysteresis loops can be regarded as a measure of economic recovery. This is because the lengths of the vertical chords represent the difference in the unemployment rate during a recession and subsequent recovery, and they reveal the level of persistent unemployment. Since the vertical chords' lengths are identical for all macroeconomic hysteresis loops formed for the same two consecutive input extrema u_+ and u_- (see formula (4.50)), **this implies that the recovery dependence on the past is controlled by the last two shocks corresponding to u_+ and u_-, while all other past shocks have no lasting effect on recovery.** In this respect, the vertical chords represent a **universal** measure of economic recovery. This is a universal measure in the sense that it does not depend on other past dominant shocks, although these shocks may affect the output values $f(u_+)$ and $f(u_-)$.

It is interesting to point out that according to formula (4.50), the length of the vertical chords of macroeconomic hysteresis loops can be determined if microeconomic data on $\mu(\alpha, \beta, u)$ is available. By using these data and formula (4.50), **the unemployment persistence for cyclical unemployment can be predicted.**

It has been proven that (see [72] and [73]) the ERASURE PROPERTY and the PROPERTY OF EQUAL VERTICAL CHORDS are characteristic properties of the hysteresis model (4.30) in the sense that the following theorem is valid.

REPRESENTATION THEOREM: The Erasure Property and the Property of Equal Vertical Chords constitute the necessary and sufficient conditions for the representation of an actual multibranch hysteresis nonlinearity by the model (4.30).

In natural sciences, the stated theorem clearly establishes the experimentally verifiable limits of applicability of the hysteresis model (4.30). Within these limits the hysteresis model (4.30) has a predictive power for

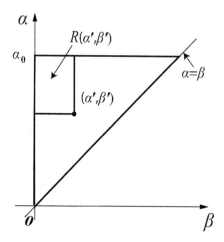

Fig. 4.20

history dependent branching. In the case of economics, the direct empirical verification of the equal vertical chord property may be very difficult.

In the case of the Preisach model discussed in the previous chapter, the equal vertical chord property is valid as well. This property follows from the Congruency Property of the Preisach model for macroeconomic hysteresis loops formed for input variations between the same consecutive extrema u_+ and u_-. As discussed later, the congruency property is not valid for the model (4.30). Nevertheless, the equal vertical chord property still holds despite the fact that the Preisach model and model (4.30) are based on the aggregation of heterogeneous microeconomic hysteresis described by microeconomic loops of different nature. This suggests that **the property of equal vertical chords is not sensitive to the underlying structure of microeconomic hysteresis subject to aggregation.**

Next, we consider an algebraic form of the aggregation model (4.30). This is the form in which the output $f(t)$ is explicitly expressed in terms of a function

$$G(\alpha', \beta', u) = \iint\limits_{R(\alpha', \beta')} \mu(\alpha, \beta, u) d\alpha d\beta. \tag{4.51}$$

Here, $R(\alpha', \beta')$ is a rectangle shown in Fig. 4.20.

To derive this algebraic form, consider a general (α, β)-diagram corresponding to time-monotonically increasing input $u(t)$. This diagram is shown in Fig. 4.21. According to this figure, the output is given by the

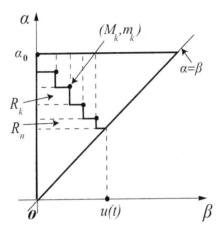

Fig. 4.21

formula

$$f(t) = \iint\limits_{S_+(t)} \mu\big(\alpha, \beta, u(t)\big)d\alpha d\beta, \qquad (4.52)$$

where $S_+(t)$ is the region consisting of points (α, β) for which the output of the corresponding rectangular loop $\hat{\gamma}_{\alpha\beta}u(t)$ is equal to one.

According to Fig. 4.21, the region $S_+(t)$ can be subdivided into $n(t)$ rectangles R_k, which means that

$$S_+(t) = \sum_{k=1}^{n(t)} R_k, \qquad (4.53)$$

and

$$f(t) = \sum_{k=1}^{n(t)} \iint\limits_{R_k} \mu\big(\alpha, \beta, u(t)\big)d\alpha d\beta. \qquad (4.54)$$

It is clear from Figs. 4.20 and 4.21 that

$$R_k = R(M_{k+1}, m_k) - R(M_k, m_k) \text{ for } k = 1, 2, \ldots (n-1). \qquad (4.55)$$

Consequently, for the above values of k we find

$$\iint\limits_{R_k} \mu\big(\alpha, \beta, u(t)\big)d\alpha d\beta = \iint\limits_{R(M_{k+1}, m_k)} \mu\big(\alpha, \beta, u(t)\big)d\alpha d\beta - \iint\limits_{R(M_k, m_k)} \mu\big(\alpha, \beta, u(t)\big)d\alpha d\beta.$$

$$(4.56)$$

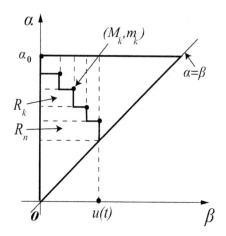

Fig. 4.22

Now, by using formula (4.51), the last expression can be written as follows:

$$\iint_{R_k} \mu(\alpha, \beta, u(t)) d\alpha d\beta = G(M_{k+1}, m_k, u(t)) - G(M_k, m_k, u(t)). \qquad (4.57)$$

It is clear from Fig. 4.21, that for the last rectangle R_n formula (4.55) can be written as:

$$R_n = R(u(t), m_n) - R(M_n, m_n). \qquad (4.58)$$

Consequently,

$$\iint_{R_n} \mu(\alpha, \beta, u(t)) d\alpha d\beta = G(u(t), m_n, u(t)) - G(M_n, m_n, u(t)). \qquad (4.59)$$

Finally, using formulas (4.54), (4.57) and (4.59) we arrive at the following result:

$$f(t) = \sum_{k=1}^{n(t)-1} \Big[G(M_{k+1}, m_k, u(t)) - G(M_k, m_k, u(t)) \Big]$$
$$+ \Big[G(u(t), m_n, u(t)) - G(M_n, m_n, u(t)) \Big]. \qquad (4.60)$$

The last formula has been derived for the monotonically increasing input $u(t)$. For monotonically decreasing inputs, the diagram shown in Fig. 4.21 is replaced by the diagram shown in Fig. 4.22. This implies that formula (4.58) must be replaced by the following formula:

$$R_n = R(u(t), u(t)) - R(M_n, u(t)). \qquad (4.61)$$

This suggests that

$$\iint\limits_{R_n} \mu\big(\alpha, \beta, u(t)\big)\, d\alpha d\beta = G(u(t), u(t), u(t)) - G(M_n, u(t), u(t)). \quad (4.62)$$

This in turn means that for the case of monotonically decreasing inputs formula (4.60) must be modified as follows:

$$f(t) = \sum_{k=1}^{n(t)-1} \Big[G(M_{k+1}, m_k, u(t)) - G(M_k, m_k, u(t)) \Big]$$
$$+ \Big[G(u(t), u(t), u(t)) - G(M_n, u(t), u(t)) \Big]. \quad (4.63)$$

Formulas (4.60) and (4.63) provide the complete reduction of the integral form of the generalized macroeconomic model (4.30) to the equivalent algebraic form. The derived algebraic expressions (4.60) and (4.63) may be useful for numerical implementation of the generalized model (4.30) of macroeconomic hysteresis. Indeed, once the function G is precomputed by using its definition (4.51), the above algebraic expressions can be used for any shape of interface $L(t)$, i.e., for any alternating sequence of past dominant extrema M_k and m_k. Furthermore, formulas (4.60) and (4.63) may provide the predictions for future branching of macroeconomic hysteresis. These predictions can be only made if the function G is precomputed. This is possible if sufficient information concerning $\mu\big(\alpha, \beta, u\big)$ is available. The latter requires detailed knowledge of the structure of the underlying microeconomic hysteresis.

It is interesting to compare algebraic forms for $f(t)$ obtained for the Preisach model (see formulas (3.80) and (3.81)) with the algebraic forms obtained for the generalized model (4.30) (see formulas (4.60) and (4.63)). The main and very important distinction is that in the case of the Preisach model only one or two of the last terms in formulas (3.80) and (3.81)may depend on $u(t)$. These terms describe only **one** last branch of macroeconomic hysteresis. This is illustrated by Fig. 4.23. The geometric shape of this last branch does not depend on past alternating dominant input extrema M_k and m_k for $k < n$. On the other hand, in the case of the generalized model (4.30), **all** terms in formulas (4.60) and (4.63)) depend on $u(t)$. This implies that there are numerous possible last branches of macroeconomic hysteresis. This is illustrated by Fig. 4.24. Geometric shapes of these branches depend on particular past histories determined by particular sets of past alternating dominant input extrema M_k and m_k. The above discussion implies that the generalized model (4.30) **is endowed with a much**

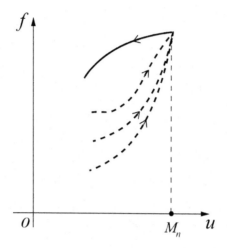

Fig. 4.23

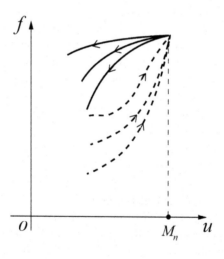

Fig. 4.24

more general mechanism of branching than the Preisach model. The above discussion also reveals that **in the case of the generalized model (4.30) macroeconomic hysteresis loops formed for identical cyclical variations of input are not congruent.**

Although the above macroeconomic hysteresis loops are not congruent, they nevertheless have the same areas. The latter follows from the Property of Equal Vertical Chords and the well known Cavalieri's Principle. These equal areas are controlled by the last two input extrema. The above area equality of comparable macroeconomic loops implies the same economic hysteresis losses caused by sunk adjustment costs (see [1] and [56]).

4.3 Macroeconomic Hystersis Models Based on the Aggregation of Heterogeneous Microeconomic "Play" Hysteresis

The play hysteresis has been briefly mentioned in Sec. 2.2. This type of hysteresis is geometrically represented by Fig. 4.25. It is clear from this figure that there is a continuous set of parallel inner lines within the major loop outlined by bold lines. Only one of these lines passes through each point inside the major loop. These lines are fully **reversible** and they can be traced in opposite directions for monotonically increasing and decreasing inputs, respectively. This type of microeconomic hysteresis may accurately describe the patterns of gradual investment undertaken by individual firms. These patterns can be described as follows. No investment is made until the input $u(t)$ is monotonically increased and reaches some trigger value α_1. A subsequent monotonic increase in input results in a gradual business investment g described as a linear function of u. This business action is represented by line 1 in Fig. 4.25. The full investment $g = m$ can be achieved when the input reaches some trigger value α_2. This implies that if input $u(t)$ increases above α_2, no additional investments are made. However, if the input $u(t)$ achieves some maximum value smaller than α_2 and subsequently undergoes some monotonic decrease, then the investment process is aborted. This business action is represented by line 2 in Fig. 4.25. This line is fully reversible. This implies that if the input $u(t)$ achieves some minimum value before line 3 is reached and then starts to monotonically increase again, then line 2 can be traced in the opposite direction until line 1 is reached. After this moment in time, the further monotonic increase in the input results in the renewal of the investment process. The latter is represented by further upward tracing of line 1 until the investment is completed when the input reaches value α_2. On the other hand, if the above monotonic decrease in the input is not interrupted, then line 2 is completely traversed in the leftward direction until line 3 is reached. The further monotonic decrease in the input results in gradual business disinvestment. The latter proceeds along line 3 in Fig. 4.25. This disinvestment process is completed when the input reaches the value $\alpha_1 - w_1$. On the other hand,

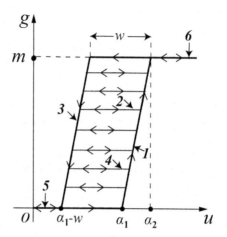

Fig. 4.25

if the above monotonic decrease in the input ends before the value $\alpha_1 - w_1$ is reached, and it is followed by a subsequent monotonic increase of input, then the reversal line 4 will be traced. If this monotonic input increase continues until line 1 is reached and proceeds further in time, then the investment process is renewed and line 1 is traced upwards.

It is apparent that the described play microeconomic hysteresis accounts for gradual and prudent investment actions. These actions are more realistic and sophisticated than the investment actions described by rectangular loops or by loops of the type shown in Fig. 4.1. It is clear that along the inner parallel lines no investment actions occur. For this reason, these inner reversible lines can be viewed as numerous **bands of inaction**. Whereas, the intervals

$$\alpha_1 < u(t) < \alpha_2 \text{ and } \alpha_1 - w < u(t) < \alpha_2 - w \qquad (4.64)$$

are the bands of gradual actions.

Despite its complexity, play hysteresis is **Markovian** (i.e., weak) hysteresis. In other words, this is a hysteresis with **local memory**. The latter implies that the value of output $g(t_0)$ at any instant of time t_0 and the value of input $u(t)$ at all subsequent instants of time $t > t_0$ uniquely define the values of output at all $t > t_0$. In other words, in the case of play hysteresis the past exerts its influence on the future through the current value $g(t_0)$ of the output. This means that for any point on the $u - g$ plane there is only one curve (i.e., combination of lines) that may represent the future time evolution of output for any specific input $u(t)$.

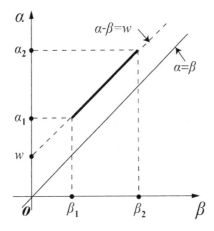

Fig. 4.26

It turns out that the play hysteresis can be represented in terms of rectangular hysteresis loops. This representation is given by the following formula:

$$g(t) = \frac{m}{\alpha_2 - \alpha_1} \int_{\alpha_1}^{\alpha_2} \hat{\gamma}_{\alpha,\alpha-w} u(t) d\alpha, \qquad (4.65)$$

where, as before, the symbol $\hat{\gamma}_{\alpha,\alpha-w}$ stands for rectangular hysteresis loops with switching up and down trigger values α and $\alpha - w$, respectively. It is apparent that parameters α_1, α_2, w and m completely define the play hysteresis (see Fig. 4.25).

The integral representation (4.65) of play hysteresis in terms of rectangular loops is very instrumental for the aggregation construction of the macroeconomic hysteresis model. As it is shown later in this section, the aggregation of heterogeneous play microeconomic hysteresis results in the Preisach model of macroeconomic hysteresis. This implies that macroeconomic hysteresis models based on the aggregation of two **very different types** of microeconomic hysteresis described by rectangular hysteresis loops, on the one hand, and by Fig. 4.25, on the other hand, have identical properties such as the Property of History Dependent Branching, the Erasure Property and the Congruency Property of macroeconomic hysteresis loops. This once again suggests that these properties are not **sensitive to the nature of the underlying microeconomic hysteresis subject to aggregation.**

Next, we proceed to the proof of formula (4.65). This proof is based on the diagram technique presented in Sec. 3.2 and frequently used in the subsequent discussion. The first step of the proof is to point out that the region of integration in formula (4.65) can be represented by the bold line segment shown in Fig. 4.26. Indeed, the points of this line segment have α- and β-coordinates coinciding with α- and β-switching values of rectangular hysteresis loops $\hat{\gamma}_{\alpha,\alpha-w}$ in formula (4.65). This is true, because the bold segment is a part of the line defined by the equation

$$\alpha - \beta - w = 0. \tag{4.66}$$

Consequently, for each point of this segment

$$\beta = \alpha - w \tag{4.67}$$

and $\hat{\gamma}_{\alpha,\alpha-w}$ is equivalent to $\hat{\gamma}_{\alpha\beta}$. Equation (4.66) also implies that

$$\beta_1 = \alpha_1 - w \tag{4.68}$$

and

$$\beta_2 = \alpha_2 - w. \tag{4.69}$$

Now, we assume that initially the value of the input $u(t)$ is equal to zero and, consequently, the output values of all rectangular loops $\hat{\gamma}_{\alpha,\alpha-w}$ are also equal to zero. This implies that the output value $g(t)$ is equal to zero, as well. Next, we consider the monotonic input increase from zero to some value $u(t)$ such that

$$u(t) < \alpha_1. \tag{4.70}$$

This implies that rectangular loops $\hat{\gamma}_{\alpha,\alpha-w}$ corresponding to the points on the bold line segment in Fig. 4.27 are not affected by the above monotonic input increase. Consequently, the output remains unchanged and

$$g(t) = 0. \tag{4.71}$$

This implies that the bold line 5 in Fig. 4.25 is traced in the rightward direction for the above monotonic input increase until the trigger value α_1 is reached. Next, we consider the case when the input $u(t)$ is further monotonically increased above the trigger value α_1:

$$u(t) > \alpha_1. \tag{4.72}$$

This is illustrated by the diagram shown in Fig. 4.28. It is clear from this diagram that all rectangular loops $\hat{\gamma}_{\alpha,\alpha-w}$ for which

$$\alpha_1 < \alpha < u(t), \tag{4.73}$$

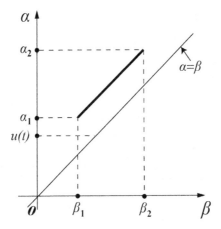

Fig. 4.27

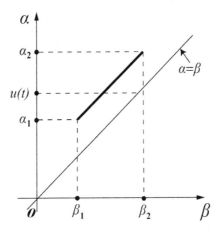

Fig. 4.28

are switched upwards and their output values are equal to one. On the other hand, all rectangular loops $\hat{\gamma}_{\alpha,\alpha-w}$ for which

$$u(t) < \alpha < \alpha_2, \tag{4.74}$$

remain in the downward position with their output values equal to zero. Consequently, according to formula (4.65), we find:

$$g(t) = \frac{m}{\alpha_2 - \alpha_1} \int_{\alpha_1}^{u(t)} d\alpha = m\,\frac{u(t) - \alpha_1}{\alpha_2 - \alpha_1}. \tag{4.75}$$

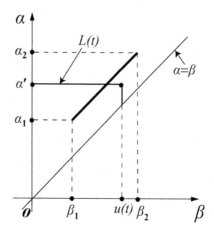

Fig. 4.29

The above formula suggests that the above monotonic increase of input results in the linear relation g vs. u, which is identical to the output vs. input relation represented by line 1 in Fig. 4.25. The latter means that line 1 is traced during the above monotonic input increase.

Now, consider the case when the input $u(t)$ achieves its maximum value α' and then is monotonically decreased in time. This monotonic decrease results in the formation of the vertical link of $L(t)$ which moves leftwards, as shown in Fig. 4.29. It is clear that if during the above monotonic decrease the following inequality is valid:

$$u(t) > \alpha' - w, \tag{4.76}$$

then rectangular loops $\hat{\gamma}_{\alpha,\alpha-w}$ corresponding to the points of the bold line segment on Fig. 4.29 are not affected by the above monotonic input decrease. Consequently, the output $g(t)$ remains constant and, according to formula (4.75), the output is equal to:

$$g(t) = m\,\frac{\alpha' - \alpha_1}{\alpha_2 - \alpha_1} = \text{const.} \tag{4.77}$$

The latter means that line 2 in Fig. 4.25 is traced leftwards. However, if the input $u(t)$ is further monotonically decreased, then the vertical link of $L(t)$ moves further leftwards and crosses the bold line segment as shown in Fig. 4.30.

It is clear from this figure that the first crossing point a occurs when

$$u(t) = \alpha' - w, \tag{4.78}$$

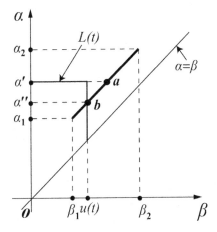

Fig. 4.30

which follows from equation (4.67). The further monotonic input decrease results in the downward movement of the crossing point along the bold line segment. This results in the downward switching of all rectangular loops $\hat{\gamma}_{\alpha,\alpha-w}$ corresponding to the points of the bold line segment between the first crossing point a and the current crossing point b. This means that only rectangular loops $\hat{\gamma}_{\alpha,\alpha-w}$ corresponding to the values of α between α_1 and α'' remain in the upward positions with their output values equal to one. As a result, from formula (4.65) we find:

$$g(t) = \frac{m}{\alpha_2 - \alpha_1} \int_{\alpha_1}^{\alpha''} d\alpha = m \, \frac{\alpha'' - \alpha_1}{\alpha_2 - \alpha_1}. \tag{4.79}$$

According to equation (4.66), we have:

$$\alpha'' = u(t) + w. \tag{4.80}$$

From the last two formulas, we obtain:

$$g(t) = m \, \frac{u(t) - (\alpha_1 - w)}{\alpha_2 - \alpha_1}. \tag{4.81}$$

The last equation is identical to the equation of line 3 on Fig. 4.25. This means that after the first crossing point a, the monotonic input decrease results in the downward tracing of line 3 in Fig. 4.25. This tracing ends when the input reaches the value $\alpha_1 - w$. At the time instant when this occurs, the output value is equal to zero (see formula (4.81). For further

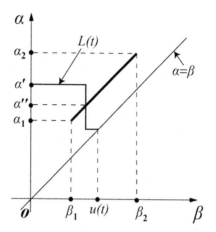

Fig. 4.31

monotonic decrease of the input, the leftward moving vertical link of $L(t)$ does not cross the bold line segment in Fig. 4.30. Consequently, the output values of all rectangular loops $\hat{\gamma}_{\alpha,\alpha-w}$ remain equal to zero. According to formula (4.65), this means that

$$g(t) = 0, \tag{4.82}$$

which implies that line 5 in Fig. 4.25 is traced in the leftward direction. However, if the input $u(t)$ reaches its minimum value

$$u(t) = \alpha'' - w, \tag{4.83}$$

which is smaller than $\alpha_1 - w$, and then is monotonically increased in time, then the final horizontal link of $L(t)$ is formed and it moves upwards. This is illustrated in Fig. 4.31. This upwards motion of the horizontal link does not affect rectangular loops $\hat{\gamma}_{\alpha,\alpha-w}$ corresponding to the points of the bold line segment. Consequently, the value of output $g(t)$ will remain constant and equal to the value defined by formula (4.79):

$$g(t) = m\,\frac{\alpha'' - \alpha_1}{\alpha_2 - \alpha_1} = \text{const.} \tag{4.84}$$

This implies that for the above monotonic increase of input line 4 in Fig. 4.25 is traced in the rightward direction until line 1 is reached. The last situation is illustrated by Fig. 4.32. After that time instant, the further monotonic increase of input will result in upward switching of rectangular loops $\hat{\gamma}_{\alpha,\alpha-w}$ for which $\alpha < u(t)$. This upward switching is a result of the

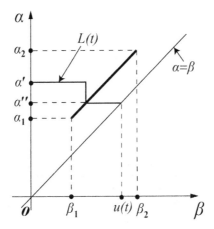

Fig. 4.32

upward motion of the final horizontal link of $L(t)$ (see Fig. 4.33). It is clear that all rectangular loops $\hat{\gamma}_{\alpha,\alpha-w}$, for which inequality (4.73) is valid, will be in the upward state with their output values equal to one. The latter means that formula (4.75) is valid for the output of $g(t)$. This in turn implies that line 1 will be traced upwards for the above monotonic input increase. This tracing ends when the input reaches the value α_2. This is because for the further monotonic increase of input, the upward moving horizontal link of $L(t)$ does not cross the bold line segment (see Fig. 4.34). Consequently, the output values of all rectangular loops $\hat{\gamma}_{\alpha,\alpha-w}$ remain equal to one. According to formula (4.65), this means that

$$g(t) = m = \text{ const.} \qquad (4.85)$$

This implies that line 6 shown in Fig. 4.25 will be traced in the rightward direction.

Thus, we have established that formula (4.65) describes the proper tracing of all lines of play hysteresis shown in Fig. 4.25. This concludes the proof of the validity of formula (4.65).

It is clear from formula (4.65) that play hysteresis can be viewed as an aggregation of hysteresis represented by rectangular loops $\hat{\gamma}_{\alpha,\alpha-w}$. This is a very special aggregation when all these rectangular loops correspond to the points of the line $\alpha - \beta - w = 0$, which is parallel to the line $\alpha = \beta$. This special aggregation results in weak (i.e, Markovian) hysteresis. For this reason, play hysteresis can be used for the description of microeconomic hysteresis, however, it cannot be used for the modelling of strong

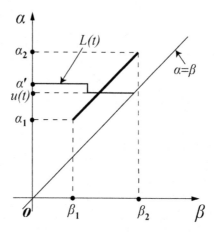

Fig. 4.33

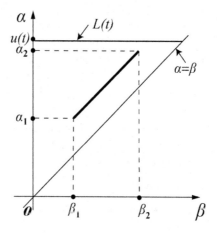

Fig. 4.34

macroeconomic hysteresis. The latter can be achieved through the aggregation of play hysteresis.

Next, we proceed to the mathematical analysis of aggregation of heterogeneous microeconomic play hysteresis. We consider the aggregation with respect to the parameter w, which can be viewed as the width of generalized bands of inaction. We also assume that in the case of play hysteresis the maximum m of investment is a function of w. The latter is quite natural from the microeconomics point of view. Thus, equation (4.65) can be written as follows:

$$g(t) = \frac{m(w)}{\alpha_2 - \alpha_1} \int_{\alpha_1}^{\alpha_2} \hat{\gamma}_{\alpha,\alpha-w} u(t) d\alpha. \tag{4.86}$$

Now, the macroeconomic hysteresis resulting in the aggregation of heterogeneous microeconomic play hysteresis with respect to w can be represented by the following formula:

$$f(t) = \frac{1}{\alpha_2 - \alpha_1} \int_{\alpha_1}^{\alpha_2} \left(\int_{w_{\min}}^{w_{\max}} m(w) \hat{\gamma}_{\alpha,\alpha-w} u(t) dw \right) d\alpha. \tag{4.87}$$

The above aggregation is performed by assuming that α_1 and α_2 are fixed, and only w and m are different for various businesses (i.e., firms). Consequently, according to Fig. 4.35, we find that

$$w_{\max} = \alpha_1, \tag{4.88}$$

while

$$w_{\min} = 0. \tag{4.89}$$

Next, we perform the change of variables from w to β. To do this, we recall equation (4.66) and find that

$$w = \alpha - \beta, \tag{4.90}$$

and, consequently,

$$dw = -d\beta. \tag{4.91}$$

Furthermore, it is clear from Fig. 4.35 as well as equations (4.88) and (4.89) that:

$$\beta = 0 \text{ for } w = w_{\max} \tag{4.92}$$

and

$$\beta = \beta_1 = \alpha_1 \text{ for } w = w_{\min}. \tag{4.93}$$

This means that the integral with respect to w in formula (4.87) can be transformed as follows:

$$\int_{w_{\min}}^{w_{\max}} m(w) \hat{\gamma}_{\alpha,\alpha-w} u(t) dw = \int_0^{\alpha_1} m(\alpha - \beta) \hat{\gamma}_{\alpha\beta} u(t) d\beta. \tag{4.94}$$

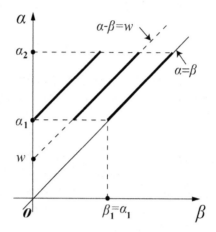

Fig. 4.35

From the last formula and equation (4.87), we find:

$$f(t) = \frac{1}{\alpha_2 - \alpha_1} \int_{\alpha_1}^{\alpha_2} \left(\int_0^{\alpha_1} m(\alpha - \beta)\hat{\gamma}_{\alpha\beta}u(t)d\beta \right) d\alpha. \tag{4.95}$$

Now, it is clear that formula (4.95) can be represented in the form

$$f(t) = \frac{1}{\alpha_2 - \alpha_1} \iint_{R_{\alpha_1\alpha_2}} m(\alpha - \beta)\hat{\gamma}_{\alpha\beta}u(t)d\alpha d\beta, \tag{4.96}$$

where the double integral is taken over the rectangle $R_{\alpha_1\alpha_2}$ shown in Fig. 4.36. By introducing the characteristic function $\chi(\alpha_1, \alpha_2)$ for the above rectangle, defined by the formula

$$\chi(\alpha_1, \alpha_2) = \begin{cases} 1, & \text{if } (\alpha, \beta) \in R_{\alpha_1\alpha_2} \\ 0, & \text{if } (\alpha, \beta) \notin R_{\alpha_1\alpha_2} \end{cases} \tag{4.97}$$

as well as the function μ

$$\mu(\alpha, \beta, \alpha_1, \alpha_2) = \frac{\chi(\alpha_1, \alpha_2)}{\alpha_2 - \alpha_1} m(\alpha - \beta), \tag{4.98}$$

equation (4.96) can be written as follows

$$f(t) = \iint_{\alpha \geq \beta} \mu(\alpha, \beta, \alpha_1, \alpha_2)\hat{\gamma}_{\alpha\beta}u(t)d\alpha d\beta. \tag{4.99}$$

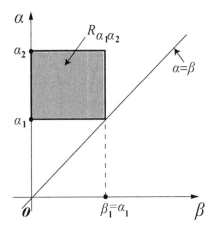

Fig. 4.36

According to formula (4.99), it is apparent that the macroeconomic hysteresis emerging as a result of the aggregation of heterogeneous microeconomic play hysteresis is mathematically identical to the macroeconomic hysteresis described by the classical Preisach model, which is obtained as a result of aggregation of heterogeneous rectangular hysteresis loops. This implies that the Preisach macroeconomic hysteresis model and the macroeconomic model based on the aggregation of play hysteresis have **identical** properties. This further suggests that these properties are not very sensitive to the specific nature of the underlying microeconomic hysteresis and that **their emergence is by and large the aggregation effect**.

In the derivation of formula (4.99), the aggregation only with respect to w was used, while parameters α_1 and α_2 were regarded as fixed. In general, the additional aggregation with respect to α_1 and α_2 must be carried out. The derivation of the final result of this aggregation is mathematically somewhat convoluted and omitted here. However, it is intuitively clear that this derivation will again lead to the Preisach model for macroeconomic hysteresis. This is because it will result in the linear superposition of rectangular loops $\hat{\gamma}_{\alpha\beta}u(t)$ which is the hallmark of the Preisach model.

We conclude this section by considering a generalization of the play hysteresis. This generalization is illustrated by Fig. 4.37. It is clear from the above figure that as before there is a continuous (i.e. infinite) set of parallel fully reversible inner lines within the major loop outlined by bold lines. The main difference between the play hysteresis shown in Fig. 4.25 and the

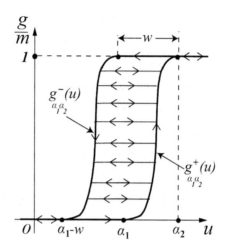

Fig. 4.37

generalized play hysteresis shown in Fig. 4.37 is that the ascending $g^+_{\alpha_1\alpha_2}(u)$ and descending $g^-_{\alpha_1\alpha_2}(u)$ branches of the latter hysteresis are **curved** lines rather than being straight lines. This difference provides better means to account for various gradual investment patterns.

The ascending and descending branches are geometrically translated (along the u-axis) versions of one another. This means that they are mathematically related by the formula

$$g^-_{\alpha_1\alpha_2}(u) = g^+_{\alpha_1\alpha_2}(u+w), \qquad (4.100)$$

where, as before, w is the width of generalized bands of inaction.

It turns out that the generalized play hysteresis can be represented in terms of rectangular hysteresis loops as well as by using the formula:

$$g(t) = m \int_{\alpha_1}^{\alpha_2} \frac{dg^+_{\alpha_1\alpha_2}}{d\alpha}(\alpha)\hat{\gamma}_{\alpha,\alpha-w}u(t)d\alpha. \qquad (4.101)$$

The proof of the last formula is based on the diagram technique and it is very similar to the proof of (4.65). The first step in this proof is to point out that the region of integration in formula (4.101) can be represented by the bold segment shown in Fig. 4.38. Next, we assume that the initial input value is equal to zero and, consequently, the output values of all rectangular loops $\hat{\gamma}_{\alpha,\alpha-w}$ are equal to zero as well. This implies that $g(t) = 0$. Subsequently, the input is monotonically increased in time but does not exceed α_1. Then, according to the diagram shown in Fig. 4.27

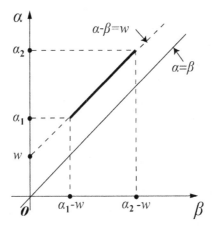

Fig. 4.38

the rectangular loops $\hat{\gamma}_{\alpha,\alpha-w}$ corresponding to the points of the bold line segment in Fig. 4.38 are not affected by this increase. Consequently, the output $g(t)$ remains equal to zero. However, in the case when the input $u(t)$ exceeds α_1, then all rectangular loops $\hat{\gamma}_{\alpha,\alpha-w} u(t)$ for which

$$\alpha_1 < \alpha < u(t) \tag{4.102}$$

are switched upwards and their output values are equal to one. Then, according to formula (4.101) we find

$$g(t) = m \int_{\alpha_1}^{u(t)} \frac{dg_{\alpha_1\alpha_2}^{+}}{d\alpha}(\alpha)d\alpha = m \, g_{\alpha_1\alpha_2}^{+}(u(t)). \tag{4.103}$$

This means that the ascending branch $g_{\alpha_1\alpha_2}^{+}(u)$ is traced upwards during the above monotonic increase.

Next, consider the case when the input $u(t)$ achieves its maximum value α' and then it is monotonically decreased. It is clear from Fig. 4.29 that if during the above monotonic decrease the following inequality

$$u(t) > \alpha' - w \tag{4.104}$$

is valid, then none of the rectangular loops $\hat{\gamma}_{\alpha,\alpha-w} u(t)$ corresponding to the points of the bold line segment in Fig. 4.38 are affected by the above monotonic decrease. This means that the output remains constant and, according to formula (4.103), this output is equal to

$$g(t) = m \, g_{\alpha_1\alpha_2}^{+}(\alpha') = \text{const.} \tag{4.105}$$

This implies that the corresponding horizontal inner line is traced leftwards. However, if the $u(t)$ is further monotonically decreased, then according to Fig. 4.30 and formulas (4.79) and (4.80) we find

$$g(t) = m \int_{\alpha_1}^{u(t)+w} \frac{dg_{\alpha_1\alpha_2}^+}{d\alpha}(\alpha)d\alpha = m\, g_{\alpha_1\alpha_2}^+\big(u(t)+w\big). \qquad (4.106)$$

According to formula (4.100), this implies that

$$g(t) = m\, g_{\alpha_1\alpha_2}^-\big(u(t)\big). \qquad (4.107)$$

This means that the descending branch $mg_{\alpha_1\alpha_2}^-(u)$ is traced downwards during the above monotonic input decrease.

By using the same line of reasoning as above, it can easily be established that formula (4.101) describes the proper tracing of all branches of generalized play hysteresis shown in Fig. 4.37.

Having established the validity of formula (4.101), the aggregation of heterogeneous generalized microeconomic play hysteresis can be discussed. This discussion closely parallels the derivation of formula (4.99). Indeed, by assuming that investment maximum m is a function of w and performing aggregation with respect to w, we derive that

$$f(t) = \int_{\alpha_1}^{\alpha_2} \left(\int_{w_{\min}}^{w_{\max}} m(w) \frac{dg_{\alpha_1\alpha_2}^+}{d\alpha}(\alpha)\hat{\gamma}_{\alpha,\alpha-w}u(t)dw \right) d\alpha. \qquad (4.108)$$

Next, the change of variables from w to β in formula (4.108) leads to the expression

$$f(t) = \int_{\alpha_1}^{\alpha_2} \left(\int_0^{\alpha_1} m(\alpha-\beta) \frac{dg_{\alpha_1\alpha_2}^+}{d\alpha}(\alpha)\hat{\gamma}_{\alpha\beta}u(t)d\beta \right) d\alpha. \qquad (4.109)$$

Finally, by using the same line of reasoning as in the derivation of formula (4.99), we obtain

$$f(t) = \iint_{\alpha \geq \beta} \mu\big(\alpha,\beta,\alpha_1,\alpha_2\big)\hat{\gamma}_{\alpha\beta}u(t)d\alpha d\beta, \qquad (4.110)$$

where

$$\mu\big(\alpha,\beta,\alpha_1,\alpha_2\big) = \chi(\alpha_1,\alpha_2)\frac{dg_{\alpha_1\alpha_2}^+}{d\alpha}(\alpha)m(\alpha-\beta). \qquad (4.111)$$

It is apparent that formula (4.111) is reduced to formula (4.98) because for the case of play hysteresis shown in Fig. 4.25 we find that

$$\frac{dg_{\alpha_1\alpha_2}^+}{d\alpha}(\alpha) = \frac{1}{\alpha_2 - \alpha_1}. \qquad (4.112)$$

It is interesting to point out in the conclusion of this section that models based on the aggregation of play hysteresis are extensively used in the study of mechanical hysteresis. In the corresponding literature, this model is referred to as the Prandtl-Ishlinskii model. It is clear from the discussion in this section, that the Prandtl-Ishlinskii model can be always reduced to the Preisach model. Such a reduction of the Prandtl-Ishlinskii model can be very attractive due to the most elementary nature of rectangular hysteresis loops $\hat{\gamma}_{\alpha\beta}$ used in the Preisach model. Furthermore, the above reduction implies that all the properties established for the Preisach model are also valid for the Prandtl-Ishlinskii model.

4.4   Feedback and Multi-Input Models of Macroeconomic Hysteresis

At the end of the first chapter, it was mentioned that Baldwin and Krugman had pointed out (see [11]) on the existence of a feedback between the output and input in the case of macroeconomic hysteresis. In foreign trade hysteresis, this is the feedback between the trade volume and the exchange rate. In cyclic unemployment hysteresis, this may be the feedback between the unemployment rate and the interest rate.

   In the Preisach model of macroeconomic hysteresis

$$f(t) = \iint\limits_{\alpha \geq \beta} \mu(\alpha, \beta)\hat{\gamma}_{\alpha\beta}u(t)d\alpha d\beta \qquad (4.113)$$

this feedback is neglected. Mathematically, this feedback can be accounted for by using the following modification of the Preisach macroeconomic hysteresis model

$$\tilde{f}(t) = \iint\limits_{\alpha \geq \beta} \mu(\alpha, \beta)\hat{\gamma}_{\alpha\beta}\left[u(t) - K\tilde{f}(t)\right]d\alpha d\beta, \qquad (4.114)$$

where K can be viewed as a feedback strength.

   It is apparent that the feedback Preisach model can be represented by the input-output diagram shown in Fig. 4.39, which is a modification of the diagram shown in Fig. 3.3. The comprehensive analysis of the feedback model (4.114) is mathematically complicated. The purpose of our subsequent discussion is to demonstrate that this analysis is still doable in the case when the feedback constant K is relatively small. In the latter case, the feedback Preisach model (4.114) can be mathematically construed as a perturbation of the classical Preisach model (4.113).

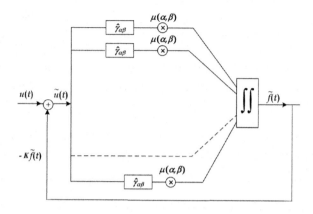

Fig. 4.39

The perturbation analysis of the feedback model (4.114) is based on the algebraic form of the classical Preisach model discussed in Sec. 3.4. This algebraic form is represented in terms of the function $\mathfrak{F}(\alpha, \beta)$ defined by the formula

$$\Im(\alpha, \beta) = \iint\limits_{T(\alpha,\beta)} \mu(\alpha', \beta') d\alpha' d\beta', \qquad (4.115)$$

and illustrated by Fig. 4.40.

It is shown in Sec. 3.4, that this algebraic form is given by the following equation:

$$f(t) = \sum_{k=1}^{n(t)-1} \left[\Im(M_k, m_{k-1}) - \Im(M_k, m_k) \right] + \Im(u(t), m_{n-1}), \qquad (4.116)$$

in the case of monotonically increasing input $u(t)$, and by the equation

$$f(t) = \sum_{k=1}^{n(t)-1} \left[\Im(M_k, m_{k-1}) - \Im(M_k, m_k) \right] + \Im(M_n, m_{n-1}) - \Im(M_n, u(t)), \qquad (4.117)$$

in the case of monotonically decreasing input. In the above formulas, $\{M_k, m_k\}$ is (as before) the alternating sequence of past dominant input extrema.

It turns out that similar formulas can be written for the feedback model (4.114). Indeed, by introducing the notation

$$\tilde{u}(t) = u(t) - K\tilde{f}(t), \qquad (4.118)$$

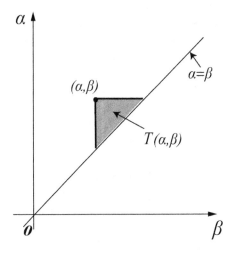

Fig. 4.40

the feedback model can be represented in the following form:

$$\tilde{f}(t) = \iint\limits_{\alpha \geq \beta} \mu(\alpha, \beta) \hat{\gamma}_{\alpha\beta} \tilde{u}(t) d\alpha d\beta, \qquad (4.119)$$

which is mathematically identical to the Preisach model (4.113). This implies that the following formulas are valid:

$$\tilde{f}(t) = \sum_{k=1}^{n(t)-1} \left[\Im(\tilde{M}_k, \tilde{m}_{k-1}) - \Im(\tilde{M}_k, \tilde{m}_k) \right] + \Im(\tilde{u}(t), \tilde{m}_{n-1}), \qquad (4.120)$$

for monotonically increasing input $\tilde{u}(t)$, and

$$\tilde{f}(t) = \sum_{k=1}^{n(t)-1} \left[\Im(\tilde{M}_k, \tilde{m}_{k-1}) - \Im(\tilde{M}_k, \tilde{m}_k) \right] + \Im(\tilde{M}_n, \tilde{m}_{n-1}) - \Im(\tilde{M}_n, \tilde{u}(t)),$$

$$(4.121)$$

for monotonically decreasing input $\tilde{u}(t)$. Here, $\{\tilde{M}_k, \tilde{m}_k\}$ is the alternating sequence of past dominant extrema of input $\tilde{u}(t)$. It is clear from formula (4.118) that

$$\tilde{M}_k = M_k - K \tilde{f}_k^+, \qquad (4.122)$$

$$\tilde{m}_k = m_k - K \tilde{f}_k^-, \qquad (4.123)$$

where $\tilde{f}_k^+$ and $\tilde{f}_k^-$ are the values of output $\tilde{f}(t)$ of the feedback model, when the input $\tilde{u}(t)$ of this model assumes the values $\tilde{M}_k$ and $\tilde{m}_k$, respectively.

Next, by subtracting formula (4.116) from formula (4.120), we find

$$\delta f(t) = \sum_{k=1}^{n(t)-1} \left\{ \left[\Im\left(\tilde{M}_k, \tilde{m}_{k-1}\right) - \Im\left(M_k, m_{k-1}\right) \right] \right.$$

$$\left. + \left[\Im\left(\tilde{M}_k, \tilde{m}_k\right) - \Im\left(M_k, m_k\right) \right] \right\},$$

$$+ \left[\Im\left(\tilde{u}(t), \tilde{m}_{n-1}\right) - \Im\left(u(t), m_{n-1}\right) \right], \tag{4.124}$$

where

$$\delta f(t) = \tilde{f}(t) - f(t). \tag{4.125}$$

Since the feedback constant K is assumed to be relatively small, then $\tilde{M}_k$ and $\tilde{m}_k$ can be treated as perturbations of M_k and m_k, respectively. This suggests that only two terms of Taylor's expansions can be used in evaluating the differences in formula (4.124). Namely,

$$\Im\left(\tilde{M}_k, \tilde{m}_k\right) - \Im\left(M_k, m_k\right) = \left.\frac{\partial \Im}{\partial \alpha}\right|_{M_k, m_k} \cdot \delta M_k + \left.\frac{\partial \Im}{\partial \beta}\right|_{M_k, m_k} \cdot \delta m_k, \tag{4.126}$$

and

$$\Im\left(\tilde{u}(t), \tilde{m}_{n-1}\right) - \Im\left(u(t), m_{n-1}\right) = \left.\frac{\partial \Im}{\partial \alpha}\right|_{u(t), m_{n-1}} \cdot \delta u(t) + \left.\frac{\partial \Im}{\partial \beta}\right|_{u(t), m_{n-1}} \cdot \delta m_{n-1}. \tag{4.127}$$

By using the last two expressions in equation (4.124) and taking into account that according to relations (4.122) and (4.123)

$$\delta M_k = -K\tilde{f}_k^+, \tag{4.128}$$

$$\delta m_k = -K\tilde{f}_k^-, \tag{4.129}$$

we arrive at the formula:

$$\delta f(t) = -K \sum_{k=1}^{n(t)-1} \left[\left.\frac{\partial \Im}{\partial \alpha}\right|_{M_k, m_{k-1}} \cdot \tilde{f}_k^+ + \left.\frac{\partial \Im}{\partial \beta}\right|_{M_k, m_{k-1}} \cdot \tilde{f}_{k-1}^- + \left.\frac{\partial \Im}{\partial \alpha}\right|_{M_k, m_k} \cdot \tilde{f}_k^+ + \left.\frac{\partial \Im}{\partial \beta}\right|_{M_k, m_k} \cdot \tilde{f}_k^- \right]$$

$$+ \left.\frac{\partial \Im}{\partial \alpha}\right|_{u(t), m_{n-1}} \cdot \delta u(t) - K \left.\frac{\partial \Im}{\partial \beta}\right|_{u(t), m_{n-1}} \cdot \tilde{f}_{n-1}^- \tag{4.130}$$

Finally, by using formula (4.125) and the fact that according to equation (4.118)

$$\delta u(t) = -Kf(t), \tag{4.131}$$

we obtain:

$$\tilde{f}(t) = \left(1 - K \left.\frac{\partial \Im}{\partial \alpha}\right|_{u(t),m_{n-1}}\right) f(t)$$

$$- K \sum_{k=1}^{n(t)-1} \left[\left.\frac{\partial \Im}{\partial \alpha}\right|_{M_k,m_{k-1}} \cdot \tilde{f}_k^+ + \left.\frac{\partial \Im}{\partial \beta}\right|_{M_k,m_{k-1}} \cdot \tilde{f}_{k-1}^- + \left.\frac{\partial \Im}{\partial \alpha}\right|_{M_k,m_k} \cdot \tilde{f}_k^+ + \left.\frac{\partial \Im}{\partial \beta}\right|_{M_k,m_k} \cdot \tilde{f}_k^- \right]$$

$$- K \left.\frac{\partial \Im}{\partial \beta}\right|_{u(t),m_{n-1}} \cdot \tilde{f}_{n-1}^- . \tag{4.132}$$

The derivation of the last formula is based on equations (4.116) and (4.120). Consequently, this formula is valid for monotonically increasing input $u(t)$. By using equations (4.117) and (4.121) and by literally repeating the same line of reasoning as in the derivation of the last formula, we arrive at the following expression, which is valid for a monotonically decreasing input:

$$\tilde{f}(t) = \left(1 - K \left.\frac{\partial \Im}{\partial \beta}\right|_{M_n,u(t)}\right) f(t)$$

$$- K \sum_{k=1}^{n(t)-1} \left[\left.\frac{\partial \Im}{\partial \alpha}\right|_{M_k,m_{k-1}} \cdot \tilde{f}_k^+ + \left.\frac{\partial \Im}{\partial \beta}\right|_{M_k,m_{k-1}} \cdot \tilde{f}_{k-1}^- + \left.\frac{\partial \Im}{\partial \alpha}\right|_{M_k,m_k} \cdot \tilde{f}_k^+ + \left.\frac{\partial \Im}{\partial \beta}\right|_{M_k,m_k} \cdot \tilde{f}_k^- \right]$$

$$- K \left[\left.\frac{\partial \Im}{\partial \alpha}\right|_{M_n,m_{n-1}} \cdot \tilde{f}_n^+ + \left.\frac{\partial \Im}{\partial \beta}\right|_{M_n,m_{n-1}} \cdot \tilde{f}_{n-1}^- + \left.\frac{\partial \Im}{\partial \alpha}\right|_{M_n,u(t)} \cdot \tilde{f}_n^+ \right]. \tag{4.133}$$

Now, the question can be asked how formulas (4.132) and (4.133) can be used for the evaluation of the output $\tilde{f}(t)$ of the feedback model (4.114). First, the output $f(t)$ of the classical Preisach model in formulas (4.132) and (4.133) can be found by using equations (4.116) and (4.117) for monotonically increasing and decreasing input $u(t)$, respectively. Then, the output of the feedback model (4.114) can be evaluated if the values of $\tilde{f}_k^+$ and $\tilde{f}_k^-$ are known. These values can be sequentially computed by using formulas (4.132) and (4.133) for sequential time intervals of monotonic input variations. Indeed, consider the time interval when the input $u(t)$ is monotonically increased from zero to its maximum value M_1. Then, the first term in formula (4.132) can be used for the evaluation of $\tilde{f}(t)$:

$$\tilde{f}(t) = \left(1 - K \left.\frac{\partial \Im}{\partial \alpha}\right|_{u(t),0}\right) f(t). \tag{4.134}$$

Consequently, the output of the feedback model can be computed at the time-instant t_1^+ when $u(t)$ reaches its maximum value M_1:

$$\tilde{f}_1^+ = \tilde{f}(t_1^+) = \left(1 - K \left.\frac{\partial \Im}{\partial \alpha}\right|_{M_1,0}\right) f(t_1^+), \tag{4.135}$$

and

$$\tilde{M}_1 = M_1 - K f_1^+. \tag{4.136}$$

Next, consider the time interval when the input is monotonically decreased and reaches its minimum value at the time-instant t_1^-. Then, the output of the feedback model can be computed by using the first term in formula (4.133):

$$\tilde{f}(t) = \left(1 - K \left.\frac{\partial \Im}{\partial \beta}\right|_{M_1,u(t)}\right) f(t), \tag{4.137}$$

and

$$\tilde{f}_1^- = \tilde{f}(t_1^-) = \left(1 - K \left.\frac{\partial \Im}{\partial \beta}\right|_{M_1,m_1}\right) f(t_1^-), \tag{4.138}$$

which results in

$$\tilde{m}_1 = m_1 - K f_1^-. \tag{4.139}$$

Now, consider the time interval when the input $u(t)$ is monotonically increased again and reaches its maximum value M_2 at the instant of time t_2^+. Then, by using formula (4.132) for $n(t) = 2$, we can find

$$\tilde{f}(t) \text{ for } t_1^- \leq t \leq t_2^+, \tag{4.140}$$

$$\tilde{f}_2^+ = \tilde{f}(t_2^+), \quad \tilde{M}_2 = M_2 - K \tilde{f}_2^+. \tag{4.141}$$

Similarly, for the next time interval when the input is monotonically decreased and reaches its minimum value m_2 at the time instant t_2^-, formula (4.133) for $n(t) = 2$ can be used to find

$$\tilde{f}(t) \text{ for } t_2^+ \leq t \leq t_2^-, \tag{4.142}$$

$$\tilde{f}_2^- = \tilde{f}(t_2^-), \quad \tilde{m}_2 = m_2 - K \tilde{f}_2^-. \tag{4.143}$$

Now, it is apparent that by using formulas (4.132) and (4.133) for subsequent time intervals of monotonic variations of input (i.e. for $n(t) > 2$), the output value of the feedback model (4.114) can be found for those time intervals along with the values of $\tilde{f}_k^+$, $\tilde{f}_k^-$, $\tilde{M}_k$ and $\tilde{m}_k$.

In formulas (4.132) and (4.133), derivatives $\frac{\partial \Im}{\partial \alpha}$ and $\frac{\partial \Im}{\partial \beta}$ are involved. For this reason, it is desirable to provide formulas for these derivatives. This can be done by using the definition (4.115) for $\Im(\alpha, \beta)$ as well as Fig. 4.40. According to this figure, it is easy to see that the following expressions are valid:

$$\Im(\alpha, \beta) = \int_{\beta}^{\alpha} \left(\int_{\beta}^{\alpha'} \mu(\alpha', \beta') d\beta' \right) d\alpha', \tag{4.144}$$

and

$$\Im(\alpha, \beta) = \int_{\beta}^{\alpha} \left(\int_{\beta'}^{\alpha} \mu(\alpha', \beta') d\alpha' \right) d\beta'. \tag{4.145}$$

By differentiating both sides of formula (4.144) with respect to α, we find:

$$\frac{\partial \Im}{\partial \alpha} = \int_{\beta}^{\alpha} \mu(\alpha, \beta') d\beta'. \tag{4.146}$$

Similarly, from formula (4.145) we derive:

$$\frac{\partial \Im}{\partial \beta} = -\int_{\beta}^{\alpha} \mu(\alpha', \beta) d\alpha'. \tag{4.147}$$

Formulas (4.146) and (4.147) can be used in performing analysis on the basis of equations (4.132) and (4.133).

In the presented discussion, the numerical analysis of the Preisach feedback model (4.114) has been carried out by using the perturbation technique, which is valid for relatively small feedback constants K. It turns out that the above limitation can be removed by using analog electronic circuit modeling. Such a modeling is based on the realization of the input-output diagram shown in Fig. 4.39 by an electronic circuit. In this circuit, rectangular loops $\hat{\gamma}_{\alpha\beta}$ can be realized by using Schmitt triggers, and the analog modeling can be performed for different feedback constants K and different inputs $u(t)$.

It is worthwhile to mention that circuit realizations of the Preisach model can be used for the development of novel data storage devices as well as hardware-based global optimizers [76].

Now, we shall move to another topic. In all our previous discussions, we considered firms whose market entries and exits depend on a single input. This may be possible for firms with only one business segment. However, many firms may have several distinct business segments. For example, Apple Inc. has many business segments. The most prominent of them are such segments as Mac personal computer, iPhone, iPad (tablet computer), wearables (for instance, Apple Watch) and services (App Store and Apple Music). For distinct business segments the structures of entry sunk costs (i.e., market entry investments) are usually quite different. This may cause different microeconomic hysteresis structures for distinct business segments. Furthermore, the market entries and exits for distinct business segments may depend on different exogenous inputs. This suggests the existence of macroeconomic hysteresis with many inputs. This type of hysteresis is discussed below.

For the sake of simplicity of our discussion, we first consider economic hysteresis with two distinct inputs $u(t)$ and $v(t)$. On the microeconomic level, this hysteresis may be described by the following formula:

$$g\big(u(t), v(t)\big) = \mu\big(\alpha, \beta, v(t)\big)\hat{\gamma}_{\alpha\beta}u(t) + \nu\big(\alpha', \beta', u(t)\big)\hat{\gamma}_{\alpha'\beta'}v(t). \quad (4.148)$$

Here: $g\big(u(t), v(t)\big)$ is the output (i.e., the total investment of a firm with two business segments), rectangular loops $\hat{\gamma}_{\alpha\beta}$ and $\hat{\gamma}_{\alpha'\beta'}$, describe two distinct microeconomic hysteresis corresponding to these segments, while functions $\mu\big(\alpha, \beta, v(t)\big)$ and $\nu\big(\alpha', \beta', u(t)\big)$ describe different scales of investments for the respective business segments.

The dependence of functions μ and ν on inputs $v(t)$ and $u(t)$, respectively, reflects the possible coupling between two business segment investments. One example of such a coupling may be the transfer of workers and/or capital from one business sector to another within the same firm caused by exogenous input variations.

The next step is the aggregation of heterogeneous two input microeconomic hysteresis represented by the formula (4.148). This aggregation is performed by using the integrations with respect to (α, β) and (α', β'). As a result of the above integrations, we arrive at the following two input macroeconomic hysteresis model:

$$f\big(u(t), v(t)\big) = \iint\limits_{\alpha \geq \beta} \mu\big(\alpha, \beta, v(t)\big)\hat{\gamma}_{\alpha\beta}u(t)d\alpha d\beta$$

$$+ \iint\limits_{\alpha' \geq \beta'} \nu\big(\alpha', \beta', u(t)\big)\hat{\gamma}_{\alpha'\beta'}v(t)d\alpha'd\beta'. \quad (4.149)$$

The two integral terms in formula (4.149) are very similar to the integral term in the classical Preisach model. This fact suggests that by using the diagram technique for each integral term in (4.149) we can establish the following:

ERASURE PROPERTY: Only the alternating sequences $\{M_k^{(u)}, m_k^{(u)}\}$ and $\{M_k^{(v)}, m_k^{(v)}\}$ of past dominant extrema of inputs $u(t)$ and $v(t)$ are stored by the two input aggregation model (4.149), while all other past extrema of $u(t)$ and $v(t)$ are erased.

This means that the past extrema $\{M_k^{(u)}, m_k^{(u)}\}$ and $\{M_k^{(v)}, m_k^{(v)}\}$ can be viewed as the dominant economic shocks which control the branching of integral terms in formula (4.149) and, consequently the branching of the output $f(u(t), v(t))$. As before, it is clear that the sequences of alternating dominant extrema are modified with time. This means that new dominant extrema (i.e., new shocks) can be introduced as a result of subsequent variations of inputs $u(t)$ and $v(t)$, while some previous dominant extrema may be erased.

Next, we consider another characteristic property of the two input macroeconomic hysteresis which is valid for periodic (i.e., cyclic) variations of inputs $u(t)$ and $v(t)$.

PROPERTY OF EQUAL VERTICAL CHORDS: All macroeconomic hysteresis loops corresponding to periodic variations of input $u(t)$ between the same consecutive extremum values and the same fixed value of v(t) have equal vertical chords regardless of the past history of variations of $u(t)$ and $v(t)$. The same is true for macroeconomic hysteresis loops formed as a result of back-and-forth variations of $v(t)$ for any fixed value of $u(t)$.

The proof of the above property is very similar to the proof of the congruency property for the classical Preisach model discussed in Sec. 4.2.

It turns out that the two input model of macroeconomic hysteresis has the following distinct property:

PATH INDEPENDENCE PROPERTY: Consider two points (u_1, v_1) and (u_2, v_2) on the (u, v)-plane and a set of paths connecting these two points and corresponding to monotonic variations of both inputs $u(t)$ and $v(t)$ (see **Fig. 4.41**). Then, the output increment predicted by the two input macroeconomic hysteresis model (4.149) does not depend on a monotonic path between the points (u_1, v_1) and (u_2, v_2).

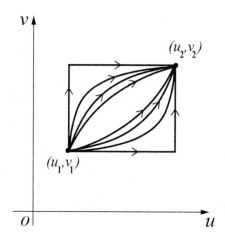

Fig. 4.41

The proof of this property is based on the following formula:

$$f\big(u(t),v(t)\big) = \iint\limits_{S^+(t)} \mu\big(\alpha,\beta,v(t)\big)\hat{\gamma}_{\alpha\beta}u(t)d\alpha d\beta$$

$$+ \iint\limits_{\Omega^+(t)} \nu\big(\alpha',\beta',u(t)\big)\hat{\gamma}_{\alpha'\beta'}v(t)d\alpha'd\beta'. \qquad (4.150)$$

This formula follows from the fact that the regions of integration with respect to α and β, and α' and β' can always be subdivided into regions $S^+(t)$ and $S^0(t)$ where $\hat{\gamma}_{\alpha\beta}u(t)$ is equal to one and zero, respectively, as well as into regions $\Omega^+(t)$ and $\Omega^0(t)$ where $\hat{\gamma}_{\alpha'\beta'}v(t)$ is equal to one and zero, respectively.

In Figs. 4.42 and 4.43 are shown the diagrams corresponding to the initial instant of time t_1 when

$$u(t_1) = u_1 \text{ and } v(t_1) = v_1. \qquad (4.151)$$

According to formula (4.150), we find that

$$f\big(u_1,v_1\big) = \iint\limits_{S^+(t_1)} \mu\big(\alpha,\beta,v_1\big)d\alpha d\beta + \iint\limits_{\Omega^+(t_1)} \nu\big(\alpha',\beta',u_1\big)d\alpha'd\beta'. \quad (4.152)$$

As a result of the monotonic increase of $u(t)$ and $v(t)$, the final horizontal links for the staircase interface line $L_u(t)$ and $L_v(t)$ will be created and they will be moved upwards until some instant of time t_2, where:

$$u(t_2) = u_2 \text{ and } v(t_2) = v_2. \qquad (4.153)$$

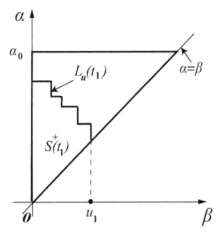

Fig. 4.42

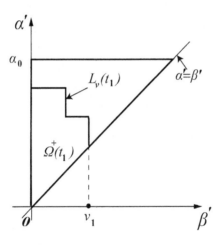

Fig. 4.43

These result in the modifications of the diagrams shown in Figs. 4.42 and 4.43. The modified diagrams are shown in Figs. 4.44 and 4.45. According to formula (4.150), we find

$$f(u_2, v_2) = \iint\limits_{S^+(t_2)} \mu(\alpha, \beta, v_2)\, d\alpha d\beta + \iint\limits_{\Omega^+(t_2)} \nu(\alpha', \beta', u_2)\, d\alpha' d\beta'. \quad (4.154)$$

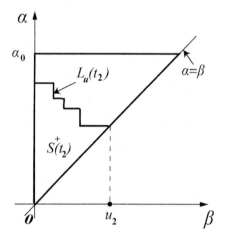

Fig. 4.44

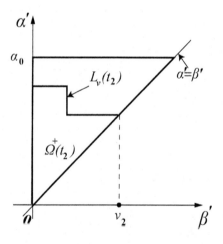

Fig. 4.45

It is clear from formula (4.154) that the output value $f(u_2, v_2)$ does not depend on a particular monotonic path between points (u_1, v_1) and (u_2, v_2). This is because all monotonic paths lead to the same modified diagrams shown in Figs. 4.44 and 4.45. Thus, it can be concluded that

$$\Delta f = f(u_2, v_2) - f(u_1, v_1) \tag{4.155}$$

is "path independent", which is stated in the "Path Independence Property".

It has been proven (see Mayergoyz [75]) that the Erasure Property, the Property of Equal Vertical Chords and the Path Independence Property are the characteristic properties for the two input macroeconomic hysteresis model (4.149) in the sense that the following theorem is valid.

REPRESENTATION THEOREM: The Erasure Property, the Property of Equal Vertical Chords and the Path Independence Property constitute the necessary and sufficient conditions for the representation of the actual two input macroeconomic hysteresis by the model (4.149).

Up to this point, we have discussed the macroeconomic hysteresis with two inputs. However, the above discussion can be easily extended to the case of many inputs., that is to the case of firms with many business segments. For instance, in the case of three inputs $u(t)$, $v(t)$ and $w(t)$ corresponding to three business segments, the macroeconomic hysteresis model similar to model (4.149) can be mathematically stated as follows:

$$
\begin{aligned}
f\big(u(t), v(t), w(t)\big) = &\iint\limits_{\alpha \geq \beta} \mu\big(\alpha, \beta, v(t), w(t)\big)\hat{\gamma}_{\alpha\beta} u(t)\,d\alpha\,d\beta \\
&+ \iint\limits_{\alpha' \geq \beta'} \nu\big(\alpha', \beta', u(t), w(t)\big)\hat{\gamma}_{\alpha'\beta'} v(t)\,d\alpha'\,d\beta' \\
&+ \iint\limits_{\alpha'' \geq \beta''} \xi\big(\alpha'', \beta'', u(t), v(t)\big)\hat{\gamma}_{\alpha''\beta''} w(t)\,d\alpha''\,d\beta''.
\end{aligned}
$$

$$(4.156)$$

It is apparent now, that a macroeconomic hysteresis model with any number of inputs can be written in the analogous way. It can be shown that the multi-input model has the same properties as the two input model (4.149).

We conclude this section with the following remark. It would be interesting to investigate the possibility of using multi-input hysteresis models for the generalizations of Leontief multi-sector input-output models of economy. In such generalizations, some sectors may be represented by multi-input hysteresis models instead of constant anhysteretic matrix coefficients.

Chapter 5

Hysteresis Driven by Random Processes

5.1 Basic Facts About Random Processes

In the previous two chapters, macroeconomic hysteresis has been studied in the case of deterministic inputs. The purpose of this chapter is to remove this limitation and to consider the macro-aggregation under stochastic conditions.

This chapter is the most sophisticated and advanced from the mathematical point of view. To make this chapter more accessible to a broad audience of readers, the very basic facts of the theory of random processes are summarized in this short section without going into subtle mathematical discussions and proofs.

We begin with the definition of stochastic processes. A stochastic process is an infinite collection (set) of random variables indexed by time (or an integer). This implies that stochastic processes can be used to describe systems which evolve probabilistically in time and this evolution can be represented by random functions of time. The notation x_t is usually employed for these functions to distinguish them from deterministic functions $x(t)$. There are infinite number of random realizations (random samples) of stochastic processes. Typical realizations in the case of time-continuous processes are shown in Fig. 5.1. Since realizations of stochastic processes are random, a probability measure is usually introduced to compute the probabilities of various subsets of realizations of random process x_t. The given descriptive (not mathematically rigorous) definition suggests that stochastic processes are sets of functions (i.e., realizations) with probabilistic measures on them.

Another mathematical way to describe stochastic processes is by using joint probability densities. Namely, consider random variables $x_1, x_2, \ldots, x_n$

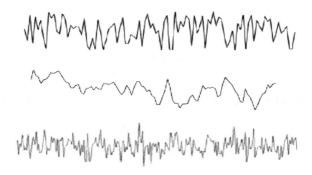

Fig. 5.1

which are random values of x_t at time instants $t_1, t_2, \ldots t_n$, respectively. Then, the joint probability density

$$\rho\big(x_1, t_1; x_2, t_2; \cdots x_n, t_n\big) \tag{5.1}$$

can be introduced. In this way, stochastic processes can be characterized by a set of joint probability densities constructed for different times $t_1, t_2, \ldots, t_n$ and different n. A very simple case of stochastic processes is when random variables $x_1, x_2, \ldots, x_n$ are independent. In this case, we find that

$$\rho\big(x_1, t_1; x_2, t_2; \cdots x_n, t_n\big) \;=\; \prod_k \rho\big(x_k, t_k\big). \tag{5.2}$$

A more complicated case is the Markov stochastic process. To define this process, we introduce the time instants

$$t_1 > t_2 > \cdots > t_n \;>\; \tilde{t}_1 > \tilde{t}_2 > \cdots > \tilde{t}_m \tag{5.3}$$

and the conditional probability density

$$\rho\big(x_1, t_1; x_2, t_2; \cdots x_n, t_n \big| \tilde{x}_1, \tilde{t}_1; \tilde{x}_2, \tilde{t}_2; \cdots \tilde{x}_m, \tilde{t}_m\big). \tag{5.4}$$

For Markov processes, the following property is valid:

$$\rho\big(x_1, t_1; x_2, t_2; \cdots x_n, t_n \big| \tilde{x}_1, \tilde{t}_1; \tilde{x}_2, \tilde{t}_2; \cdots \tilde{x}_m, \tilde{t}_m\big)$$
$$= \rho\big(x_1, t_1; x_2, t_2; \cdots x_n, t_n \big| \tilde{x}_1, \tilde{t}_1\big). \tag{5.5}$$

This property reveals that Markov processes have a short memory. Namely, only the last past measurement of $\tilde{x}_1$ at $\tilde{t}_1$ affects the conditional probability density of future measurements $x_1, x_2, \ldots, x_n$ at time instants $t_1, t_2, \ldots, t_n$, respectively. By using property (5.5), it can be proven that

$$\rho\big(x_1, t_1; x_2, t_2; \cdots x_n, t_n\big)$$
$$= \rho\big(x_1, t_1 \big| x_2, t_2\big)\rho\big(x_2, t_2 \big| x_3, t_3\big) \cdots \rho\big(x_{n-1}, t_{n-1} \big| x_n, t_n\big)\rho\big(x_n, t_n\big). \tag{5.6}$$

This means that the transition probability density $\rho(x, t|y, \tau)$ completely defines a Markov process.

We next consider Markov processes with continuous in time samples (realizations). The simplest and most studied example of such processes is the Wiener process W_t. This is the stochastic process with independent increments which are Gaussian random variables. More precisely, the following properties define the Wiener process:

(a)

$$W_0 = 0; \tag{5.7}$$

(b) independent (uncorrelated) increments:

$$E\left[(W_{t_1} - W_{t_2})(W_{t_3} - W_{t_4})\right] = 0, \tag{5.8}$$

where

$$t_4 < t_3 < t_2 < t_1, \tag{5.9}$$

and $E[\ ]$ is the notation for the expected (mean) value;

(c) $W_{t_1} - W_{t_2}$ (for any $t_1 > t_2 \geq 0$) is a Gaussian random variable with zero mean

$$E\left[W_{t_1} - W_{t_2}\right] = 0 \tag{5.10}$$

and the variance:

$$E\left[(W_{t_1} - W_{t_2})^2\right] = t_1 - t_2. \tag{5.11}$$

It can be shown that the Wiener process has continuous in time samples. However, these samples are not differentiable at any instant of time t. Nevertheless, it can be shown that the realizations of the Wiener process satisfy with probability one the following Hölder condition:

$$\left|W_t - W_s\right| < C|t - s|^\lambda, \tag{5.12}$$

where C is some constant and

$$0 < \lambda \leq 0.5. \tag{5.13}$$

It is interesting to point out that the last fact is consistent with the property (see (5.11)):

$$E\left[dW_t^2\right] = dt, \tag{5.14}$$

which implies that the differential dW_t is not proportional to dt.

It turns out that by using the Wiener process W_t, the broad class of Markov processes can be generated and studied by using the following **stochastic differential equation**:

$$\frac{dx_t}{dt} = b(x_t, t) + \sigma(x_t, t)\frac{dW_t}{dt}. \tag{5.15}$$

These are processes with continuous in time samples, and they are called diffusion processes. The reason for the last terminology is the fact that the term

$$\sigma(x_t, t)\frac{dW_t}{dt} \tag{5.16}$$

describes random diffusion. Using a physical analogy, the latter means that the random movement (diffusion) of particles is from high density regions to lower density regions.

Equation (5.15) is often written in the following form:

$$dx_t = b(x_t, t)dt + \sigma(x_t, t)dW_t. \tag{5.17}$$

Now, it is important to point out that there are technical difficulties related to the mathematical interpretation of equation (5.15). These difficulties are related to the meaning of the derivative dW_t/dt in view of the fact that the Wiener process W_t is not differentiable in time. To circumvent these difficulties, the stochastic differential equation (5.15) is replaced by the following integral equation:

$$x_{t+s} - x_t = \int_t^{t+s} b(x_\lambda, \lambda)d\lambda + \int_t^{t+s} \sigma(x_\lambda, \lambda)dW_\lambda, \tag{5.18}$$

and the solution of equation (5.15) is defined as the solution of the above integral equation.

The second integral in equation (5.18) is called a stochastic integral. It can be approximated by an integral sum and defined as a limit of this sum. Namely,

$$\int_t^{t+s} \sigma(x_\lambda, \lambda)dW_\lambda = \lim_{n\to\infty} \sum_{k=1}^{n} \sigma(x_{\tilde{\lambda}_k}, \tilde{\lambda}_k)(W_{\lambda_{k+1}} - W_{\lambda_k}). \tag{5.19}$$

It turns out that this limit depends on the choice of $\tilde{\lambda}_k$. The simplest choice is when

$$\tilde{\lambda}_k = \lambda_k. \tag{5.20}$$

For this choice $\sigma(x_{\tilde{\lambda}_k}, \tilde{\lambda}_k)$ is uncorrelated with the Wiener process increment $W_{\lambda_{k+1}} - W_{\lambda_k}$. This choice leads to the so-called Itô stochastic integral and the Itô solution of equation (5.15). There is another choice

$$\tilde{\lambda}_k = (\lambda_{k+1} + \lambda_k)/2. \tag{5.21}$$

and it leads to the Stratonovich solution of stochastic differential equation (5.15). The detailed discussion of these issues can be found in books with mathematically rigorous expositions of the stochastic process theory. This discussion is beyond the scope of this brief review. We shall only mention that the Itô solution can be reduced to the Stratonovich solution by properly modifying the drift term in stochastic differential equation (5.15). In the discussion below, it is assumed that the solution of equation (5.15) is defined in the Itô sense.

The Markov process defined by equation (5.15) can be also characterized by the transition probability density $\rho(x,t|y,\tau)$. This probability has the "forward" (x,t) and "backward" (y,τ) coordinates. It can be shown that $\rho(x,t|y,\tau)$ satisfies the following partial differential equation with respect to the forward variables x and t:

$$\frac{\partial}{\partial t}\rho(x,t|y,\tau) = -\frac{\partial}{\partial x}\Big[b(x,t)\rho(x,t|y,\tau)\Big] + \frac{1}{2}\frac{\partial^2}{\partial x^2}\Big[\sigma^2(x,t)\rho(x,t|y,\tau)\Big].$$
(5.22)

This equation is called the forward Kolmogorov equation. It turns out that there is also a partial differential equation with respect to the backward coordinates y and τ. This equation can be written as follows.

$$\frac{\partial}{\partial \tau}\rho(x,t|y,\tau) = -b(x,t)\frac{\partial}{\partial y}\rho(x,t|y,\tau) - \frac{1}{2}\sigma^2(x,t)\frac{\partial^2}{\partial y^2}\rho(x,t|y,\tau).$$ (5.23)

The last equation is often called the backward Kolmogorov equation.

It is clear from the presented discussion that stochastic processes can be studied on two equivalent levels. They can be studied on the level of random realizations (samples) by solving the **nonlinear stochastic ordinary differential equation** (5.15). This is typically done by using Monte Carlo simulations. On the other hand, diffusion stochastic processes can also be studied on the level of the transition probability density function $\rho(x,t|y,\tau)$. This requires the solution of **linear** and **deterministic** equations (5.22) or (5.23). However, these are **partial differential equations**. Our subsequent analysis will be by and large carried out in terms of transition probability density.

In mathematics, the Wiener process and its time derivative (i.e., white noise) are used to generate a class of diffusion processes described by stochastic differential equation (5.15). In physics, the last term in equation (5.15) is used for the description of thermal noise, and the equation of the similar type as (5.15) is usually called the Langevin equation. The corresponding equation (5.22) for the transition probability density is known in physics as the Fokker-Planck equation.

It is interesting to point out that the mathematical structure of the forward Kolmogorov equation is **consistent** with the probabilistic meaning of the solutions of this equation. According to this meaning, the following equality must be valid for any probabilistically relevant solution of equation (5.22) at any instant of time $t > \tau$:

$$\int_{-\infty}^{\infty} \rho(x, t | y, \tau) dx = 1. \tag{5.24}$$

To prove that this is the case, we integrate both sides of the forward Kolmogorov equation with respect to x from $-\infty$ to ∞. This leads to:

$$\frac{\partial}{\partial t} \left[\int_{-\infty}^{\infty} \rho(x, t | y, \tau) dx \right]$$
$$= \left[-b(x, t)\rho(x, t | y, \tau) + \frac{1}{2} \frac{\partial}{\partial x} \left[\sigma^2(x, t)\rho(x, t | y, \tau) \right] \right]_{x=-\infty}^{x=\infty}. \tag{5.25}$$

Since $\rho(x, t | y, \tau)$ and its x-derivative tend to zero at $\pm\infty$, we find from the last formula that for $t > \tau$:

$$\int_{-\infty}^{\infty} \rho(x, t | y, \tau) dx = c = \text{const.} \tag{5.26}$$

According to the probabilistic nature of the initial condition at $t = \tau$, we find that c in the above equation is equal to one. This establishes the validity of equality (5.24). This equality implies that probabilistically relevant solutions of the forward Kolmogorov equations belong to the **unit sphere** of the L_1 space of Lebesgue integrable (i.e., summable) functions.

Furthermore, for any probabilistically relevant solution of the forward Kolmogorov equation (5.22), the initial condition for transition probability density ρ must be positive. Since equation (5.22) is a linear partial differential equation of parabolic type, this implies that ρ is strictly positive for all $t > \tau$. Thus, probabilistically relevant solutions of the forward Kolmogorov equation belong to the set of positive functions on the unit sphere in L_1.

Next, we consider one very special diffusion process which has important applications in physics and economics. This is the Ornstein-Uhlenbeck process. This is the stationary Gaussian Markov process. This process is very unique because, as it is often stated, this is the only stationary Gaussian Markov process in one real variable. The term stationary means that all properties of the process are **invariant with respect to time translations** (i.e., they are time-invariant).

The Ornstein-Uhlenbeck process is described by the following stochastic differential equation:

$$dx_t = -kx_t dt + \sigma dW_t, \tag{5.27}$$

where k and σ are positive constants.

In terms of the transition probability density, the Ornstein-Uhlenbeck process is described by the following forward Kolmogorov equation:

$$\frac{\partial \rho}{\partial t} = \frac{\partial}{\partial x}(kx\rho) + \frac{\sigma^2}{2}\frac{\partial^2 \rho}{\partial x^2}. \tag{5.28}$$

We want to derive the expression for the **stationary** distribution ρ_{st} of this process. This distribution does not depend on time. For this reason, it depends only on x:

$$\rho_{st} = \rho_{st}(x). \tag{5.29}$$

Consequently,

$$\frac{\partial \rho_{st}}{\partial t} = 0. \tag{5.30}$$

This implies that equation (5.28) is reduced to the following ordinary differential equation for $\rho_{st}(x)$:

$$\frac{d}{dx}\left[kx\rho_{st} + \frac{\sigma^2}{2}\frac{d\rho_{st}}{dx}\right] = 0, \tag{5.31}$$

which leads to

$$kx\rho_{st} + \frac{\sigma^2}{2}\frac{d\rho_{st}}{dx} = 0. \tag{5.32}$$

The right-hand side of the last equation is chosen to be zero instead of some constant because ρ_{st} and its x-derivative must tend to zero at infinity. The last equation can be written as:

$$d(\ln \rho_{st}) = -\frac{k}{\sigma^2}d(x^2). \tag{5.33}$$

By integrating equation (5.33) and using the proper normalization for ρ_{st}, we finally arrive at the following Gaussian stationary distribution:

$$\rho_{st}(x) = \sqrt{\frac{k}{\pi\sigma^2}}\exp\left(-\frac{kx^2}{\sigma^2}\right). \tag{5.34}$$

This is the distribution with **zero mean** and variance $\frac{\sigma^2}{2k}$.

In economics, the Ornstein-Uhlenbeck process with nonzero mean is used. The stochastic differential equation for this process is the following modification of equation (5.27):

$$dx_t = k(\mu - x_t)dt + \sigma dW_t, \tag{5.35}$$

where μ is some positive constant. By introducing the notation

$$\tilde{x}_t = x_t - \mu, \tag{5.36}$$

equation (5.35) can be reduced to

$$d\tilde{x}_t = -k\tilde{x}_t dt + \sigma dW_t \tag{5.37}$$

which is mathematically identical to equation (5.27). Consequently, formula (5.34) can be used for $\tilde{x}$. This leads to the following expression for the stationary distribution:

$$\rho_{st}(x) = \sqrt{\frac{k}{\pi\sigma^2}} \exp\left(-\frac{k(x-\mu)^2}{\sigma^2} \right). \tag{5.38}$$

Thus, the modified Ornstein-Uhlenbeck process x_t defined by stochastic differential equation (5.35) has nonzero mean equal to μ.

It is interesting to point out that by using the **nonstationary** Wiener process, the stationarity of the Ornstein-Uhlenbeck process has been achieved by introducing the linear drift term $-kx_t$ (or $k(\mu - x_t)$).

In economics, the Ornstein-Uhlenbeck process defined by equation (5.35) has been used to model the stochasticity of interest rates, currency exchange rates and commodity prices. This approach was introduced in 1977 by Oldřich Alfons Vašíček [90], and it captures **mean reversion** in interest rate fluctuations.

In the Vašíček model (5.35), μ represents the mean value of interest rate around which current values of interest rate randomly evolve. The parameter σ reflects the degree of random volatility of the interest rate, while the constant k characterizes the speed at which the random interest rate returns to its mean value μ. In the absence of randomness ($dW_t = 0$), the interest rate x_t remains constant and, according to equation (5.35), it is equal to its mean value

$$x_t = \mu. \tag{5.39}$$

If the interest rate x_t falls below its mean value μ due to random volatility, then the drift term $k(\mu - x_t)$ becomes positive resulting in the tendency for the interest rate to rise (toward its mean value). Similarly, if the interest rate rises above its mean value μ, then the drift term becomes negative resulting in the tendency for the interest rate to fall towards its mean value. This is the mechanism of mean reversion.

It is clear that the parameters σ and k reflect opposite tendencies of random interest rate variations. This is clearly reflected in the expression for the variance $\frac{\sigma^2}{2k}$ of the interest rate under stationary conditions.

The main disadvantage of the Vašíček model is the possibility for the interest rate to become negative. Various models have been proposed (see, for instance, the Hull-White model [57]) to eliminate the above possibility. It is worthwhile to mention here that the possibility of negative interest rate values can be removed by considering the forward Kolmogorov equation for the Vašíček model in the semi-infinite interval $0 < x < \infty$ and by imposing the reflecting boundary condition:

$$\left[b(x,t)\rho(x,t|y,\tau) - \frac{1}{2}\frac{\partial}{\partial x}\left[\sigma^2(x,t)\rho(x,t|y,\tau) \right] \right]\Bigg|_{x=0} = 0. \qquad (5.40)$$

We conclude this section by outlining how hysteresis driven by stochastic processes will be analyzed in the subsequent sections. The starting point of this analysis will be the study of random output i_t of rectangular loop hysteresis driven by a diffusion process x_t:

$$i_t = \hat{\gamma}_{\alpha\beta} x_t. \qquad (5.41)$$

Two techniques will be developed for this purpose. The first technique will treat random triggering (i.e., random switching of rectangular loops) as an **exit problem** for diffusion processes [59]. The second entirely different approach will be based on the **theory of stochastic processes on graphs** [50]. This theory was originally developed to study random perturbations of Hamiltonian dynamical systems [49]. It turns out that the mathematical machinery of this theory is naturally suitable for the analysis of random non-Markovian outputs i_t of randomly driven rectangular hysteresis loops. As soon as the techniques for the analysis of i_t defined by formula (5.41) are developed, they can be applied to the solution of more complex problems. This is because, as discussed in the previous chapters, complex hysteresis can be represented in terms of rectangular loop hysteresis. For instance, consider the Preisach model of macroeconomic hysteresis driven by stochastic input x_t:

$$f_t = \iint\limits_{\alpha \geq \beta} \mu(\alpha, \beta)\hat{\gamma}_{\alpha\beta} x_t \, d\alpha \, d\beta. \qquad (5.42)$$

Then, for the expected value $\bar{f}_t$ we find

$$\bar{f}_t = \iint\limits_{\alpha \geq \beta} \mu(\alpha, \beta) E\left(\hat{\gamma}_{\alpha\beta} x_t\right) d\alpha d\beta. \tag{5.43}$$

Thus, the analysis of the random process i_t defined by formula (5.41) allows one to easily compute the expected value $\bar{f}_t$ of the much more complex random process specified by formula (5.42). Similar results will be obtained in subsequent sections for other economic hysteresis models discussed in the previous chapters.

5.2   Random Triggering (Switching) as an Exit Problem

We start with the case of the rectangular loop shown in Fig. 5.2 driven by the stochastic process defined as:

$$x_t = u_0 + X_t. \tag{5.44}$$

Here, u_0 is the mean value of the input, while X_t is a stationary diffusion process specified by the stochastic differential equation

$$dX_t = b\left(X_t\right)dt + \sigma\left(X_t\right)dW_t, \ (X_0 = 0). \tag{5.45}$$

The random output i_t (see formula (5.41)) is a random binary process shown in Fig. 5.3. Our goal is to completely characterize this random non-Markovian process generated as a result of random triggering (switching) of rectangular loop $\hat{\gamma}_{\alpha\beta}$. This will be accomplished by treating random switching as a set of exit problems for the random process X_t. Indeed, consider the case when the initial values of input and output are as follows:

$$u_0 < \alpha \text{ and } i_0 = 0. \tag{5.46}$$

Then, it is clear that the random upward switching of the rectangular loop $\hat{\gamma}_{\alpha\beta}$ occurs when the stochastic process X_t starting from the point

$$X_0 = 0 \tag{5.47}$$

exits for **the first time** the bold semi-infinite line shown in Fig. 5.4a at the point $\alpha - u_0$. As a result of this exit, the process i_t switches from 0 to 1. The second random and downward switching of the rectangular loop $\hat{\gamma}_{\alpha\beta}$ occurs when the stochastic process X_t starting from the point $\alpha - u_0$ exits the bold semi-infinite line shown in Fig. 5.4b at the point $\beta - u_0$. As a result of this exit, downward switching of the rectangular loop $\hat{\gamma}_{\alpha\beta}$ from 1 to 0 happens. The third random and upward switching

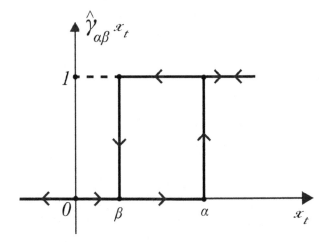

Fig. 5.2

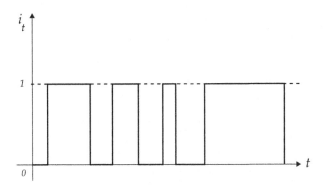

Fig. 5.3

of the rectangular loop $\hat{\gamma}_{\alpha\beta}$ from 0 to 1 occurs when the stochastic process X_t starting from the point $\beta - u_0$ exits the bold semi-infinite line shown in Fig. 4.4c at the point $\alpha - u_0$. It is clear that all subsequent even switchings occur in the same way as the previously described second switching, while all subsequent random odd switchings occur in the same manner as the previously described third switching. Thus it can be concluded that the random switchings of rectangular hysteresis loops $\hat{\gamma}_{\alpha\beta}$ can be mathematically framed as the aforementioned sequence of exit problems for the stochastic process X_t.

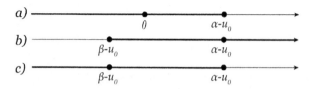

Fig. 5.4

The described exit problems are characterized by the following three random exit times:

$$\tau_0^+, \ \tau_{\alpha-u_0}^0, \ \tau_{\beta-u_0}^+, \tag{5.48}$$

where subscripts correspond to the initial points, while superscripts "+" and "0" indicate upward and downward switchings, respectively, caused by exits of the stochastic process X_t. It is apparent that the random time $\tau_{\alpha-u_0}^0$ determines the random width of rectangular pulses shown in Fig. 5.3, while random time $\tau_{\beta-u_0}^+$ determines the random separation between rectangular pulses. For this reason, the statistics of random exit times τ_0^+, $\tau_{\alpha-u_0}^0$ and $\tau_{\beta-u_0}^+$ completely characterize the random binary process shown in Fig. 5.3.

In our previous discussion, we considered the case when the initial values of input and output are specified by formula (5.46). Another possible case for initial values of the input and output can be specified by the following formula

$$u_0 > \beta \text{ and } i_0 = 1. \tag{5.49}$$

By using the same line of reasoning as before, it can be shown that the binary output process i_t is completely characterized by the statistics of random exit times

$$\tau_0^0, \ \tau_{\beta-u_0}^+, \ \tau_{\alpha-u_0}^0 \tag{5.50}$$

from the semi-infinite bolder lines shown in Figs. 5.5a, b and c, respectively.

Next, we shall describe the mathematical technique for the determination of the statistics of the random exit times. To this end, we first introduce the function

$$v^+(x,t) = P\left(\tau_x^+ \geq t\right), \tag{5.51}$$

where symbol P stands for probability, and τ_x^+ is a random exit time for upward switching corresponding to initial (starting) point x. Furthermore, we also introduce the function

$$V^+(x,t) = e(t) - v^+(x,t), \tag{5.52}$$

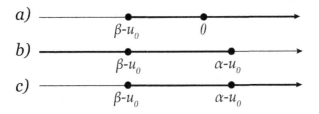

Fig. 5.5

where $e(t)$ is the unit step function. It is clear from the last two formulas that

$$V^+(x,t) = P(\tau_x^+ < t). \tag{5.53}$$

It is apparent that $V^+(x,t)$ has the meaning of the probability distribution function of the random exit time τ_x^+. Thus, if the function $v^+(x,t)$ is found, then the statistics of random time τ_x^+ can be determined by using formula (5.52).

Next, we derive the initial boundary value problem for the function $v^+(x,t)$. The derivation proceeds as follows. Let $\rho(\tilde{x},t|x,0)$ be the transition probability density for the process X_t inside the semi-infinite interval $(-\infty, \alpha - u_0]$. Then, according to formula (5.51), $v^+(x,t)$ is equal to the probability that no exit of X_t from the above semi-infinite interval occurred before time t. Consequently,

$$v^+(x,t) = \int_{-\infty}^{\alpha-u_0} \rho(\tilde{x},t|x,0)d\tilde{x}. \tag{5.54}$$

The mathematical structure of the stochastic differential equation (5.45) is invariant with respect to time translation. This implies that $\rho(\tilde{x},t|x,0)$ must be invariant with respect to time translation as well. Consequently,

$$\rho(\tilde{x},t|x,0) = \rho(\tilde{x},0|x,-t). \tag{5.55}$$

According to formula (5.54), this leads to the following expression

$$v^+(x,t) = \int_{-\infty}^{\alpha-u_0} \rho(\tilde{x},0|x,-t)d\tilde{x}. \tag{5.56}$$

Now, we shall use the following backward Kolmogorov equation for $\rho(\tilde{x},0|x,-t)$ corresponding to the stochastic differential equation (5.45):

$$\frac{\partial \rho(\tilde{x},0|x,-t)}{\partial t} = b(x)\frac{\partial}{\partial x}\rho(\tilde{x},0|x,-t) + \frac{\sigma^2(x)}{2}\frac{\partial^2}{\partial x^2}\rho(\tilde{x},0|x,-t). \tag{5.57}$$

It is also clear that the transition probability density $\rho(\tilde{x}, 0|x, -t)$ satisfies the following initial condition:

$$\rho(\tilde{x}, 0|x, 0) = \delta(x - \tilde{x}), \qquad (5.58)$$

where the right-hand side is the Dirac δ-function.

By integrating the last two equations with respect to $\tilde{x}$ from $-\infty$ to $\alpha - u_0$ and taking into account the formula (5.54), we respectively derive that

$$\frac{\partial v^+(x, t)}{\partial t} = b(x) \frac{\partial v^+(x, t)}{\partial x} + \frac{\sigma^2(x)}{2} \frac{\partial^2 v^+(x, t)}{\partial x^2}, \qquad (5.59)$$

$$v^+(x, 0) = 1. \qquad (5.60)$$

It is also clear that the function $v^+(x, t)$ satisfies the following absorbing boundary condition:

$$v^+(\alpha - u_0, t) = 0. \qquad (5.61)$$

This is because the process X_t cannot reenter the semi-infinite interval $(-\infty, \alpha - u_0]$ through the boundary point $\alpha - u_0$ after upward switching and, consequently,

$$\rho(\tilde{x}, t|\alpha - u_0, 0) = 0. \qquad (5.62)$$

According to formula (5.56), this leads to the boundary condition (5.61). Thus, the calculation of the function $v^+(x, t)$ is reduced to the solution of the initial boundary value problem (5.59), (5.60) and (5.61). As soon as this problem is solved, the probability distribution function $V^+(x, t)$ for random exit times τ_x^+ can be found by using formula (5.52).

Next, we consider the similar problem of computing the probability distribution function $V^0(x, t)$ for random exit times τ_x^0 resulting in downward switching of rectangular loops $\hat{\gamma}_{\alpha\beta}$. To this end, functions $v^0(x, t)$ and $V^0(x, t)$ are introduced by formulas similar to equations (5.51) and (5.52), respectively:

$$v^0(x, t) = P\left(\tau_x^0 \geq t\right), \qquad (5.63)$$

$$V^0(x, t) = e(t) - v^0(x, t), \qquad (5.64)$$

which means that

$$V^0(x, t) = P\left(\tau_x^0 < t\right). \qquad (5.65)$$

Furthermore, the following formula is valid for $v^0(x,t)$:

$$v^0(x,t) = \int_{\beta-u_0}^{\infty} \rho(\tilde{x},t|x,0)d\tilde{x}, \qquad (5.66)$$

where $\rho(\tilde{x},t|x,0)$ is the transition probability density function of the process X_t defined on the semi-infinite interval $[\beta-u_0,\infty)$ with absorbing boundary condition at $\beta - u_0$. Now, by almost literally repeating the same line of reasoning that was used above for the function $v^+(x,t)$, we derive the following initial-boundary value problem for $v^0(x,t)$:

$$\frac{\partial v^0(x,t)}{\partial t} = b(x)\frac{\partial v^0(x,t)}{\partial x} + \frac{\sigma^2(x)}{2}\frac{\partial^2 v^0(x,t)}{\partial x^2}, \qquad (5.67)$$

$$v^0(x,0) = 1, \qquad (5.68)$$

$$v^0(\beta - u_0, t) = 0. \qquad (5.69)$$

By solving the last problem and finding the function $v^0(x,t)$, the probability distribution function $V^0(x,t)$, for the random exit time τ_x^0 can be found by using formula (5.64).

Equations (5.59) and (5.67) are valid for the general diffusion process described by the stochastic differential equation (5.45). However, as discussed in the previous section, in economics random volatility of forcing input is often described by the Ornstein-Uhlenbeck process. For this process:

$$b(x) = -kx, \quad k > 0 \qquad (5.70)$$

and

$$\sigma(x) = \sigma = \text{ const.} \qquad (5.71)$$

Under the above conditions, equations (5.59) and (5.67) are reduced to:

$$\frac{\partial v^{\binom{+}{0}}(x,t)}{\partial t} = -kx\frac{\partial v^{\binom{+}{0}}(x,t)}{\partial x} + \frac{\sigma^2}{2}\frac{\partial^2 v^{\binom{+}{0}}(x,t)}{\partial x^2}. \qquad (5.72)$$

Formula (5.70) corresponds to the Ornstein-Uhlenbeck process with zero mean. In economics, the Ornstein-Uhlenbeck process with nonzero mean is instrumental (see previous section). For this process, formula (5.70) is replaced by the following relation:

$$b(x) = -k(x - \mu), \qquad (5.73)$$

where $\mu = u_0$ is the process mean value. For this case, by using the variable

$$x' = x - \mu \qquad (5.74)$$

instead of x, equations (5.59) and (5.67) can be again reduced to the equation (5.72). This is an equation with a variable with respect to the x coefficient. Nevertheless, the analytical solution of this equation can be obtained by using the Laplace transform

$$\tilde{v}^{\binom{+}{0}}(x,s) = \int_0^\infty v^{\binom{+}{0}}(x,t)e^{-st}dt, \quad (\Re e(s) \geq 0), \tag{5.75}$$

which reduces the initial-boundary value problems (5.59)–(5.61) and (5.67)–(5.69) for partial differential equations to the following boundary value problem for the ordinary differential equation:

$$\frac{\sigma^2}{2}\frac{d^2\tilde{v}^{\binom{+}{0}}(x,s)}{dx^2} - kx\frac{d\tilde{v}^{\binom{+}{0}}(x,s)}{dx} - s\tilde{v}^{\binom{+}{0}}(x,s) = -1, \tag{5.76}$$

$$\tilde{v}^{\binom{+}{0}}\left(c^{\binom{+}{0}}, s\right) = 0, \tag{5.77}$$

$$\lim_{|x|\to\infty} \tilde{v}^{\binom{+}{0}}(x,s) = \frac{1}{s}, \tag{5.78}$$

where the following notation is used for abbreviation purposes:

$$c^+ = \alpha - u_0 \quad \text{and} \quad c^0 = \beta - u_0. \tag{5.79}$$

It turns out that the analytical solutions to the boundary value problems (5.76)–(5.79) can be represented in terms of parabolic cylinder functions. Namely,

$$\tilde{v}^{\binom{+}{0}}(x,s) = \frac{1}{s}\left[1 - \exp\left(\frac{x^2 - \left(c^{\binom{+}{0}}\right)^2}{4\lambda^2}\right)\frac{\mathcal{D}_{-s/k}\left(\frac{x}{\lambda}\right)}{\mathcal{D}_{-s/k}\left(\frac{c^{\binom{+}{0}}}{\lambda}\right)}\right], \tag{5.80}$$

and

$$\lambda = \sigma/\sqrt{2k}. \tag{5.81}$$

Here, $\mathcal{D}_{-s/k}$ are parabolic cylinder functions which are extensively studied in mathematics [53].

It is also interesting to consider the probability density functions

$$g^+(x,t) = \frac{dV^+(x,t)}{dt} \tag{5.82}$$

and

$$g^0(x,t) = \frac{dV^0(x,t)}{dt} \tag{5.83}$$

for the random exit times τ_x^+ and τ_x^0, respectively. From formulas (5.52), (5.64), (5.80), (5.82) and (5.83), we find that

$$\tilde{g}^{\left(\substack{+\\0}\right)}(x,s) = s\tilde{V}^{\left(\substack{+\\0}\right)}(x,s) = 1 - s\tilde{v}^{\left(\substack{+\\0}\right)}(x,s), \qquad (5.84)$$

and

$$\tilde{g}^{\left(\substack{+\\0}\right)}(x,s) = \exp\left(\frac{x^2 - \left(c^{\left(\substack{+\\0}\right)}\right)^2}{4\lambda^2}\right) \frac{\mathcal{D}_{-s/k}\left(\frac{x}{\lambda}\right)}{\mathcal{D}_{-s/k}\left(\frac{c^{\left(\substack{+\\0}\right)}}{\lambda}\right)}. \qquad (5.85)$$

The above two exit problems resulting in random upward and downward switching of rectangular loops $\hat{\gamma}_{\alpha\beta}$, respectively, may be instrumental in microeconomic hysteresis analysis under uncertainty briefly discussed in Secs. 2.2 and 2.3. Indeed, in microeconomics, a firm's market entry and market exit are often characterized by two trigger values α and β, which may be identified with switching thresholds of rectangular loops $\hat{\gamma}_{\alpha\beta}$. The market entry may occur when the stochastic input reaches some specific threshold α chosen on the basis of microeconomic analysis. This implies that a firm, which is ready to invest at some time when the input is equal to u_0, has to wait until exogenous input reaches the threshold α. This waiting time is equal to the random exit time resulting in upward switching of a rectangular loop. The statistics of this random time is determined by the function $V^+(x,t)$ which can be found by solving the exit problem (5.59)–(5.61). If the solution of this problem suggests very long waiting times for market entry, this may lead to the adjustment of the microeconomic analysis resulting in the selection of the α trigger.

On the other hand, the firm market exit time occurs when the stochastic input x_t reaches some value β. This implies that the time when a firm remains in the market is equal to the random exit time resulting in the downward switching of the rectangular loop $\hat{\gamma}_{\alpha\beta}$. The statistics of this random time is fully determined by the function $V^0(x,t)$ which can be found by solving the exit problem (5.67)–(5.69). This statistic can be used to determine the average time the firm remains in the market. In turn, this may lead to the estimate of the expected value of the firm's revenue. It is apparent that the wider the rectangular loop $\hat{\gamma}_{\alpha\beta}$, the longer on average the firm remains in the market and higher the expected revenue. This suggests that investment under uncertainty may benefit from the broadening of the "band of inaction" which is equal to $\alpha - \beta$.

The numerical calculation of the exit time probability density functions given in expressions (5.84) and (5.85) is significantly facilitated by employing the Fourier transform method. By setting $s = j\omega$, these expressions

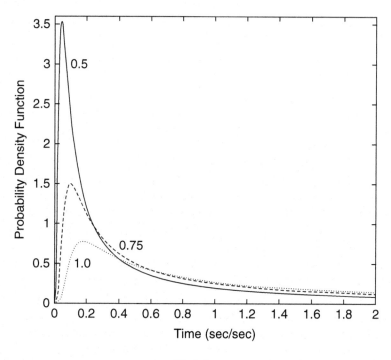

Fig. 5.6

can be used to calculate the Fourier transforms of the exit time probability density functions, which in turn can be used to calculate the exit time probability density functions by using their inverse Fourier transforms. The details of this approach can be found in the earlier publication of the authors [59]. As an illustration, Fig. 5.6 shows the calculation of the exit time probability density functions for three different initial values for the semi-infinite interval $(-\infty, \beta)$.

The exit problems discussed above can also be used to compute the average (expected) output values of rectangular loops driven by stochastic diffusion processes

$$q_{\alpha\beta}(t) = E\big(\hat{\gamma}_{\alpha\beta}x_t\big), \tag{5.86}$$

which can then be instrumental for evaluating the expected value of the output of the macroeconomic hysteresis $\bar{f}_t$ (see formula (5.43)). It is apparent that

$$q_{\alpha\beta}(t) = P\big(\hat{\gamma}_{\alpha\beta}x_t = 1\big). \tag{5.87}$$

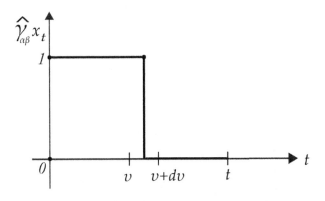

Fig. 5.7

It turns out that $q_{\alpha\beta}(t)$ can be expressed in terms of the following switching probabilities $P_k^+(t)$ and $P_k^0(t)$ defined as follows:

$$P_k^+(t) = P\left(k \text{ switchings during } (0,t) \,\middle|\, \hat{\gamma}_{\alpha,\beta} x_0 = 1\right), \qquad (5.88)$$

$$P_k^0(t) = P\left(k \text{ switchings during } (0,t) \,\middle|\, \hat{\gamma}_{\alpha,\beta} x_0 = 0\right). \qquad (5.89)$$

It is clear that

$$q_{\alpha\beta}(t) = \sum_{k=0}^{\infty} P_{2k}^+(t), \text{ if } \hat{\gamma}_{\alpha,\beta} x_0 = 1 \qquad (5.90)$$

and

$$q_{\alpha\beta}(t) = \sum_{k=0}^{\infty} P_{2k+1}^0(t), \text{ if } \hat{\gamma}_{\alpha,\beta} x_0 = 0. \qquad (5.91)$$

First, consider the case when $\hat{\gamma}_{\alpha,\beta} x_0 = 1$. It is clear from the definition of $v^0(x,t)$ that

$$P_0^+(t) = v^0(0,t). \qquad (5.92)$$

It is apparent from Fig. 5.7, that the occurrence of exactly one downward switching is the union of the following disjoint elementary events: downward switching occurrence in the time interval $(\nu, \nu + d\nu)$ and then no upward switching occurrence up to the time t. The probability of this elementary event, $\rho_1^+ d\nu$, is given by the formula:

$$\rho_1^+ d\nu = g^0(0,\nu)v^+(\beta - u_0, t - \nu)d\nu. \qquad (5.93)$$

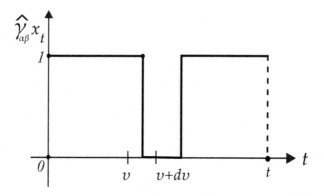

Fig. 5.8

Now, the probability of exactly one downward switching during the time interval $(0, t)$ can be found as:

$$P_1^+(t) = \int_0^t g^0(0, \nu) v^+(\beta - u_0, t - \nu) d\nu. \qquad (5.94)$$

It is clear that $P_1^+(t)$ is the convolution of $g^0(0, t)$ and $v^+(\beta - u_0, t)$. Consequently, it can be written in a concise form as

$$P_1^+(t) = g^0(0, t) * v^+(\beta - u_0, t). \qquad (5.95)$$

By using the same line of reasoning, we find that in the case when $\hat{\gamma}_{\alpha, \beta} x_0 = 0$, the following formulas are valid:

$$P_0^0(t) = v^+(0, t) \qquad (5.96)$$

and

$$P_1^0(t) = g^+(0, t) * v^0(\alpha - u_0, t). \qquad (5.97)$$

Next, consider the probability of occurrence of exactly one switching starting from the initial state $\hat{\gamma}_{\alpha, \beta} x_0 = 1$. According to Fig. 5.8, this occurrence can be viewed as the union of the following disjoint elementary events: downward switching occurrence in the time interval $(\nu, \nu + d\nu)$ and then exactly one upward switching occurrence up to the time t. The probability of such elementary events, $\rho_2^0 d\nu$, is given by the formula:

$$\rho_2^0 d\nu = g^0(0, \nu) P_1^0(t - \nu) d\nu. \qquad (5.98)$$

Now, the probability of exactly two switchings can be found by the following convolution:

$$P_2^+(t) = g^0(0, t) * P_1^0(t). \qquad (5.99)$$

By using formula (5.99), the last equation can be represented as:

$$P_2^+(t) = g^0(0,t) * g^+(\beta - u_0, t) * v^0(\alpha - u_0, t). \qquad (5.100)$$

For the sake of conciseness, we introduce the following notation:

$$g^+(0,t) = g_0^+(t), \quad g^0(0,t) = g_0^0(t), \qquad (5.101)$$

$$g^+(\beta - u_0, t) = g^+(t), \quad g^0(\alpha - u_0, t) = g^0(t), \qquad (5.102)$$

$$v^+(0,t) = v_0^+(t), \quad v^0(0,t) = v_0^0(t), \qquad (5.103)$$

$$v^+(\beta - u_0, t) = v^+(t), \quad v^0(\alpha - u_0, t) = v^0(t), \qquad (5.104)$$

Now, by using induction arguments and the same line of reasoning as before, it easy to demonstrate the validity of the following formula:

$$P_{2k}^+(t) = g_0^0(t) * g^+(t) * \overbrace{g^0(t) * g^+(t) * \cdots * g^0(t) * g^+(t)}^{(2k-2) \text{ terms}} * v^0(t). \qquad (5.105)$$

Now, formulas (5.90), (5.92) and (5.105) can be written as follows:

$$\tilde{q}_{\alpha\beta}(s) = \sum_{k=0}^{\infty} \tilde{P}_{2k}^+(s), \quad \text{if } \hat{\gamma}_{\alpha,\beta}x_0 = 1, \qquad (5.106)$$

$$\tilde{P}_0^+(s) = \tilde{v}_0^+(s), \qquad (5.107)$$

$$\tilde{P}_{2k}^+(s) = \tilde{g}_0^0(s)\tilde{g}^+(s)\tilde{v}^0(s)\left[\tilde{g}^0(s)\tilde{g}^+(s)\right]^{k-1}, \qquad (5.108)$$

where $\tilde{q}_{\alpha\beta}(s)$, $\tilde{P}_{2k}^+(s)$, $\tilde{v}_0^+(s)$, $\tilde{g}_0^0(s)$, $\tilde{g}^0(s)$ and $\tilde{g}^+(s)$ are one-sided Laplace transforms of the functions $q_{\alpha\beta}(t)$, $P_{2k}^+(t)$, $v_0^+(t)$, $g_0^0(t)$, $g^0(t)$ and $g^+(t)$, respectively.
It can be proven that

$$\left|\tilde{g}^0(s)\right| < 1, \quad \left|\tilde{g}^+(s)\right| < 1. \qquad (5.109)$$

Indeed, according to (5.82) and the probabilistic meaning of $V^+(x,t)$, we find that:

$$\tilde{g}^+(s) = \int_0^\infty \frac{dV^+(x,t)}{dt} e^{-st} dt. \qquad (5.110)$$

and

$$\frac{dV^+(x,t)}{dt} \geq 0 \qquad (5.111)$$

Taking into account that

$$\left|e^{-st}\right| = e^{-at}, \quad (a = \Re e(s)), \qquad (5.112)$$

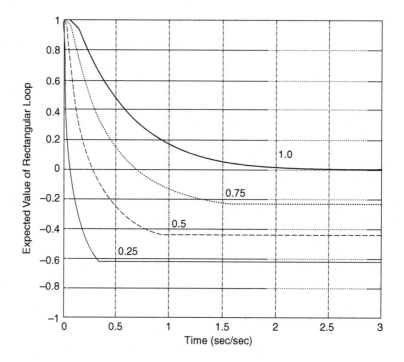

Fig. 5.9

we derive:

$$|\tilde{g}^+(s)| < \int_0^\infty \frac{dV^+(x,t)}{dt} dt = 1. \qquad (5.113)$$

The first inequality in (5.109) is similarly established.

By substituting formulas (5.107) and (5.108) into (5.106), we find that:

$$\tilde{q}_{\alpha\beta}(s) = \tilde{v}_0^0(s) + \tilde{g}_0^0(s)\tilde{g}^+(s)\tilde{v}^0(s) \sum_{k=1}^\infty \left[\tilde{g}^0(s)\tilde{g}^+(s)\right]^{k-1}. \qquad (5.114)$$

It is clear from inequalities (5.109) that the infinite sum in the last formula is a converging geometric series. Consequently,

$$\tilde{q}_{\alpha\beta}(s) = \tilde{v}_0^0(s) + \frac{\tilde{g}_0^0(s)\tilde{g}^+(s)\tilde{v}^0(s)}{1 - \tilde{g}^0(s)\tilde{g}^+(s)}, \quad \text{if } \hat{\gamma}_{\alpha,\beta}x_0 = 1. \qquad (5.115)$$

A similar expression can be derived for $\tilde{q}_{\alpha\beta}(s)$ in the case when $\hat{\gamma}_{\alpha,\beta}x_0 = 0$.

The above expressions can be used for the calculation of the time evolution of the expected value of output $q_{\alpha\beta}(t)$. Similar to the calculations of the exit time probability density functions, the numerical calculation of the

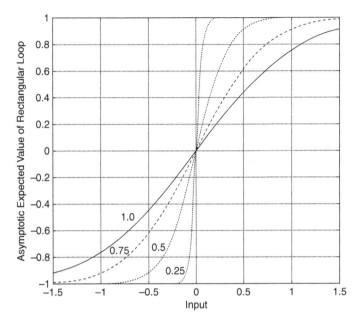

Fig. 5.10

expected value of output given in expression (5.115) can be significantly facilitated by employing the Fourier transform method. Again, by setting $s = j\omega$, this expression can be used to calculate the Fourier transform of the time evolution of the expected value of output. This Fourier transform, in turn, can be used to calculate the expected value of the output by taking the inverse Fourier transform. The detailed demonstration of this approach can be found in [59]. Fig. 5.9 shows the time evolution of the expected value of the output of the rectangular hysteresis loop with ±1 values. The time evolution of the expected value of the output is shown for various mean input values above β when the output is initially in the +1 state. For such mean values of input, it is clear that the expected value of the output should approach −1 as the mean value approaches β from above because the output is most likely to switch down and remain there with high probability. (Note that, in this sample calculation, a symmetric loop around the origin of $\alpha = 1$ and $\beta = -1$ is used). Fig. 5.10 reveals asymptotic variations of the expected value as a function of the mean value of the input for several decreasing values of the variance. The asymptotic value of the expected value is computed by employing the final value theorem of

Fourier transform theory. It can be seen in the figure that the asymptotic expected value of the output is closer to the $+1$ state when the mean input is greater than zero, zero when the mean input is equal to zero and closer to the -1 state when the mean input is less than zero. The figure also shows that as the value of the variance decreases, the asymptotic expected value of the output approaches a step function.

5.3 Noise in Hysteretic Systems and Stochastic Processes on Graphs

In this section, another approach is developed for the analysis of randomness in hysteretic systems. This approach is based on the theory of stochastic processes on graphs [50]. The foundation of this approach is based on the following simple fact. The output i_t of a randomly driven rectangular hysteresis loop is a random binary process. This process is not Markovian. However, the two component process

$$\vec{y}_t = \begin{bmatrix} i_t \\ x_t \end{bmatrix} \tag{5.116}$$

is Markovian. This is because the rectangular loop operators describe hysteresis with local memory. This means that joint specifications of current values of input and output uniquely define the states of this hysteresis. It turns out that the two-component process (5.116) is defined on the four-edge graph shown in Fig. 5.11 for a rectangular loop with output values of ± 1.

Here, we consider symmetric rectangular loops, because this simplifies the mathematical treatment of the problem. The presented analysis can be used for nonsymmetric rectangular loops of the type shown in Fig. 5.2. This is because symmetric rectangular loops can be obtained from the above nonsymmetric loops by shifting them downward by one half and subsequently vertically scaling them by two.

It is apparent that the binary process i_t assumes constant value on each edge I_k, $(k = 1, 2, 3, 4)$ of the graph shown in Fig. 5.11. Furthermore, the two component Markovian process $\vec{y}_t$ can be characterized by the transition probability density function:

$$\rho(\vec{y}, t | \vec{y}_0, t_0) \tag{5.117}$$

defined on all edges of the graph shown in Fig. 5.11. This justifies the following notation:

$$\rho(\vec{y}, t | \vec{y}_0, t_0)\big|_{\vec{y} \in I_k} = \rho^{(k)}(x, t | \vec{y}_0, t_0). \tag{5.118}$$

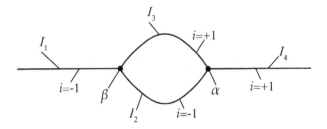

Fig. 5.11

It is clear that

$$\rho^{(1)} = \rho, \text{ for } x \leq \beta, \tag{5.119}$$

$$\rho^{(4)} = \rho, \text{ for } x \geq \alpha, \tag{5.120}$$

and

$$\rho^{(2)} + \rho^{(3)} = \rho, \text{ for } \beta \leq x \leq \alpha, \tag{5.121}$$

where ρ is the transition probability density of the process x_t.

It is also clear that on each edge of the graph the following forward Kolmogorov equation is valid:

$$\frac{\partial \rho^{(k)}}{\partial t} = \frac{1}{2}\frac{\partial^2}{\partial x^2}\left[\sigma^2(x)\rho^{(k)}\right] - \frac{\partial}{\partial x}\left[b(x)\rho^{(k)}\right], \quad (k = 1, 2, 3, 4). \tag{5.122}$$

The Markovian nature of the process $\vec{y}_t$ on the entire graph implies certain boundary conditions for $\rho^{(k)}$ at graph vertices [49]. It is evident that these vertex boundary conditions should impose the continuity of transition probability density when the transition through a vertex from one edge of the graph to another occurs without a rectangular loop switching. This implies that zero vertex boundary conditions are imposed on other graph edges. Namely, for edge I_3 we have:

$$\rho^{(3)}\Big|_{x=\beta} = 0, \tag{5.123}$$

while

$$\rho^{(3)}\Big|_{x=\alpha} = \rho\Big|_{x=\alpha}. \tag{5.124}$$

Similarly, for edge I_2 we find:

$$\rho^{(2)}\Big|_{x=\beta} = \rho\Big|_{x=\beta}, \tag{5.125}$$

while

$$\rho^{(2)}\Big|_{x=\alpha} = 0. \tag{5.126}$$

Furthermore, the probability current

$$J_k(x) = -\frac{\sigma^2(x)}{2}\frac{\partial \rho^{(k)}}{\partial x} + b(x)\rho^{(k)}(x) \tag{5.127}$$

must be conserved at each vertex. According to formulas (5.123)–(5.127), this implies the following boundary conditions:

$$\frac{\partial \rho}{\partial x}\Big|_{x=\beta} = \frac{\partial \rho^{(2)}}{\partial x}\Big|_{x=\beta} + \frac{\partial \rho^{(3)}}{\partial x}\Big|_{x=\beta}, \tag{5.128}$$

$$\frac{\partial \rho}{\partial x}\Big|_{x=\alpha} = \frac{\partial \rho^{(2)}}{\partial x}\Big|_{x=\alpha} + \frac{\partial \rho^{(3)}}{\partial x}\Big|_{x=\alpha}. \tag{5.129}$$

Finally, the following initial condition is valid

$$\rho(x,0|x',0) = \delta_{kk'}\delta(x - x'). \tag{5.130}$$

Equations (5.122) along with boundary conditions (5.123)–(5.126) and (5.128)–(5.129) as well as initial condition (5.130) completely define the dynamics of the transitional probability density for the two component Markovian process $\vec{y}_t$ defined on the graph shown in Fig. 5.11. This initial-boundary value problem can be solved numerically, and then the probabilities of different values of the binary process i_t can be found by proper integration of the probability densities $\rho^{(k)}$.

It is clear that the presented approach of "stochastic processes on graphs" is quite different from the "stochastic process exit" approach discussed in the previous section. Indeed, the **stochastic process exit** approach is based on the solution of the backward Kolmogorov equation, while the **stochastic processes on graph approach** is based on the solution of the forward Kolmogorov equation. The latter approach is especially convenient for the calculation of stationary densities $\rho_{st}^{(3)}$ and $\rho_{st}^{(2)}$. Indeed, in order to find $\rho_{st}^{(3)}$ we have to solve the following boundary value problem for the ordinary differential equation:

$$\frac{1}{2}\frac{d^2}{dx^2}\left[\sigma^2(x)\rho_{st}^{(3)}(x)\right] - \frac{d}{dx}\left[b(x)\rho_{st}^{(3)}(x)\right] = 0 \tag{5.131}$$

subject to the boundary conditions

$$\rho_{st}^{(3)}(\beta) = 0, \tag{5.132}$$

and

$$\rho_{st}^{(3)}(\alpha) = \rho_{st}(\alpha). \tag{5.133}$$

The above boundary conditions follow from formulas (5.123) and (5.124).

Having solved the boundary value problem (5.131)–(5.133), $\rho_{\text{st}}^{(2)}$ can be found from formula (5.121) as

$$\rho_{\text{st}}^{(2)}(x) = \rho_{\text{st}}(x) - \rho_{\text{st}}^{(3)}(x). \tag{5.134}$$

The last equation implies that the boundary conditions (5.128) and (5.129) will be satisfied.

The analytical solution to the boundary value problem (5.131)–(5.133) can be found for any stationary diffusion process x_t. However, having in mind economic applications, we present below the solution for the case of the Ornstien-Uhlenbeck process.

By integrating equation (5.131) corresponding to this process, we find:

$$\frac{\sigma^2}{2} \frac{d\rho_{\text{st}}^{(3)}}{dx} + kx\rho_{\text{st}}^{(3)}(x) = C = \text{const.}. \tag{5.135}$$

We look for the solution of equation (5.135) in the following form

$$\rho_{\text{st}}^{(3)}(x) = \rho_{\text{st}}(x)\varphi(x), \tag{5.136}$$

where $\rho_{\text{st}}(x)$ is the Gaussian stationary distribution for the Ornstein-Uhlenbeck process (see Sec. 5.1), while $\varphi(x)$ must be determined. By substituting the last formula into equation (5.135), we find:

$$\frac{\sigma^2}{2}\rho_{\text{st}}(x)\frac{d\varphi(x)}{dx} + \varphi(x)\left[\frac{\sigma^2}{2}\frac{d\rho_{\text{st}}(x)}{dx} + kx\rho_{\text{st}}(x)\right] = C. \tag{5.137}$$

For the stationary Ornstein-Uhlenbeck process, the probability current (see expression (5.127)) is equal to zero. This implies that

$$\frac{\sigma^2}{2}\frac{d\rho_{\text{st}}(x)}{dx} + kx\rho_{\text{st}}(x) = 0. \tag{5.138}$$

From the last two equations, we obtain:

$$\frac{\sigma^2}{2}\rho_{\text{st}}(x)\frac{d\varphi(x)}{dx} = C. \tag{5.139}$$

By integrating the last equation and taking into account the boundary condition (5.132) and formula (5.136), we obtain:

$$\varphi(x) = \frac{2C}{\sigma^2}\int_\beta^x \frac{dy}{\rho_{\text{st}}(y)}. \tag{5.140}$$

From boundary condition (5.133) and formula (5.136), it further follows that

$$\varphi(\alpha) = 1. \tag{5.141}$$

From equations (5.140) and (5.141), we obtain:

$$1 = \frac{2C}{\sigma^2} \int_\beta^\alpha \frac{dy}{\rho_{\text{st}}(y)}, \tag{5.142}$$

which leads to

$$\frac{2C}{\sigma^2} = \frac{1}{\displaystyle\int_\beta^\alpha \frac{dy}{\rho_{\text{st}}(y)}}. \tag{5.143}$$

Now, by recalling from expression (5.140), we derive

$$\varphi(x) = \frac{\displaystyle\int_\beta^x \frac{dy}{\rho_{\text{st}}(y)}}{\displaystyle\int_\beta^\alpha \frac{dy}{\rho_{\text{st}}(y)}}, \tag{5.144}$$

which according to equation (5.136) results in:

$$\rho_{\text{st}}^{(3)}(x) = \rho_{\text{st}}(x)\frac{\displaystyle\int_\beta^x \frac{dy}{\rho_{\text{st}}(y)}}{\displaystyle\int_\beta^\alpha \frac{dy}{\rho_{\text{st}}(y)}}, \tag{5.145}$$

where, as before, $\rho_{\text{st}}(x)$ is the Gaussian stationary distribution for the Ornstein-Uhlenbeck process.

By using the last formula, the stationary expected value of the random process $i_t = \hat{\gamma}_{\alpha\beta}\, x_t$ and its variance $\sigma_{i_t}^2$ can be calculated. Indeed, it is clear that

$$\bar{i}_t = E_{\text{st}}\big\{\hat{\gamma}_{\alpha\beta}\, x_t\big\} = P_{\text{st}}\big\{i_t = 1\big\} - P_{\text{st}}\big\{i_t = -1\big\}. \tag{5.146}$$

Since

$$P_{\text{st}}\big\{i_t = 1\big\} + P_{\text{st}}\big\{i_t = 1\big\} - 1, \tag{5.147}$$

we find

$$\bar{i}_t = 2P_{\text{st}}\big\{i_t = 1\big\} - 1. \tag{5.148}$$

Further, it is clear that

$$P_{\text{st}}\big\{i_t = 1\big\} = \int_\beta^\alpha \rho_{\text{st}}^{(3)}(x)dx + \int_\alpha^\infty \rho_{\text{st}}(x)dx. \tag{5.149}$$

Consequently,

$$\bar{i}_t = 2\left[\int_\beta^\alpha \rho_{\text{st}}^{(3)}(x)dx + \int_\alpha^\infty \rho_{\text{st}}(x)dx\right] - 1. \tag{5.150}$$

Once $\bar{i}_t$ is computed by using formulas (5.145) and (5.150), the variance $\sigma_{i_t}^2$ can be calculated as well. This is done by using the well-known relation

$$\sigma_{i_t}^2 = \bar{i_t^2} - \left(\bar{i}_t\right)^2 \tag{5.151}$$

and the fact that

$$\bar{i_t^2} = 1. \tag{5.152}$$

Consequently,

$$\sigma_{i_t}^2 = 1 - \left(\bar{i}_t\right)^2. \tag{5.153}$$

The last formula along with equation (5.150) can be used for the computation of the variance $\sigma_{i_t}^2$. These computations are facilitated by the observation that

$$\int_0^x e^{y^2}\,dy = \frac{\sqrt{\pi}}{2}\mathrm{erfi}(x) \tag{5.154}$$

and

$$\int e^{-x^2}\mathrm{erfi}(x)dx = \frac{x^2}{\pi}\,{}_2F_2\left(1,1;\frac{3}{2},2;-x^2\right). \tag{5.155}$$

Here, $\mathrm{erfi}(x)$ and ${}_2F_2$ are the "imaginary error function" and the "generalized hypergeometric function," respectively.

By employing formulas (5.145), (5.150), and (5.153), the stationary expected value $\bar{i}_t$ and variance $\sigma_{i_t}^2$ have been computed as functions of the expected value x_0 of the input Ornstein-Uhlenbeck process x_t for symmetric rectangular loops $\hat{\gamma}_{\alpha,-\alpha} = \hat{\gamma}_\alpha$. The results of computations are presented in Figs. 5.12 and 5.13, respectively. These results are plotted for normalized x_0-values $\nu = x_0/\alpha$ and normalized values of switching thresholds $\tilde{\alpha} = \alpha/\lambda$, where $\lambda^2 = \sigma^2/b$ is the variance of the stationary distribution of Ornstein-Uhlenbeck process x_t.

The results obtained for the binary process $i_t = \hat{\gamma}_{\alpha\beta}$ can be used to compute the stationary expected value of the output random process $\bar{f}_t^{\mathrm{st}}$. Indeed, it is clear that

$$\bar{f}_t^{\mathrm{st}} = \iint_{\alpha\geq\beta} \mu(\alpha,\beta)E_{\mathrm{st}}\left(\hat{\gamma}_{\alpha,\beta}x_t\right)d\alpha d\beta. \tag{5.156}$$

It turns out that the stationary values of the second moment $E_{\mathrm{st}}(f_t^2)$ and the variance of f_t can also be computed by using the mathematical

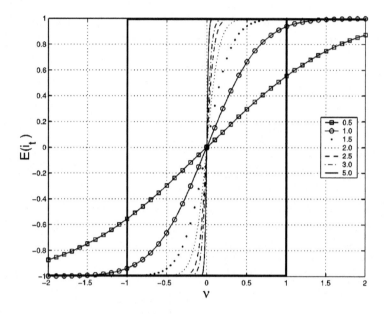

Fig. 5.12

machinery of stochastic processes on graphs. The starting point of these computations is the following formula:

$$f_t^2 = \iint\limits_{\alpha_1 \geq \beta_1} \mu(\alpha_1, \beta_1) \hat{\gamma}_{\alpha_1 \beta_1} x_t d\alpha_1 d\beta_1 \cdot \iint\limits_{\alpha_2 \geq \beta_2} \mu(\alpha_2, \beta_2) \hat{\gamma}_{\alpha_2 \beta_2} x_t d\alpha_2 d\beta_2,$$

(5.157)

which leads to the following formula:

$$E_{\mathrm{st}}\left(f_t^2\right) = \iint\limits_{\alpha_1 \geq \beta_1} \iint\limits_{\alpha_2 \geq \beta_2} E_{\mathrm{st}}\left(i_t^{(1)} i_t^{(2)}\right) \mu(\alpha_1, \beta_1) \mu(\alpha_2, \beta_2) d\alpha_1 d\beta_1 d\alpha_2 d\beta_2,$$

(5.158)

where

$$i_t^{(1)} = \hat{\gamma}_{\alpha_1, \beta_1} x_t,$$

(5.159)

$$i_t^{(2)} = \hat{\gamma}_{\alpha_2, \beta_2} x_t.$$

(5.160)

To evaluate the expected value $E_{\mathrm{st}}(i_t^{(1)} i_t^{(2)})$, we introduce the three component Markov process $\vec{z}_t$ defined by the formula

$$\vec{z}_t = \begin{bmatrix} i_t^{(1)} \\ i_t^{(2)} \\ x_t \end{bmatrix}.$$

(5.161)

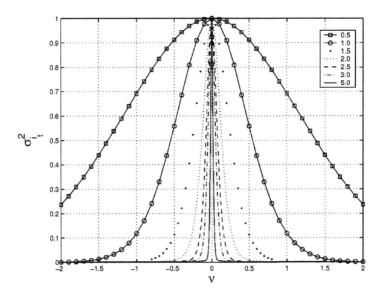

Fig. 5.13

This process is defined on graphs whose structures depend on relations between $\alpha_1, \alpha_2, \beta_1, \beta_2$. It turns out that there are three distinct cases. The first case is realized for the following inequalities:

$$\beta_1 < \alpha_1 < \beta_2 < \alpha_2. \tag{5.162}$$

For this case, the rectangular loops $\hat{\gamma}_{\alpha_1,\beta_1}$ and $\hat{\gamma}_{\alpha_2,\beta_2}$ do not overlap (see Fig. 5.14). This implies that the three component Markov process $\vec{z}_t$ is defined on the graph shown in Fig. 5.15. As before, we introduce the following notation:

$$\rho_{\text{st}}\left(\vec{z}_t\right)\big|_{I_k} = \rho_{\text{st}}^{(k)}(x). \tag{5.163}$$

It is clear from Fig. 5.15 that

$$\rho_{\text{st}}^{(k)}(x) = \rho_{\text{st}}(x) \quad \text{for} \quad k = 1, 4 \text{ and } 7, \tag{5.164}$$

while

$$\rho_{\text{st}}^{(3)}(x) = \rho_{\text{st}}(x)\varphi_3(x), \tag{5.165}$$

$$\rho_{\text{st}}^{(2)}(x) = \rho_{\text{st}}(x) - \rho_{\text{st}}^{(3)}(x), \tag{5.166}$$

$$\rho_{\text{st}}^{(6)}(x) = \rho_{\text{st}}(x)\varphi_6(x), \tag{5.167}$$

$$\rho_{\text{st}}^{(5)}(x) = \rho_{\text{st}}(x) - \rho_{\text{st}}^{(6)}(x). \tag{5.168}$$

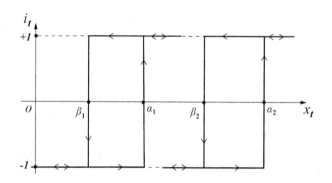

Fig. 5.14

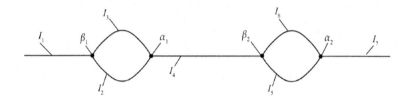

Fig. 5.15

By using the same line of reasoning as before, it can be shown that $\varphi_3(x)$ and $\varphi_6(x)$ can be determined by using formula (5.144) by replacing in that formula α and β by α_2 and β_2 and α_1 and β_1, respectively.

The second case is specified by the inequalities

$$\beta_1 < \beta_2 < \alpha_2 < \alpha_1 \qquad (5.169)$$

and it is realized when rectangular loops $\hat{\gamma}_{\alpha_1,\beta_1}$ and $\hat{\gamma}_{\alpha_2,\beta_2}$ completely overlap (see Fig. 5.16). In this case, the three component Markov process is defined on the graph shown in Fig. 5.17.
From this figure we find that

$$\rho_{\text{st}}^{(k)}(x) = \rho_{\text{st}}(x) \ \text{ for } \ k = 1 \text{ and } 10, \qquad (5.170)$$

while

$$\rho_{\text{st}}^{(3)}(x) = \rho_{\text{st}}(x)\varphi_3(x), \qquad (5.171)$$

$$\rho_{\text{st}}^{(2)}(x) = \rho_{\text{st}}(x) - \rho_{\text{st}}^{(3)}(x), \qquad (5.172)$$

$$\rho_{\text{st}}^{(5)}(x) = \rho_{\text{st}}^{(3)}(x)\varphi_5(x), \qquad (5.173)$$

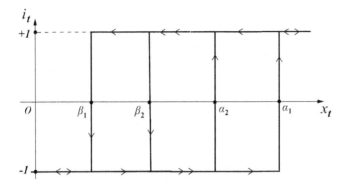

Fig. 5.16

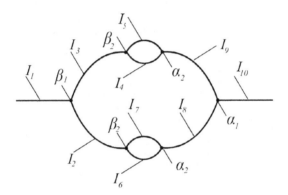

Fig. 5.17

$$\rho_{\text{st}}^{(4)}(x) = \rho_{\text{st}}^{(3)}(x) - \rho_{\text{st}}^{(5)}(x), \qquad (5.174)$$

$$\rho_{\text{st}}^{(7)}(x) = \rho_{\text{st}}^{(2)}(x)\varphi_7(x), \qquad (5.175)$$

$$\rho_{\text{st}}^{(6)}(x) = \rho_{\text{st}}^{(2)}(x) - \rho_{\text{st}}^{(7)}(x), \qquad (5.176)$$

$$\rho_{\text{st}}^{(9)}(x) = \rho_{\text{st}}^{(3)}(x), \qquad (5.177)$$

$$\rho_{\text{st}}^{(8)}(x) = \rho_{\text{st}}^{(2)}(x). \qquad (5.178)$$

In the above equations, the functions $\varphi_3(x)$, $\varphi_5(x)$ and $\varphi_7(x)$ are determined by using the same line of reasoning as in the derivation of formula (5.144). The resulting formulas for the above functions are similar to formula (5.144) but use different limits of integration.

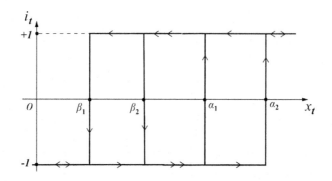

Fig. 5.18

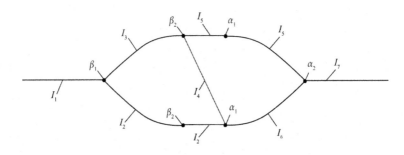

Fig. 5.19

Finally, we consider the third case specified by the following inequalities:

$$\beta_1 < \beta_2 < \alpha_1 < \alpha_2. \tag{5.179}$$

This case is realized when rectangular loops $\hat{\gamma}_{\alpha_1,\beta_1}$ and $\hat{\gamma}_{\alpha_2,\beta_2}$ partially overlap (see Fig. 5.18). This is the most intricate case. In this case, the three component process $\vec{z}_t$ is defined on the graph shown in Fig. 5.19. The unique feature of this case is the absence of the graph edge corresponding to $i_t^{(1)} = -1$ and $i_t^{(2)} = 1$. This is because these simultaneous values of $i_t^{(1)}$ and $i_t^{(2)}$ are not consistent with the definition of rectangular loops $\hat{\gamma}_{\alpha_1,\beta_1}$ and $\hat{\gamma}_{\alpha_2,\beta_2}$ specified by inequalities (5.179).

By using Fig. 5.18) it can be concluded that the edges in Fig. 5.19 are characterized by specific values of the binary processes $i_t^{(1)}$ and $i_t^{(2)}$ specified in the following formulas:

$$I_1: \quad i_t^{(1)} = i_t^{(2)} = -1, \tag{5.180}$$

$$I_2 : \quad i_t^{(1)} = i_t^{(2)} = -1, \tag{5.181}$$

$$I_3 : \quad i_t^{(1)} = 1, \ i_t^{(2)} = -1, \tag{5.182}$$

$$I_4 : \quad i_t^{(1)} = 1, \ i_t^{(2)} = -1, \tag{5.183}$$

$$I_5 : \quad i_t^{(1)} = i_t^{(2)} = 1, \tag{5.184}$$

$$I_6 : \quad i_t^{(1)} = 1, \ i_t^{(2)} = -1, \tag{5.185}$$

$$I_7 : \quad i_t^{(1)} = i_t^{(2)} = 1. \tag{5.186}$$

By using the graph shown in Fig. 5.19 and the same line of reasoning as before, we find that

$$\rho_{\mathrm{st}}^{(k)}(x) = \rho_{\mathrm{st}}(x) \quad \text{for} \quad k = 1 \text{ and } 7, \tag{5.187}$$

$$\rho_{\mathrm{st}}^{(2)}(x) = \rho_{\mathrm{st}}(x)\varphi_2(x), \tag{5.188}$$

$$\rho_{\mathrm{st}}^{(3)}(x) = \rho_{\mathrm{st}}(x) - \rho_{\mathrm{st}}^{(2)}(x), \tag{5.189}$$

$$\rho_{\mathrm{st}}^{(5)}(x) = \rho_{\mathrm{st}}(x)\varphi_5(x), \tag{5.190}$$

$$\rho_{\mathrm{st}}^{(6)}(x) = \rho_{\mathrm{st}}(x) - \rho_{\mathrm{st}}^{(5)}(x), \tag{5.191}$$

and

$$\rho_{\mathrm{st}}^{(4)}(x) = \rho_{\mathrm{st}}(x) - \rho_{\mathrm{st}}^{(2)}(x) - \rho_{\mathrm{st}}^{(5)}(x). \tag{5.192}$$

The last formula follows from the relation

$$\rho_{\mathrm{st}}^{(4)}(x) + \rho_{\mathrm{st}}^{(2)}(x) = \rho_{\mathrm{st}}^{(6)}(x). \tag{5.193}$$

and equation (5.191). As far as the determination of functions $\varphi_2(x)$ and $\varphi_5(x)$ is concerned, it can be done by using the same line of reasoning as in the derivation of formula (5.144).

It is worthwhile to mention that the calculations of $E_{\mathrm{st}}(f_t^2)$ are considerably simplified in the particular (but important in many applications) case of the Preisach model containing only symmetric loops $\hat{\gamma}_{\alpha,-\alpha} = \hat{\gamma}_\alpha$. In this case,

$$f_t = \int_0^{\alpha_0} \mu(\alpha)\hat{\gamma}_\alpha x_t d\alpha, \tag{5.194}$$

where α_0 is the maximum value of α for symmetric rectangular loops $\hat{\gamma}_\alpha$.

From the last formula, we find:

$$\bar{f}_t^{\text{st}} = \int_0^{\alpha_0} \mu(\alpha) E_{\text{st}}\left(\hat{\gamma}_\alpha x_t\right) d\alpha \tag{5.195}$$

and

$$E_{\text{st}}\left(f_t^2\right) = 2 \int_0^{\alpha_0} \mu(\alpha) \left(\int_0^\alpha \mu(\alpha') E_{\text{st}}\left(\hat{\gamma}_\alpha x_t \hat{\gamma}_{\alpha'} x_t\right) d\alpha' \right) d\alpha. \tag{5.196}$$

The value of $E_{\text{st}}\left(\hat{\gamma}_\alpha x_t\right)$ can be evaluated in the same way as in the case of formula (5.146). The value of $E_{\text{st}}\left(\hat{\gamma}_\alpha x_t \hat{\gamma}_{\alpha'} x_t\right)$ can be evaluated by using the graph shown in Fig. 5.17 and the formula

$$E_{\text{st}}\left(\hat{\gamma}_\alpha x_t \hat{\gamma}_{\alpha'} x_t\right) = 2P\left(\hat{\gamma}_\alpha x_t \hat{\gamma}_{\alpha'} x_t = +1\right) - 1, \tag{5.197}$$

which leads to

$$E_{\text{st}}\left(\hat{\gamma}_\alpha x_t \hat{\gamma}_{\alpha'} x_t\right) = 2\left[\int_{-\infty}^{-\alpha} \rho_{\text{st}}(x)dx + \int_{-\alpha}^{-\alpha'} \rho_{\text{st}}^{(2)}(x)dx + \int_{-\alpha'}^{\alpha'} \rho_{\text{st}}^{(5)}(x)dx \right.$$
$$\left. + \int_{-\alpha'}^{\alpha'} \rho_{\text{st}}^{(6)}(x)dx + \int_{\alpha'}^{\alpha} \rho_{\text{st}}^{(9)}(x)dx + \int_{\alpha}^{\infty} \rho_{\text{st}}(x)dx \right] - 1. \tag{5.198}$$

The stochastic processes on graph technique lends itself to efficient numerical calculations. Figs. 5.20 and 5.21 show some sample results of calculations for $\bar{f}_t^{\text{st}}$ and $E_{\text{st}}(f_t^2)$, respectively. In these calculations it was assumed that $\mu(\alpha) = 1$. Here, $\bar{f}_t^{\text{st}}$ and $E_{\text{st}}(f_t^2)$ were computed as functions of $\nu = x_0/\alpha_0$ for various values of $\tilde{\alpha}_0 = \alpha_0/\lambda$, where as before λ^2 is the variance of the stationary distribution of Ornstein-Uhlenbeck process. Furthermore, the values of $\bar{f}_t^{\text{st}}$ and $E_{\text{st}}(f_t^2)$ have been normalized by λ and λ^2, respectively.

The technique of stochastic processes on graphs can be further extended to compute higher order moments of the random output process f_t. This extension is more or less straightforward in the case of hysteresis model (5.194). In this case, the relevant multicomponent Markovian processes are defined on the graphs similar to the graph shown in Fig. 5.17.

Thus, it can be concluded that the technique of the stochastic processes on graphs can be used for the analysis of non-Markovian stochastic processes generated by random excitation of the Preisach hysteresis model.

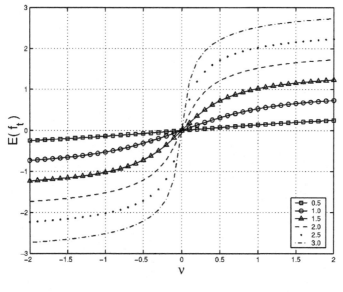

Fig. 5.20

5.4 Generalized and "Play" Economic Hysteresis Models Driven by Stochastic Processes

In the previous sections of this chapter, we considered the properties of the rectangular microeconomic hysteresis loop driven by stochastic diffusion type processes. In this section, we will extend that discussion to the analysis of the more realistic generalized hysteresis microeconomic models that were described in the previous chapter. Specifically, we will focus on the expected (mean) value of the outputs of these more general microeconomic hysteresis models driven by stochastic inputs. We will also extend this analysis to aggregate macroeconomic Preisach hysteresis models driven by stochastic inputs and show that the key calculations for macroeconomic hysteresis models are reduced to the calculation of the expected value of rectangular hysteresis loops presented in Secs. 5.1–5.3.

We will begin this section by first considering the generalized hysteresis model presented in Sec. 4.1. In that section, we constructed the aggregation of more general microeconomic hysteresis loops as shown in Figs. 4.1 or 4.3, which can be represented mathematically by the following formula:

$$\hat{\Gamma}_{\alpha\beta}(u) = \left(f_{\alpha\beta}^{-}(u) - f_{\alpha\beta}^{+}(u)\right)\hat{\gamma}_{\alpha\beta}u + f_{\alpha\beta}^{+}(u). \tag{5.199}$$

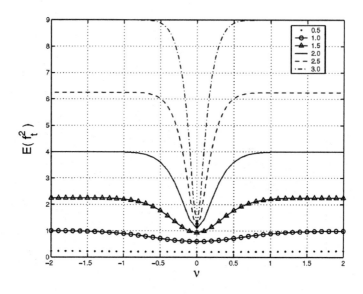

Fig. 5.21

The aggregation of such generalized microeconomic hysteresis models according to the formula

$$f(t) = \iint_{\alpha \geq \beta} \hat{\Gamma}_{\alpha\beta} u(t) d\alpha d\beta, \tag{5.200}$$

resulted in the following generalized macroeconomic hysteresis model:

$$f(t) = \iint_{R_{u(t)}} \mu(\alpha, \beta, u(t)) \hat{\gamma}_{\alpha\beta} u(t) d\alpha d\beta + \iint_{T} f^{+}_{\alpha\beta}(u(t)) d\alpha d\beta, \tag{5.201}$$

where

$$\mu(\alpha, \beta, u(t)) = f^{-}_{\alpha\beta}(u(t)) - f^{+}_{\alpha\beta}(u(t)), \tag{5.202}$$

from expressions (4.10), (4.13) and (4.29). The region of integration $R_{u(t)}$ in the first term is defined in (4.23) and is shown in Fig. 4.5. It is worthwhile to recall here that the first term of expression (5.201) represents the irreversible component of the output, while the second term represents the reversible component.

In order to analyze the above generalized macroeconomic hysteresis model driven by stochastic inputs, we employ the customary stochastic process notation and write expression (5.201) as follows:

$$f_t = \iint_{R_{x_t}} \mu(\alpha, \beta, x_t) \hat{\gamma}_{\alpha\beta} x_t d\alpha d\beta + \iint_{T} f^{+}_{\alpha\beta}(x_t) d\alpha d\beta. \tag{5.203}$$

Here, x_t denotes the stochastic input modeled by diffusion type processes considered in prior sections. We also note that the region of integration R_{x_t} in the first term in expression (5.203) depends on the stochastic input x_t. In order to simplify the subsequent analysis, it will be helpful to define the following characteristic function:

$$\chi_{\alpha\beta}(x_t) = \begin{cases} 1, & \text{if } (\alpha,\beta) \in R_{x_t} \\ 0, & \text{if } (\alpha,\beta) \notin R_{x_t}. \end{cases} \tag{5.204}$$

Based on this characteristic function, we can rewrite (5.203) as follows:

$$f_t = \iint\limits_{T} c_{\alpha\beta}(x_t)\hat{\gamma}_{\alpha\beta}x_t d\alpha d\beta + \iint\limits_{T} f_{\alpha\beta}^{+}(x_t)d\alpha d\beta. \tag{5.205}$$

Here, we note that the limits of integration in the first term are now independent of the stochastic input, and the function $c_{\alpha\beta}$ is defined as follows:

$$c_{\alpha\beta}(x_t) = \chi_{\alpha\beta}(x_t)\mu(\alpha,\beta,x_t). \tag{5.206}$$

We next proceed to the calculation of the expected value of output of the above macroeconomic generalized hysteresis model driven by stochastic inputs. Taking the expected value of both sides of expression (5.205), the expected value of the output of the macroeconomic hysteresis model can be expressed as follows:

$$\bar{f}_t \equiv E(f_t) = \iint\limits_{T} E\Big[c_{\alpha\beta}(x_t)\hat{\gamma}_{\alpha\beta}x_t\Big]d\alpha d\beta + \iint\limits_{T} E\Big[f_{\alpha\beta}^{+}(x_t)\Big]d\alpha d\beta, \tag{5.207}$$

where $\bar{f}_t$ denotes the expected value of the stochastic output process f_t.

In the subsequent analysis, we consider x_t to be a stationary diffusion type stochastic process as we did in the previous section. Employing the same notation as in the previous section, we will consider this process to have a known stationary probability density function, $\rho_{\text{st}}(x)$. Accordingly, the expected value of the second term (reversible component) can be expressed in terms of this probability density function by noting that

$$E\Big[f_{\alpha\beta}^{+}(x_t)\Big] = \int_{-\infty}^{+\infty} f_{\alpha\beta}^{+}(u)\rho_{\text{st}}(u)du. \tag{5.208}$$

Consequently, the reversible component of the output has the following expected value:

$$\iint\limits_{T} E\Big[f_{\alpha\beta}^{+}(x_t)\Big]d\alpha d\beta = \iint\limits_{T} \int_{-\infty}^{+\infty} f_{\alpha\beta}^{+}(u)\rho_{\text{st}}(u)du d\alpha d\beta. \tag{5.209}$$

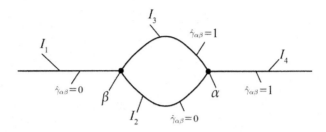

Fig. 5.22

In order to calculate the irreversible component of the output in expression (5.207), we will again employ the framework of stochastic processes on graphs. We note that the joint stochastic process $(x_t, \hat{\gamma}_{\alpha\beta}x_t)$ is defined on the graph shown in Fig. 5.22. This significantly facilitates the calculation of the expected value of the irreversible term.

We begin the calculation by first noting that the expected value of a generalized microeconomic hysteresis loop can be calculated by employing the following conditional probabilities:

$$E\Big[c_{\alpha\beta}(x_t)\hat{\gamma}_{\alpha\beta}x_t\Big] = E\Big[c_{\alpha\beta}(x_t)\hat{\gamma}_{\alpha\beta}x_t\Big|\hat{\gamma}_{\alpha\beta}x_t = 1\Big]P\Big[\hat{\gamma}_{\alpha\beta}x_t = 1\Big]$$
$$+ E\Big[c_{\alpha\beta}(x_t)\hat{\gamma}_{\alpha\beta}x_t\Big|\hat{\gamma}_{\alpha\beta}x_t = 0\Big]P\Big[\hat{\gamma}_{\alpha\beta}x_t = 0\Big].$$
(5.210)

The conditions $\hat{\gamma}_{\alpha\beta}x_t = 1$ and $\hat{\gamma}_{\alpha\beta}x_t = 0$ in the first and second terms above, respectively, imply that

$$E\Big[c_{\alpha\beta}(x_t)\hat{\gamma}_{\alpha\beta}x_t\Big] = E\Big[c_{\alpha\beta}(x_t)\Big|\hat{\gamma}_{\alpha\beta}x_t = 1\Big]P\Big[\hat{\gamma}_{\alpha\beta}x_t = 1\Big]. \qquad (5.211)$$

In order to calculate the above conditional expectation of $\hat{\gamma}_{\alpha\beta}x_t - 1$, the conditional probability density function on edges I_3 and I_4 of the graph shown in Fig. 5.22 can be used. This conditional probability density function can be expressed by the following equation

$$\rho_{x|\hat{\gamma}}(x|\hat{\gamma}_{\alpha\beta}x_t = 1) = \frac{1}{q_{\alpha\beta}}\begin{cases}\rho^{(3)}(x), & \beta < x < \alpha \\ \rho^{(4)}(x), & \alpha < x,\end{cases} \qquad (5.212)$$

where, as before, $\rho^{(3)}$ and $\rho^{(4)}$ denote the steady-state probability densities on the graph edges I_3 and I_4, respectively, while $q_{\alpha\beta}$ is the steady-state probability that $\hat{\gamma}_{\alpha\beta}x_t = 1$ as defined in (5.87). Employing the same notation as in Secs. 5.2 and 5.3, it is also clear that

$$q_{\alpha\beta} = P\Big[\hat{\gamma}_{\alpha\beta}x_t = 1\Big] = P\Big[I_3\Big] + P\Big[I_4\Big] = \int_\beta^\alpha \rho^{(3)}(u)du + \int_\alpha^\infty \rho^{(4)}(u)du.$$

$$(5.213)$$

Based on the conditional probability density function in (5.212) and the definition of $q_{\alpha\beta}$ in (5.213), the conditional expectation in (5.211) can be derived to be

$$E\Big[c_{\alpha\beta}(x_t)\hat{\gamma}_{\alpha\beta}x_t\Big] = \int_\beta^\alpha c_{\alpha\beta}(u)\rho^{(3)}(u)du + \int_\alpha^\infty c_{\alpha\beta}(u)\rho^{(4)}(u)du.$$

$$(5.214)$$

Substituting expressions (5.214) and (5.209) for the irreversible and reversible components, respectively, into formula (5.207), we can now determine the expected value of the output $\bar{f}_t$ to be given as follows:

$$\bar{f}_t = \iint_T \left(\int_\beta^\alpha c_{\alpha\beta}(u)\rho^{(3)}(u)du + \int_\alpha^\infty c_{\alpha\beta}(u)\rho^{(4)}(u)du \right) d\alpha d\beta$$

$$+ \iint_T \int_{-\infty}^{+\infty} f_{\alpha\beta}^+(u)\rho_{st}(u)dud\alpha d\beta.$$

$$(5.215)$$

This is the expected value for the generalized aggregate macroeconomic hysteresis output. From the previous analysis, it is also clear that the expected value for the generalized microscopic hysteresis loop $\hat{\Gamma}_{\alpha\beta}$ given in expression (5.199) is as follows:

$$E\Big[\hat{\Gamma}_{\alpha\beta}(x_t)\Big] = \int_\beta^\alpha c_{\alpha\beta}(u)\rho^{(3)}(u)du + \int_\alpha^\infty c_{\alpha\beta}(u)\rho^{(4)}(u)du$$

$$+ \int_{-\infty}^{+\infty} f_{\alpha\beta}^+(u)\rho_{st}(u)du.$$

$$(5.216)$$

We next proceed to the stochastic analysis of the macroeconomic hysteresis model (4.110) which is the aggregation of heterogeneous microeconomic "play" hysteresis, as presented in Sec. 4.3. This model is given by the following expression

$$f(t) = \iint_{\alpha \geq \beta} \mu(\alpha, \beta, \alpha_1, \alpha_2)\hat{\gamma}_{\alpha\beta}u(t)d\alpha d\beta,$$

$$(5.217)$$

where

$$\mu(\alpha, \beta, \alpha_1, \alpha_2) = \chi(\alpha_1, \alpha_2) \frac{dg^+_{\alpha_1 \alpha_2}}{d\alpha}(\alpha) m(\alpha - \beta). \tag{5.218}$$

Like the earlier analysis, we consider the input to this model to be a diffusion type stochastic process x_t. Accordingly, the output will be a stochastic process f_t. The stochastic analysis for this macroeconomic model is very similar to the one for the generalized macroeconomic hysteresis model presented above. Accordingly, the steady-state expected value of the output of the above macroscopic hysteresis model is

$$\bar{f}_t = \iint\limits_{\alpha \geq \beta} \mu(\alpha, \beta, \alpha_1, \alpha_2) E\left[\hat{\gamma}_{\alpha\beta} x_t\right] d\alpha d\beta. \tag{5.219}$$

From the definition of the steady state probability $q_{\alpha\beta}$ given by

$$q_{\alpha\beta} = P\left[\hat{\gamma}_{\alpha\beta} x_t = 1\right], \tag{5.220}$$

the expected value of the rectangular loop $\hat{\gamma}_{\alpha\beta} x_t$ is given as follows

$$E\left[\hat{\gamma}_{\alpha\beta} x_t\right] = q_{\alpha\beta}. \tag{5.221}$$

As a result, from (5.219) and (5.221), the expected value of the output of the macroeconomic hysteresis model based on the aggregation of heterogeneous "play" hysteresis loops is given by the following expression:

$$\bar{f}_t = \iint\limits_{\alpha \geq \beta} \mu(\alpha, \beta, \alpha_1, \alpha_2) q_{\alpha\beta} d\alpha d\beta. \tag{5.222}$$

This concludes the stochastic analysis of macroeconomic hysteresis models based on the aggregation of generalized and "play" hysteresis type heterogeneous microeconomic hysteresis models. We have shown that aggregation of microeconomic hysteresis results in Preisach type models, and that the key calculations are reduced to the stochastic analysis of rectangular microeconomic hysteresis loops. We have also shown that the framework of the stochastic processes on graphs significantly facilitates these calculations.

Bibliography

[1] J. Adamonis and Matthias Göcke, "Modelling economic hysteresis losses caused by sunk adjustment costs," Journal of Post Keynesian Economics, 42:2, 299-318, 2019, DOI: 10.1080/01603477.2017.1401902.

[2] J. Adamonis and L. Werner, "A New Measure To Quantify Hysteresis Losses: The Case Of Italian Wine Exports To The United States," Macroeconomic Dynamics, 23(7), 2787-2814, 2019, DOI:10.1017/S1365100517000967.

[3] A. A. Adly, "Efficient Unconventional Models of Multi-Component Magnetic Hysteresis," World Scientific, 2022.

[4] B. Amable, J. Henry, F. Lordon and R. Topol, "Strong Hysteresis: An Application to Foreign Trade," OFCE Working Paper No. 9103, Paris, France, 1991.

[5] B. Amable, J. Henry, F. Lordon and R. Topol, "Hysteresis: what it is and what it is not," OFCE Working Paper No. 9216, Paris, France, 1992.

[6] B. Amable, J. Henry, F. Lordon and R. Topol, "Unit Root in the Wage-Price Spiral Is Not Hysteresis in Unemployment," Journal of Economic Studies, Vol. 20 No. 1/2, 1993, https://doi.org/10.1108/01443589310038551.

[7] B. Amable, J. Henry, F. Lordon and R. Topol, "Weak and Strong Hysteresis: An Application to Foreign Trade," Economic Notes, 24 (2), 1995, pp. 353-374, 1995.

[8] B. Amable, J. Henry, F. Lordon and R. Topol, "Strong hysteresis versus zero-root dynamics," Economics Letters, Vol. 44, Issues 1–2, pp. 43-47, 1994, ISSN 0165-1765, https://doi.org/10.1016/0165-1765(93)00300-D.

[9] R. Baldwin, "Hysteresis in Import Prices: The Beachhead Effect," The American Economic Review 78, no. 4, 773–85, 1988, http://www.jstor.org/stable/1811174.

[10] R. Baldwin, "Sunk-Cost Hysteresis," National Bureau of Economic Research, Working Paper , 2911, Cambridge, MA, USA, 1989, DOI: 10.3386/w2911.

[11] R. Baldwin, and P. Krugman, "Persistent Trade Effects of Large Exchange Rate Shocks," The Quarterly Journal of Economics, 104, no. 4, 635–54, 1989, https://doi.org/10.2307/2937860.

[12] R. Baldwin and R. Lyons, "Exchange Rate Hysteresis: The Real Effects of Large vs Small Policy Misalignments," National Bureau of Economic

Research, Working Paper Series, 2828, 1989, DOI:10.3386/w2828, http://www.nber.org/papers/w2828.

[13] R. Baldwin, "Hysteresis in trade," Empirical Economics 15, 127–142, 1990, https://doi.org/10.1007/BF01973449.

[14] G. Bate, "Statistical Stability of the Preisach Diagram for Particles of γ-Fe$_2$O$_3$," Journal of Applied Physics, Vol. 33, pp. 2263-2269, 1962.

[15] S. A. Belbas and Y. H. Kim, "A Model of Hysteresis with Two Inputs," Journal of Mathematical Analysis and Applications, 366(1), 181-194, 2010, DOI: https://doi.org/10.1016/j.jmaa.2009.11.048.

[16] A. Belke and M. Göcke, "A Simple Model of Hysteresis in Employment under Exchange Rate Uncertainty," Scottish Journal of Political Economy, 46 (3), 260-28, 1999, https://doi.org/10.1111/1467-9485.00132.

[17] A. Belke and M. Göcke, "Exchange Rate Uncertainty and Employment: An Algorithm Describing 'play'," Applied Stochastic Models in Business and Industry, 17 (2), 181-204, 2001, https://doi.org/10.1002/asmb.436.

[18] A. Belke and M. Göcke, "Real Options Effects on Employment: Does Exchange Rate Uncertainty Matter for Aggregation?," German Economic Review, Volume 6, Issue 2, 185-203, 2005, https://doi.org/10.1111/j.1465-6485.2005.00126.x.

[19] A. Belke, M. Göcke and M. Günther, "Exchange Rate Bands of Inaction and Play-Hysteresis in German Exports—Sectoral Evidence For Some OECD Destinations," Metroeconomica, Volume 64, Issue 1, 152-179, 2013, https://doi.org/10.1111/meca.12000.

[20] A. Belke and M. Göcke, "Interest Rate Hysteresis in Macroeconomic Investment under Uncertainty," IZA Institute of Labor Economics, Discussion Paper Series, IZA DP No. 12566, 2019, https://docs.iza.org/dp12566.pdf.

[21] G. Bertotti, "Hysteresis in Magnetism: For Physicists, Materials Scientists, and Engineers," Academic Press, 1998.

[22] G. Biorci and D. Pescetti, "Some Remarks on Hysteresis," Journal of Applied Physics, 37, 425-427, 1966, https://doi.org/10.1063/1.1707852.

[23] O. J. Blanchard and L. H. Summers, "Hysteresis and the European Unemployment Problem," National Bureau of Economic Research, NBER Macroeconomics Annual 1986, Volume 1, 15-90, MIT Press, 1986.

[24] O. J. Blanchard, "Should We Reject the Natural Rate Hypothesis?," Journal of Economic Perspectives, 32 (1), 97-120, 2018, DOI: 10.1257/jep.32.1.97.

[25] M. Brokate and J. Sprekels, "Hysteresis and Phase Transitions," Springer, 1996.

[26] W. F. Brown, "Failure of the Local-Field Concept for Hysteresis Calculations," Journal of Applied Physics, 33, 1308-1309, 1962, https://doi.org/10.1063/1.1728706.

[27] J.-P. Bouchard, "Crises and Collective Socio-Economic Phenomena: Simple Models and Challenges," Journal of Statistical Physics, 151, 567–606, 2013, DOI: 10.1007/s10955-012-0687-3.

[28] R. Cross and A. Allan, "On the History of Hysteresis," in "Unemployment, Hysteresis, and the Natural Rate Hypothesis: Proceedings of a Conference

Held at the University of St. Andrews, Scotland, July 1986," (editor: R. Cross), Oxford: Basil Blackwell, 26-38, 1988.

[29] R. Cross, "On the Foundations of Hysteresis in Economic Systems," Economics & Philosophy, 9(1), 53-74, 1993, doi:10.1017/S0266267100005113

[30] R. Cross (editor), "The Natural Rate of Unemployment-Reflextions on 25 years of the hypothesis," Cambridge University Press, 1995.

[31] R. Cross, J. Darby, L. Piscitelli and J. Ireland, "Hysteresis and Unemployment: a Preliminary Investigation," in "The Science of Hysteresis, Volume 1," (editors: G. Bertotti and I. Mayergoyz), 667-699, 2005.

[32] R. Cross, M. Grinfeld and H. Lamba, "Hysteresis and economics," IEEE Control Systems Magazine, 29(1), 30-43, 2009, doi: 10.1109/ MCS.2008.930445.

[33] R. Cross, "Unemployment: natural rate epicycles or hysteresis?," 11(2), 136-148, 2014, DOI: https://doi.org/10.4337/ejeep.2014.02.01.

[34] K. Dahmen and J. P. Sethna, "Hysteresis, Avalanches, and Disorder-Induced Critical Scaling: A renormalization-Group Approach," Physical Review B, 53(22), 14872-14905, 1996, DOI: 10.1103/PhysRevB.53.14872.

[35] A. Damlamian and A. Visintin, "Une généralisation vectorielle du modèle de Preisach pour l'hystérésis," C.R. Acad. Sci. Paris, Série I 297, pp. 437-440, 1983.

[36] E. Della Torre, "Measurements of Interaction in an Assembly of γ-Iron Oxide Particles," Journal of Applied Physics, 36(2), 518-522, 1965, https://doi.org/10.1063/1.1714022.

[37] M. Dimian and I. D. Mayergoyz, "Spectral Density Analysis of Nonlinear Hysteretic Systems," Physical Review E, **70**, 046124, 2004, DOI: https:// doi.org/10.1103/PhysRevE.70.046124.

[38] A. Dixit, "Entry and Exit Decisions under Uncertainty," Journal of Political Economy, 97(3), 620-638, 1989, https://www.jstor.org/stable/1830458.

[39] A. Dixit, "Hysteresis, Import Penetration, and Exchange Rate Pass-Through," The Quarterly Journal of Economics, 104 (2), 205-228, May 1989, DOI: https://doi.org/10.2307/2937845.

[40] A. Dixit, "Investment and Hysteresis," Journal of Economic Perspectives, 6 (1), 107-132, 1992, DOI: 10.1257/jep.6.1.107.

[41] A. Dixit and R. S. Pindyck, "Investment Under Uncertainty," Princeton, NJ, USA, 1994.

[42] A. Dixit, "Irreversible investment with uncertainty and scale economies," Journal of Economic Dynamics and Control, 19(1–2), 327-350, 1995, ISSN 0165-1889, DOI: https://doi.org/10.1016/0165-1889(93)00784-2.

[43] J. A. Enderby, "The domain model of hysteresis. Part 2.—Interacting domains," Transactions of the Faraday Society, Vol. 52, p. 106-120, 1956.

[44] D. H. Everett and W. I. Whitton, "A general approach to hysteresis," Transactions of the Faraday Society, 48, 749-757, 1952, DOI: 10.1039/TF9524800749, http://dx.doi.org/10.1039/TF9524800749".

[45] D. H. Everett, "A general approach to hysteresis. Part 3.—A formal treatment of the independent domain model of hysteresis," Transactions of the Faraday Society, Vol. 50, pp. 1077-1096, 1954.

[46] D. H. Everett, "A general approach to hysteresis. Part 4. An alternative formulation of the domain model," Transactions of the Faraday Society, Vol. 51, pp. 1551-1557, 1955.

[47] J. A. Ewing, "On the Production of Transient Electric Currents in Iron and Steel Conductors by Twisting Them When Magnetised, or by Magnetising Them When Twisted," Proceedings of the Royal Society of London, 33, Issue 228-231, pp. 117-135, 1883, DOI: http://doi.org/10.1098/rspl.1883.0084.

[48] A. Fatás and L. H. Summers, "The Permanent Effects of Fiscal Consolidations," National Bureau of Economic Research, Working Paper 22374, 2016, DOI: 10.3386/w22374, http://www.nber.org/papers/w22374.

[49] M. E. Freidlin and A. D. Wentzell, "Diffusion Processes on Graphs and the Averaging Principle," The Annals of Probability, Vol. 21, No. 4, pp. 2215-2245, 1993.

[50] M. I. Freidlin, I. D. Mayergoyz, and R. Pfeiffer, "Noise in Hysteretic Systems and Stochastic Processes on Graphs," Physical Review E, 62(2), 1850-1855, 2000, DOI: https://doi.org/10.1103/PhysRevE.62.1850.

[51] M. Friedman, "The Role of Monetary Policy," American Economic Review 58, May, pp. 1-17, 1968.

[52] A. Friedman, "Foundation of Modern Analysis," Dover Publications, NY, 1982.

[53] C. W. Gardiner, "Handbook of stochastic methods for physics, chemistry and the natural sciences," Springer Verlag, Berlin, 1982.

[54] M. Göcke, "Various Concepts of Hysteresis Applied in Economics," Journal of Economic Surveys, 16(2), 167-188, 2002, DOI: https://doi.org/10.1111/1467-6419.00163.

[55] M. Göcke and L. Werner, "Play Hysteresis in Supply or in Demand as Part of a Market Model," Metroeconomica, 66(2), 339-374, 2015, DOI: https://doi.org/10.1111/meca.12074.

[56] M. Göcke and J. Matulaityte, "Modelling Economic Hysteresis Losses Caused by Sunk Adjustment Costs," MAGKS Papers on Economics 36, 2015, https://www.econstor.eu/bitstream/10419/125533/1/841276366.pdf.

[57] J. Hull and A. White, "Pricing Interest-Rate-Derivative Securities," Review of Financial Studies, 3 (4), pp. 573-92, 1990.

[58] C. E. Korman and I. D. Mayergoyz, "The input dependent Preisach model with stochastic input as a model for aftereffect," in IEEE Transactions on Magnetics, vol. 30, no. 6, pp. 4368-4370, Nov. 1994, doi: 10.1109/20.334090.

[59] C. E. Korman and I. D. Mayergoyz, "Switching as an Exit Problem," IEEE Transactions on Magnetics, 31(6), 3545-3547, 1995, DOI: 10.1109/20.489564.

[60] C. E. Korman and I. D. Mayergoyz, "Semiconductor Noise in the Framework of Semiclassical Transport," Physical Review B, 54(24), 17620–17627, 1996, DOI: 10.1103/PhysRevB.54.17620.

[61] C. E. Korman and I. D. Mayergoyz, "Review of Preisach Type Models Driven by Stochastic Inputs as a Model for After-Effect," Physica B, 233(4), 381-389, 1997, DOI: https://doi.org/10.1016/S0921-4526(97)00325-6.

[62] M. A. Krasnosel'skiĭ and A. V. Pokrovskiĭ, "Systems with Hysteresis," Springer, 1989.

[63] P. Krejčí, "Hysteresis, Convexity and Dissipation in Hyperbolic Equations," Gakuto Int. Series Math. Sci. and Appl., Vol. 8, Gakkotosho, Tokyo 1996.

[64] P. R. Krugman and R. E. Baldwin, "The Persistence of the U.S. Trade Deficit," Brookings Papers on Economic Activity, 1987(1), pp. 1-55, 1987, DOI: https://doi.org/10.2307/2534513.

[65] P. Krugman, "Exchange-Rate Instability," The MIT Press, 1988.

[66] W. W. Leontief, "Quantitative Input and Output Relations in the Economic Systems of the United States," The Review of Economics and Statistics, 18(3), 105-125, 1936, DOI: https://doi.org/10.2307/1927837.

[67] W. W. Leontief, "The Structure of American Economy, 1919–1939: An Empirical Application of Equilibrium Analysis (Second edition, enlarged)," New York: Oxford University Press, 1951.

[68] W. Leontief, "Input-Output Economics," Oxford University Press, 1966.

[69] A. Marshall, "Principles of Economics," Great Mind Series, 1890.

[70] I. D. Mayergoyz, "Mathematical Models of Hysteresis," Physical Review Letters, 56, 1518-1521, 1986, DOI: https://doi.org/10.1103/PhysRevLett.56.1518.

[71] I. D. Mayergoyz, "Mathematical Models of Hysteresis," IEEE Transactions on Magnetics, 22(5), 603-608, 1986, DOI: 10.1109/TMAG.1986.1064347.

[72] I. D. Mayergoyz and G. Friedman, "Generalized Preisach Model of Hysteresis," IEEE Transactions on Magnetics, 24(1), 212-217, 1988, DOI: 10.1109/20.43892.

[73] I. D. Mayergoyz, "Mathematical Models of Hysteresis," Springer, 1991.

[74] I. D. Mayergoyz and A. Adly, "Numerical Implementation of the Feedback Preisach Model," IEEE Transactions on Magnetics, 28(5), 2605-2607, 1992, DOI: 10.1109/20.179571.

[75] I. Mayergoyz, "Mathematical Models of Hysteresis and Their Applications," Elsevier, 2003.

[76] I. Mayergoyz and C. Korman, "Hysteresis and Neural Memory ," World Scientific, 2020.

[77] P. R. Mota and P. B. Vasconcelos, "Play-Hysteresis in the Joint Dynamics of Employment and Investment," Math.Comput.Sci., 16, 5, 2022, https://doi.org/10.1007/s11786-022-00523-w.

[78] P. R. Mota, "Aggregate demand uncertainty outbreaks and employment hysteresis in G7 countries," Journal of Post Keynesian Economics,2023, DOI: 10.1080/01603477.2023.2268090.

[79] L. Neel, "Sur les effets d'un couplage entre grains ferromagnétiques doués d'hystérésis," Academie des Sciences, Paris, Comptes-Rendus Hebdomaines des Seances, Vol. 246 (16), pp. 2313-2319, 1958.

[80] J. von Neumann, "Mathematical Foundations of Quantum Mechanics," Princeton Landmarks in Mathematics and Physics, 1996.

[81] E. S. Phelps, "PCs, Expectations of Inflation, and Optimal Unemployment Over Time," Economica 34, August, pp. 254-81, 1967.

[82] E. S. Phelps, "Money-wage Dynamics and Labor-Market Equilbrium," Journal of Political Economy 76, July-August, pp. 678-711, 1968.

[83] R. Pindyck, "Irreversibility, Uncertainty, and Investment," Journal of Economic Literature, Vol. XXIX, 1110-1148, 1991.

[84] H. Poincare, "Science and Hypothesis," Dover, New York, 1952.

[85] F. Preisach, "Über die magnetische Nachwirkung," Zeitschrift für Physik, 94(5–6), 277–302, 1935, DOI: https://doi.org/10.1007%2Fbf01349418.

[86] F. Preisach, "On the Magnetic Aftereffect," IEEE Transactions on Magnetics, 53(3), 1-11, Art no. 0700111, 2017, doi: 10.1109/TMAG.2016.2548379.

[87] I. W. Sandberg, "A Nonlinear Input-Output Model of a Multisectored Economy," Econometrica, Vol. 41, No. 6, 1973, pp. 1167–82. JSTOR, https://doi.org/10.2307/1914043.

[88] J. P. Sethna, K. A. Dahmen and O. Perkovic, "Random-Field Ising Models of Hysteresis," in "The Science of Hysteresis" (editors: G. Bertotti and I. Mayergoyz), Vol. 2, 107-180, 2006.

[89] L. H. Summers and A. Fatás, "Hysteresis and Fiscal Policy During the Global Crisis," VOXEU, CEPR, October 2016.

[90] O. Vasicek, "An Equilibrium Characterization of the Term Structure," Journal of Financial Economics, 5(2), 177-188, 1977, DOI: https://doi.org/10.1016/0304-405X(77)90016-2.

[91] A. Visintin, "Differential Models of Hysteresis," Springer, 1994.

Index

Printed in the United States
by Baker & Taylor Publisher Services